D1602403

Tramps,
Unfit Mothers, and
Neglected Children

Tramps, Unfit Mothers, and Neglected Children

Negotiating the Family in
Nineteenth-Century Philadelphia

SHERRI BRODER

PENN

University of Pennsylvania Press

Philadelphia

10 9 8 7 6 5 4 3 2 1

Published by
University of Pennsylvania Press
Philadelphia, Pennsylvania 19104-4011

Library of Congress Cataloging-in-Publication Data

Broder, Sherri.
    Tramps, unfit mothers, and neglected children : negotiating the family in
nineteenth-century Philadelphia / Sherri Broder.
            p.   cm.
    ISBN 0-8122-3654-8 (alk. paper)
    Includes bibliographical references and index.
    1. Family social work—Pennsylvania—Philadelphia—History—19th century.
2. Child welfare—Pennsylvania—Philadelphia—History—19th century. 3. Poor
families—Pennsylvania—Philadelphia—History—19th century. 4. Working class
families—Pennsylvania—Philadelphia—History—19th century. I. Title
HV699.4.P5 B76 2002
362.7'09748'1109034—dc21   2001052469

For Marvin

and for

Samuel

and Rebecca

and Jacob

Contents

"You take this and hock it, " frontispiece from Caroline Pemberton, *Your Little Brother James* (1896). In her novel, Philadelphia reformer Caroline Pemberton used James's mother's habit of pawning household items—a contested strategy for making ends meet relied on by many poor families—and James's reliance on his proceeds to buy food—to indict James's mother as unfit.

Introduction

IN THE CLOSING YEARS OF THE NINETEENTH CENTURY, Caroline Pemberton, daughter of a prominent "old" Philadelphia family and a child welfare reformer with over a decade's experience working among the city's "outcast children," published *Your Little Brother James* (1896), a novel that reads like a page from a reformer's case records. Eight-year-old James—introduced as "an unwanted baby that wouldn't die"—has no father and a dangerous mother who lacks maternal instinct. Having failed to kill the resilient boy in his infancy, James's mother continues to neglect him: he runs wild in the street, pawns items for his mother and other women in the neighborhood, steals a portion of his proceeds in order to eat, and attends school irregularly. James is seen on the street till midnight, except for those nights when his mother entertains gentlemen friends and he stays out all night. At nine, James is sent to the House of Refuge while his mother serves a stint in the House of Correction. When released, he joins a gang that steals and sells lead pipe. After seventeen days in jail and a trial, the young "street urchin" is committed to the custody of a charitable association that agrees to provide him with a proper home in the country. Shrewdly attempting to manipulate the feminine sensibilities of those determining his fate, James pleads to be returned to his mother. But his appeal is ignored and James is sent far beyond the reach of his unfit and "unnatural" mother and the temptations of city streets.[1]

Like other late nineteenth-century charity and child welfare reformers, Caroline Pemberton placed the erosion of—indeed the apparent lack of—the family life of the laboring poor at the heart of her analysis of urban social problems and her understanding of class relations.[2] *Your Little Brother James* takes as its central themes the relation between social classes, the dangerous family life of the poor, and the immense significance of childhood environment in determining morality. In it Pemberton tackled the belief that the children of the poor were products of innate depravity destined to fill American reformatories as children and prisons as adults. She argued that the removal of children from unfit parents and improper surroundings and their subsequent placement in new homes rather than in reform schools was critical to saving the errant children of the poor. Her novel served both as a critique of the institutionalization of juvenile offenders and as an elaboration of the unnatural family life of the poor.

While Pemberton chronicles the immoral environment in which James's boyhood is spent, the novel's paternalistic title establishes the (presumably middle- or upper-class) reader's responsibility as James's "older brother" or "sister" and asserts that the reader and James—read the upper and middle classes and the poor—are part of the same human family. James's welfare, therefore, is critical to the reader, as is the future of the entire class he represents. This familial metaphor simultaneously grants the upper and middle classes the right and the obligation to intervene in the family life of the poor.

The social project shared by charity reformers and childsavers to recast the family lives of the poor did not go uncontested, however, either ideologically or in actual practice. In Philadelphia's poorer neighborhoods, witnesses testifying on behalf of neighbors under investigation by child welfare reformers defended their own views of appropriate family life, chastising reformers who offered censure instead of praise for hardworking parents struggling to raise children in difficult circumstances. Reformers frequently encountered physical resistance too as they struggled to remove children from families deemed neglectful or surroundings deemed improper.

Charity and child welfare reformers also met ideological opposition from members of the city's organized labor movement, who—like the mainstream social welfare reformers they opposed—saw the emergence in the post-Civil War decades of a permanent wage-earning laboring class as a crisis of the family. Labor leaders, however, had a much different agenda than other reformers—and so gave the "family crisis" a much different interpretation.

Labor reformers agreed that healthy families were crucial to the health of the Republic and that laboring families were in serious trouble. Like charity and child welfare reformers, they worked to establish distinctions between "honest" laboring people (who were neither thieves nor welfare cheats) and the "degraded" poor. Labor reformers also worried that male unemployment, women's wage work, child labor and prostitution, all threatened to erode the boundaries between the laboring poor and the "dangerous" class. Yet if they shared the belief that the threatened moral deterioration of laboring poor families placed the nation in peril, they denied that all social ills had their origins in the "unnatural" family life of the poor. Countering that hardworking families were threatened rather than threatening, labor leaders traced the source of urban social problems to the changing class relations of post-Civil War society, and found the solution in their transformation.

Both the national and Philadelphia labor movements addressed the same issues—male unemployment, vagrancy, prostitution, child labor and neglect—that confronted the theorists of scientific charity and the legion of "friendly visitors," volunteer charity workers, and paid agents who staffed the city's philanthropic organizations and roamed the streets, "haunts," and houses of the laboring poor. Using the same representations of tramps, fallen women, and street waifs that so engaged charity and child welfare reformers, labor leaders fashioned competing narratives of working-class family life that challenged mainstream social welfare analyses and policies directed at transforming the lives of the poor. All the Victorian stock characters that served to depict the men, women, and children of the poor—the missing father who walks away from his role as family provider and protector (the tramp); the sexually active fallen woman (the prostitute) who irresponsibly conceives a child she never intends to raise and becomes a dangerously unfit mother; the half-orphaned waif well on his way to becoming a thief (the neglected child)—were central not only to the scientific charity and organized philanthropy that defined mainstream or orthodox liberal benevolence in the late nineteenth century, but to the organized labor movement that challenged them as well.

For labor leaders, however, the alleged disintegration of the poorest of laboring families into a motley collection of prostitutes, tramps, street children, and thieves was an indictment of late nineteenth-century American capitalism rather than a criticism of working-class people themselves. George McNeill, a prominent trade unionist and national labor reformer, expressed the view shared by many laboring people when he argued that the disintegration of the working-class family—represented by the wage labor of women and children and the under- and unemployment of men— was a direct consequence of the transformed relations between labor and capital:

We complain, that whereas labor produces all the wealth of the world, the laborer receives only as much as will keep him in the poorest condition of life to which he can be crowded down . . . his wife is forced from home, and his children from school. . . . When at work, he belongs to the lower orders, and is continually under surveillance; when out of work, he is an outlaw, a tramp,—he is a man without the rights of manhood,—the pariah of society, homeless, in the deep significance of the term.[3]

If a labor leader had written *Your Little Brother James*, perhaps James's father would have been portrayed as an honest but unemployed worker who went searching for work to support his family. Unable to find work, the demoralized man would have been arrested and jailed as a tramp. Too ashamed to return home until he could support his family, and unaware of the desperate plight they were in, the decent laborer would be transformed into a missing husband and absent father. James's mother would be an honest hardworking woman who died of overwork as she struggled to support her child, leaving James an orphan. Possibly, James might have an older sister, a seamstress at the mercy of the sweating system, who struggled to support her younger brother against all odds, and who eventually would be forced to give in to the sexual demands of the boss in order to keep her position. Meanwhile, James would have manfully tried to support his mother and sister by selling papers and doing odd jobs. As he roamed the city streets searching for ways to earn money, the well-meaning boy would nonetheless be easy prey for those who taught boys that picking pockets and running errands for the women who worked in houses of prostitution would net more income than honest labor. Both James and his older sister would end up incarcerated (if she did not die an early death from prostitution); she would be trapped in a rescue home founded by the wives and daughters of the very employers who ground her down, paying her starvation wages while their sons tried to seduce her. And James would be sent to the House of Refuge, where he would serve an apprenticeship with those who could teach him the ins and outs of a life of crime. If a happy ending graced the end of the novel, it would involve the furthering of labor organization and cooperation among the workers who made up the "family of labor," rather than the intercession of meddling "sham philanthropists" who created the very problems they and their female relatives then set out to ameliorate.

Although charity reformers and labor movement activists explicitly addressed each other's political analyses of the family crisis of the poor, the perspectives of these two groups did not dominate reform thought and practice. Evangelical Protestant women "rescue" workers concerned with the plight of single mothers and their children also addressed the apparent breakdown of working-class family life in late nineteenth-century cities. The homes for unwed mothers that they founded were one of a variety of institutions established in the late nineteenth century to redeem "wayward girls."

If a reformer who sought the salvation of unwed mothers had written

Your Little Brother James, she would have retained the notion of familial obligation that the rich owed the poor, but would have given the story a maternalistic slant, perhaps calling it *Your Fallen Sister and Her Innocent Child*. Her tale would present single motherhood as a variant of the endangered poor family with its missing father, immoral mother, and child at risk of neglect, but would also highlight the seduction of an innocent young woman at the hands of a man. James's mother would begin life as an innocent girl, only to be cruelly seduced and then abandoned by her suitor. Driven to infanticide, prostitution, suicide, or perhaps eventually all three, her death would be imminent unless she was saved by a caring "sister" whose religious and womanly sympathies obligated her to try to redeem her errant fallen sister and return her to the "holy principles of motherhood" and a proper male-headed family.

Thus charity and child welfare reformers, labor activists, and evangelical Protestant women rescue workers all used the troubled laboring family as the object of their sharply conflicting assessments of American society. But the representations of tramps, fallen women, and street waifs shared by charity and child welfare reformers, labor leaders and rescue workers— even as their meanings were contested—were also sites of cultural contention for men, women, and children outside of the arena of organized labor. So too were the reform interventions these representations legitimated.

As they responded to the presence of charity reformers and childsavers in their neighborhoods—at times actively seeking out intervention, other times shunning reformers and agents as intruders—the city's laboring men, women, and children also shared in the struggle to define norms of womanhood, manhood, and childhood and articulated their own, frequently conflicting views regarding the family. In the process, they might variously invoke, play upon, or repudiate both the dominant cultural norms of charity and child protection reformers and the working-class respectability of the labor movement. Although male and female social welfare reformers and Philadelphia's male labor reformers all claimed to represent the "plight" of the poor, their competing discourses were nonetheless challenged by the multiplicity of alternative working-class perspectives on the family—some antagonistic to both social welfare and labor reform goals—that were elaborated in poor neighborhoods.

If ordinary laboring Philadelphians had written *Your Little Brother James*, a variety of competing outlooks would have been represented. Family situations like those explored in the novel were part of everyday life in the city's laboring neighborhoods, where Philadelphia's poorer residents expressed a range of responses: they might ostracize a woman like James's mother for her faulty mothering and hoot at her in the street for her indiscreet sexual activities, or perhaps sneak a child like James food and clothing to prevent his mother from pawning them for drink. Other residents might sympathize with her plight as a single mother trying to raise an unruly boy, or share some of the very household strategies that she used to make ends meet, such as sending her young son out to scavenge what he might. Acting upon their own sense of themselves as good mothers and responsible neighbors, local women might bring James and his mother to the attention of charity workers or childsavers. Conversely, wary neighbors who defied reformers' right to "rescue" poor children might band together to prevent James and his mother from falling into the clutches of the dreaded "Cruelty" Society, as the Pennsylvania Society to Protect Children from Cruelty (SPCC) was popularly called.

In contrast to those who have put forth social control theories—or even feminist revisions and critiques of such theories—domestic ideology wasn't simply imposed on the laboring poor by middle-class reformers or political pundits; rather, working people had their say too.[4] Their beliefs and behavior shaped by more than simple acquiescence, resistance, or manipulation of reformers' assumptions, laboring Philadelphians drew on their own cultural traditions and experiences as they negotiated family life. *Tramps, Unfit Mothers, and Neglected Children* chronicles how multiple characters—from working-class leaders in the local labor movement to the concerned upper- and upper-middle-class social-scientific members of the Society to Protect Children from Cruelty, from the wealthy and devout evangelical Protestant Lady Managers of the "sisterly" Haven for Unwed Mothers and Infants and the destitute single mothers who sought their aid, to the rough and respectable neighbors and relatives in the homes and streets of Kensington and Northern Liberties and in the slums of the South Street corridor—all drew on the discourse of the family to define themselves variously as gendered members of different social classes, as respected family and community members, as political actors, and as people with claims on the state, the police, and public and private social services.[5]

This volume mines the rich case records of the Pennsylvania Society to Protect Children from Cruelty (SPCC) from its founding in 1877 through the end of the nineteenth century, to recreate neighborhood life and the controversy over the family in Philadelphia in the late Victorian era.[6] Using the published work of national and local charity reformers, the institutional records of the Pennsylvania SPCC and the Haven for Unwed Mothers and Infants, and the Philadelphia labor press, I restore a dialogue that took place over a century ago and that has been largely ignored by historians, despite its striking resonance with similar debates over "family values" in the late twentieth century.[7] While other historians have used case records from child protection agencies, charity organizations and maternity homes to analyze either domestic violence and transformations in social policy throughout American history or the relationship between social workers and their clients in the early twentieth century, here I use these records in a fresh way, to provide an overview of the wide range of gender and family issues debated in the late Victorian era and to demonstrate how late nineteenth-century debates over the family engaged not only charity and child welfare and labor reformers, but ordinary Philadelphians too.[8] By analyzing a local, multi-vocal debate over the laboring family in the late nineteenth century—a period when state intervention into family life increased—the book provides a window into Gilded Age family life on its own terms while also illuminating contemporary concerns regarding the family and social policy.[9] In doing so, this study contributes to the literature on laboring families, reform, and the state; the literature on the "gendered landscape of working-class life" and the gendering of labor protest; and the body of interdisciplinary work that is beginning to investigate how discourses and practices of motherhood and child welfare vary across cultures, class, race, and ethnicity.[10]

As they struggled to define what it meant to be a good mother or an "unnatural" one, an involuntarily idle worker or a tramp, an exploited child or a dutiful son or daughter, charity, child protection and rescue workers, labor activists and the laboring poor all contended to shape social policy, family, and community life. Institutional and case records reveal disagreement in laboring communities over these and similar issues: When is a man unemployed and when is he a tramp? If a husband doesn't turn over his wages to his wife for a year, are they still married? When can a woman legally married to one man call another man who provides for her and her children her husband? Can a good mother wash the laundry or clean the rooms of a brothel if she does so to support her children? If her daughter works there also, is she a neglected child, a dutiful daughter, or a bad girl? When is a child neglected and when is she self-reliant? When is child labor justified and when is it exploitation? Who is a legitimate mother? What constellation of people constitutes a family? Can a single mother gain respectability if she marries? Can a good mother rely on others to raise her child so she can resume wage-work? These questions are not trivial, for they were—and in some form still are—at the heart of American social policy and civic life. Their answers determined and continue to determine who loses or gains child custody, who receives aid and under what terms and in what forms such assistance is given.

The SPCC case records are particularly useful in capturing both the nature of the debate and the diversity of its participants because they address a vast array of family and community concerns and because the testimony of complainants, defendants, and witnesses interviewed by the SPCC agents offers indirect access to a variety of people—women, children, unorganized workers, African Americans and Southern and Eastern European immigrants, prostitutes, the unemployed—whose voices were seldom represented in the formal political rhetoric of the labor movement but who nonetheless were crucial participants in working-class life.[11] Yet no matter how faithful to the original testimony of agents, defendants, complainants, and witnesses, and no matter how carefully quantified—either in SPCC annual reports or in the work of other historians—the case records are necessarily subjective and incomplete and require an immense interpretive effort on the part of any historian or reader, both because they typically contain conflicting interpretations of events and because they were created by a process of shared authorship by reformers and clients in a context of investigation and interrogation.[12] In utilizing the case records as sources, I have tried to consider how the tales that were told and those that were silenced were structured by social, political, and economic inequality between "defendants" and agents and within families; how the process of shared authorship by defendants, complainants, witnesses, and agents shaped the interpretation of a case; and how both the mission of the SPCC and the needs of family members ensured that complaints were framed in certain ways.

The book is organized topically and considers the negotiation of late nineteenth-century working-class family life as it occurred in several different contexts, between classes and within working-class neighborhoods and families. Each chapter addresses a different aspect of the late Victorian debate over laboring families. Chapter 1 establishes the main characters in the late nineteenth-century family morality tale. It analyzes three representations of the urban poor—the tramp, the fallen woman, and the waif or neglected child—that were central to late Victorian political culture and investigates the ways they were used by national and local charity, child protection, and labor reformers in order to shape social policies, from vagrancy and child labor laws to demands for the family wage and eight-hour day.

The rest of the book considers laboring people as subjects rather than objects of debate and examines how ordinary Philadelphians also contributed to the public and "private" discourse over the nature of family life and its discontents. Chapters 2 and 3 explore the struggles of reformers and laboring people—first in working-class neighborhoods and then in laboring families—to implement sometimes shared, sometimes competing ideologies, as they elaborated their own distinctive views of family life. As families and communities renegotiated the limits of parental and filial obligations in the late nineteenth century, they negotiated the family in both senses of the word, working out differences and also maneuvering around expectations of appropriate behavior.

As charity, child welfare, and labor reformers and other respectable Philadelphians worked to shore up the normative family, a variety of other kinds of families were declared illegitimate. Chapters 4 and 5 add the figures of the "unwed" and "unnatural" mother to our characterizations of fallen women and consider the efforts of laboring communities and reformers to police both the concept of "family" and the boundaries of motherhood by stigmatizing single motherhood. They focus on another aspect of child nurture and motherhood in working-class Philadelphia by exploring the lives of single new mothers and their young children, inside and outside of institutions for fallen mothers. While religious reformers committed to "redemptive maternity" and the rescue of fallen women struggled to awaken new mothers to an appreciation of "holy motherhood" and the exclusivity of the mother/child bond, some laboring poor single mothers practiced a different form of motherhood that incorporated other women into a network of support for their children while they pursued wage work. Chapter 5 analyzes the controversial practice of baby farming—as the boarding of infants and toddlers was popularly known—and its relation to the childcare practices of poor and especially single wage-earning mothers. This chapter adds two more female characters—those of the mercenary baby farmer and the potentially murderous single mother who "farmed out" her infant—to the late Victorian morality tale, and considers the social meaning of the cultural anxiety over baby farming.

Social policy is embedded in cultural narratives of the family and the poor, even as it contributes to their production. The ways that people imagine what it is to be a mother, a father, a child, help create and are also shaped by social policies and laws about the family.[13] Our ideas about the family and its relationship to the state are integrally related to the ways we answer the question: to what extent should the larger society be held accountable and exercise responsibility for all of our children? By exploring the diverse ways that Gilded Age Philadelphians contributed to this ongoing discussion, I hope to enrich our own efforts to do so as well.

Chapter 1

Tramps, Fallen Women, and Neglected Children

Political Culture and the Urban Poor in the Late Nineteenth Century

IN THE LAST QUARTER OF THE NINETEENTH CENTURY, charity and child welfare reformers and labor advocates across the nation all used the troubled laboring family as the object of their sharply conflicting assessments of American society. In these years reformers of diverse political perspectives contested the meanings of family relations in order to define both the problem of the working-class family and its solution. Labor leaders, charity workers and child savers concurred that contemporary conditions—including class polarization, male unemployment, and female and child labor—threatened the laboring family's ability to transmit republican values through the nurturing of potential citizens. They argued that pervasive family crisis among the poor—indeed, the likely disintegration of the family if existing social conditions continued unchecked—was a central threat to the stability of the Republic.

Despite their political differences, mainstream social welfare reformers and labor activists alike identified several factors as central to the "crisis" of working-class families and therefore the crisis of the state: the idleness of laboring men, the troubled relationship of working-class women to domesticity, and children's presence in mills and factories and in the streets. Each group feared the erosion of the boundary they perceived between the working and the "dangerous" classes and argued that the reinstitution of the "traditional" sexual division of labor was critical to the preservation of both laboring families and the working class. Finally, the symbolic significance of the marginal unrespectable poor—the chronic unemployed, prostitutes, street children—was heightened for charity and child welfare and labor reformers, who all placed the disreputable poor at the center of their analyses of working-class identity and disintegration.

Although they drew on shared images of tramps, fallen women and deserted wives, and neglected and overworked children, labor and main-stream social welfare reformers varied tremendously in their analysis of the origins of the threat to the working-class family and in the competing social policies they elaborated as they each invoked a developing reliance on state power to implement very different agendas. By the 1890s, labor and charity and child protection reformers had articulated comprehensive analyses of post-Civil War society and proposed contrasting strategies for reclaiming the republican legacy. Labor leaders argued that capitalism destroyed fami-ly life and left the children of working parents vulnerable to "the evil associ-ations and surroundings which train them in vice and crime."[1] Mainstream social welfare reformers, however, argued that it was working-class family life that posed a challenge to respectable society. In the words of childsaver Charles Loring Brace, the improperly socialized children of the urban poor were a threat to the "property, morals, and political life of the Republic."[2]

Over the last quarter of the nineteenth century, the state emerged as a "battleground for competing claims upon its authority."[3] Charity and child protection reformers turned to the state for solutions to the problems of beg-ging, prostitution, tramping, and labor unrest, advocating vagrancy legisla-tion, regulation of the street trades, and the denial of relief to the able-bodied poor. But male labor activists attacked the system of "monop-oly" that threatened to turn honest laborers into beggars, tramps, and thieves; their wives and daughters into prostitutes, and their children into street children. They, too, turned to the state with their own legislative agenda and demanded the eight-hour day, child labor legislation, and a "living wage" that would enable men to support a family. At the same time, child protection reformers sought to suppress the "street trades" and wom-en's work in brothels. They encouraged women to press legal charges against husbands for desertion and nonsupport, but were slow to address the "involuntary idleness" of able-bodied men. Finally, while childsavers arranged for young women sentenced by the courts to be admitted to the privately sponsored rescue missions for "fallen" women run by Protestant and Catholic moral reformers, labor movement activists disdained philan-thropy and argued that the organization of women into trade unions was preventive rescue work. As labor reformer and journalist John Swinton declared, "Something other than the bogus philanthropies of the plundering classes is essential to the public salvation."[4]

The story of the Gilded Age counterpart to the late twentieth- and early twenty-first-century preoccupation in the United States with "family val-ues" and welfare reform has been fragmented, neglected by policy historians who have focused on institutional histories and legislation without placing the history of social welfare in a political context that takes labor activism into account, and by labor historians who have ignored the labor movement's dialogue with social welfare reformers regarding "private" issues of gender, sexuality, and family. Although many reformers perceived social welfare legislation and labor reform as integrally related, for the most part historians have not analyzed them in this way, nor have they interpreted the issues of tramping, prostitution, and child labor that engaged mainstream social welfare workers and the organized labor movement in the late nineteenth century as a cohesive debate regarding the family.[5] The Gilded Age labor movement addressed a wide range of issues, encompassing gender and family relations, health, infant mortality, juvenile delinquency, child labor, prostitution, unemployment, hours and wages, and the overall quality of life for working people. Furthermore, ostensibly gender-neutral issues like poverty, vagrancy, and unemployment were inseparable from working-class constructions of masculinity and femininity and from the gender politics of late Victorian American society. The late nineteenth-century American labor movement had a family policy—one formed in explicit opposition to that of mainstream social welfare reformers and that at times clashed with the diverse informal family policies of the laboring poor.

Tramps: Married Vagabonds or Involuntarily Idle Men?

In the decades following the Civil War, Americans experienced three financial contractions in the nation's economy. In 1873, 1883, and again in 1893, a panic triggered a period of prolonged economic depression accompanied by widespread unemployment and massive poverty. Antebellum Americans had considered social mobility the answer to poverty, persuading themselves that the class conflict and political strife of Europe were inconceivable in a nation in which all white men could eventually attain enough property to gain a stake in the community. In the postwar years, the growth of an urban working class posed a threat to previous conceptions of life in a Republic shared across a broad spectrum of Americans.[6] Afraid that the independent producer would be reduced to laboring for another man for his entire working life, white labor activists began to draw parallels between the war fought to abolish slavery, and what they termed the "irrepressible conflict between labor and capital."[7]

The growth of an urban working class threatened men and women of property as well: they feared mob rule and the impact of demagogues on uneducated men who had no stake in the republic since they lacked property, yet were granted the right to vote. Prosperous Americans had been horrified at the turmoil unleashed during the New York City draft riots in 1863. With the advent of the Paris Commune in 1871, fresh images of political unrest awakened memories of looting and bloodshed. When the Great Railroad Strike of 1877 shattered any claim to consensus between wage-earners and employers, the contention that an "irrepressible conflict" between labor and capital threatened to divide a formerly complacent republic into two warring classes appeared all too plausible to many Americans.[8]

It was no coincidence that the Pennsylvania Society to Protect Children from Cruelty (SPCC) was founded in 1877 in a decade when economic depression and great labor strikes swept the nation. In these turbulent years, reformers motivated by a combination of humanitarian concern and fear of social disorder founded charity organizations and childsaving societies and "rescue" institutions as a response to the social problems of the city.[9] In 1878, acting out of a mixture of humanitarian sentiment, fear of the "dangerous" class, and the desire to imbue charity with business principles, the city's Quaker and evangelical Protestant reformers founded the Society to Organize Charity, one of the nation's earliest charity organization societies. The following year Philadelphia was one of the first cities to abolish public outdoor relief in the name of charity reform.

If Philadelphia, the nation's second largest city, was an important center of the postbellum "scientific" reform of benevolence, it was also the birthplace of the Knights of Labor and the home of a vital labor movement in the mid-1880s. Although the depression of the 1870s had decimated the city's trade unions, in the 1880s the city's textile workers, shoemakers, and laborers in other trades organized craft unions and joined the Knights of Labor in response to transformations in the organization of work similar to those experienced by industrial workers across the nation.

The panic of 1873, the downturn of the mid-1880s, and the depression of the 1890s sent shock waves through Philadelphia's economy and contributed to profound transformations in the lives of many Philadelphians. Homelessness, begging, poverty, child labor, prostitution, "tramping," and unemployment were practical concerns for the new breed of "scientific" postbellum reformers and harsh realities for the urban poor. The low wages, unsteady employment, and "involuntary idleness" of male workers made women's and children's contributions to the family income critical. Nationally, the number of women and children in the labor force more than doubled between 1870 and 1890.[10] As a leading textile center, Philadelphia attracted immigrant families who traditionally expected daughters and sometimes wives to earn wages as part of their contribution to the family economy. In 1880, women were 26 percent of the city's labor force—almost twice the national average—and 46 percent of the city's textile workers. In these years Philadelphia had the highest percentage of families with more than one breadwinner of all industrial cities in the United States.[11] In this context, the issues of unemployment, female wage-labor, and child labor were of central concern to the city's laboring poor.

In the 1870s, Americans began to rely on the term "tramp" to refer with misgivings to the roving unemployed.[12] During the lean years of the 1870s and mid-1880s, an increasing number of working-class men took to the roads in search of work or hand-outs when work evaded them. More prosperous Americans responded with alarm to the geographic mobility and apparent rootlessness of the poor.[13] Tramps and "married vagabonds" aroused dread and anxiety for several reasons: they were perceived as propertyless men who lacked commitment to both work and family, the two pillars of Victorian culture.

Married Vagabonds: What the Reformers Said

In the decades following the Civil War, Gilded Age charity reformers interpreted the poverty and unemployment so evident in America's major cities as a consequence of the collective moral failings of the individual members of an entire class. Charity reformers insisted on the significance of class as a moral marker that distinguished the productive workers from the lazy idlers, and argued that they could make "scientific" distinctions between those who were poor through misfortune and therefore worthy of aid, and the "unworthy poor" distinguished by their laziness, intemperance, and unwillingness to work. This attempt to winnow out the deserving from the undeserving poor remained the dominant response to the poverty engendered by the nation's volatile economy throughout the Gilded Age.[14]

Although expressed in ostensibly gender-neutral terms, this distinction between the "workers" and the "idlers" nonetheless had great significance for the way charity reformers perceived the family relations of the poor. In

Victorian America, labor was defined in gendered terms. As work performed for wages outside one's household became the standard by which all labor was judged, middle-class women's unwaged domestic labor within their families was naturalized as a labor of love. By the end of the antebellum period, as historian Jeanne Boydston has argued, a "gender division of labor" had become "a gendered definition of labor."[15] Work—gainful productive labor—defined men as manly individuals, just as the performance of wage work jeopardized women's womanliness.

For charity reformers, two related issues provided the key to the demoralization of working-class family life: the alleged unwillingness of working-class men to be manly providers and the lack of clearly defined family and gender roles within the poorest working-class families. Unemployment, "tramping," even the pauperism of entire families could be traced back to the refusal of laboring men to behave as men and support their families. When "married vagabonds" deserted their families, they forced women and children either to assume the man's role of breadwinning, or to turn to the charities for the economic support they should have found at home. And once a family began to rely on the charities, all of its members—fathers, mothers, and children—took the first step toward pauperism, the ultimate state of demoralization.

Scientific charity theorists' consideration of pauperism also posed a sharp critique of the sexual division of labor in laboring and destitute families. Mary Richmond—a national leader in charity reform and later in scientific social work, who worked with the Society to Organize Charity in Philadelphia at the turn of the century—suggested that one way to deal effectively with the problem of "married vagabonds" who had neglected their familial responsibilities was to insist that all applications for charity be made by the man of the family. She noted that the "married vagabond" often left the home "when the charity agent calls . . . in response to the appeals of his family." Such men were "rather shy of appearing at all, unless in dull times they take the trouble to pose as industrious artisans out of work." As a result, public and private relief officials had "drifted into the habit of receiving and filling applications for relief made by the mothers and children of needy families." For their part, poor families preferred the "pernicious practice of sending children [or mothers] to charity offices."[16]

Although charity reformers believed they were witnessing the breakdown of gender roles in the working-class family, they were instead observing a gendered division of labor common to the poorest of working-class families. Charity agents believed that it was easier for poor women to beg than to work. But, as the phrase "working the charities" implied, applying for aid to public and private relief officials was hard work. Moreover, poor families considered it not only work, but women's work.[17] This failure to recognize the attempts of poor women to provide for their families as work was paralleled by a similar failure to perceive the "tramping" of unemployed working-class men as a genuine search for employment. Although desertion was a common mode of informal divorce in all regions of the United States throughout the nineteenth century—indeed the labor press frequently printed letters from wives searching for missing spouses—men did not always undertake "tramping" in order to avoid domestic responsibilities. Unemployed men might also leave home so that charity officials would deem their wives and children deserted—and therefore deserving.

Charity reformers believed that any provision of aid and personal contact between charity workers and poor families necessarily had as its goal the reinstitution of working-class manhood. Forcing the man of the family "not only [to] do all the asking, but . . . [to] show good cause why he should receive" would restore the husband and father to his proper role of family provider. Reformers argued that if a man knew that his wife and children could not rely on public or private relief, he would be less likely to leave the home to wander about the country, ostensibly searching for work. And those families headed by men who truly were unable to work could still retain the dignity of having a man arrange for their material comfort. This was particularly important so that the boys of the family could learn to be breadwinners and the girls could learn to be homemakers rather than wage-earners. Richmond explained, "There is little use in telling our boys in Sunday schools and boys' brigades that they must respect and protect all women, if we let them go home to a father who is a loafer, and a mother who takes in washing in order to support the family. Such object lessons undo all our teaching."[18]

Thus, until the panic of 1893 and the ensuing depression forced a reevaluation of the causes of "involuntary idleness," charity reformers focused their energies on preventing pauperism rather than investigating the causes of unemployment, on teaching the poor the discipline of work, rather than providing work for the unemployed, and on inculcating proper gender roles. Those who betrayed signs of pauperization, or a marked dislike for honest labor, had to be taught the discipline of work before they infected the rest of society. Henry Boies, a member of the Pennsylvania Board of Public

Charities, contended that "It may be asserted with assurance that no sound man, woman, or child in good health in this country need ever be a pauper. ... The ... hereditary or incorrigible beggar, tramp, vagrant, or idler, should be . . . passed into the State reformatory for convicts, to be treated; and either transformed into honest self-supporters (sic) or transferred into the State penientiary [sic], for life."[19]

Charity organizers advised an end to "indiscriminate" charity—including almsgiving, the admission of all who came to soup kitchens, and free lodging in bunks or on the floor of police station houses for homeless men, women and children. In Philadelphia, the Society to Organize Charity (SOC) abolished public outdoor relief in 1879.[20] The Society also systematized the city's ward charity societies in order to prevent people from applying for aid in more than one ward. This measure was directed at those women thought to prefer dependence on charity to hard work: to reveal too much knowledge about the available public and private sources of "relief" could render a woman ineligible for aid, if agents determined she was "working the charities."[21] To this end, the SOC carried out thorough investigations of all who applied for aid. The Society also established "friendly inns and provident woodyards" as well as a Wayfarer's Lodge for male workers who had traveled to the city in search of work. As the Society to Organize Charity explained, the Wayfarer's Lodge used a "work test" to distinguish between the deserving and the undeserving poor, by requiring all those who sought shelter to chop a certain amount of wood.[22]

In the 1880s, numerous states began to pass punitive "antitramp" laws, which in effect criminalized those traveling to find work, which were much harsher than the traditional vagrancy statutes that had previously regulated the mobility of the poor. Through efforts to organize charity and legislation such as the tramp acts, more prosperous citizens sought to reassert control over the apparent chaos of working-class life.

The panic of 1893, however, awakened at least some previously orthodox liberals and charity workers to the causes of "involuntary idleness" or unemployment. While some responded to the labor unrest of the early 1890s with more conservative rhetoric and a desire to exert more control over the immigrant and African American working class, others who would later become prominent in Progressive reform began to reconsider their approach to pauperism, poverty and unemployment. As an intern at the New England Hospital in Boston, Alice Hamilton (who later became the founder of industrial medicine and an influential Progressive reformer) discovered the involuntary nature of "idleness" as she came into contact with many of the city's unemployed. In a letter home in January 1894 she noted her changing perception of men who were out of work, commenting, "We always used to feel that a family with an able-bodied man in it were poor only from laziness or drunkenness. . . . It is the greatest exception when I find a family whose father is doing steady work."[23]

In the early 1890s, charity reformer Amos Warner still believed that day laborers and "others of a similar class" had earned their low position in the "industrial scale" because of their own "sensuality," which was in marked contrast to the sexual self-control middle-class manhood demanded. Yet even Warner acknowledged the impact of unemployment on working-class life when he commented, "The weightiest charge which many contented and discontented vagabonds might bring against the modern industrial organization is that they have become what they are through the effect of involuntary idleness; for idleness, voluntary or involuntary, tends to produce a degeneration, physical, mental, and moral, which perpetuates the condition that begets it."[24]

Josephine Shaw Lowell had come to a similar realization by 1889, when she relinquished her position on the New York State Board of Charities to tackle the problem of class antagonism between labor and capital. In a letter explaining her decision she declared, "If the working people had all they ought to have, we should not have the paupers and the criminals. It is better to save them before they go under, than to spend your life fishing them out when they're half drowned and taking care of them afterwards!"[25] Although Lowell is best known as a founder of scientific charity, her shift from concern over pauperization to the material conditions of working-class life foreshadowed the transformation of nineteenth-century liberalism into early twentieth-century Progressive reform.

"Involuntary Idleness": The Labor Movement Weighs In

Like charity reformers, labor activists were also concerned with the distinction they perceived between the "workers" and the "idlers." Throughout the nineteenth century, republican political culture contrasted those honest laborers who produced the nation's wealth with those "idle rich" and "idle poor" who did no work themselves but fed off the wealth of others. Notions of masculinity, honor, and the dignity of labor were bound up in the labor movement's depiction of the skilled white male worker. Each issue of *The Trades*, a Philadelphia labor paper and the local organ of the Knights of Labor in the late 1870s, asserted:

> Whom do we call our heroes?
> To whom our praises sing?
> The pampered child of fortune,
> The titled lord or king?
>
> They live by others' labor.
> Take all, and nothing give;
> The noblest types of manhood,
> Are those who work to live.[26]

Although the Knights of Labor—the dominant voice of organized labor in the 1880s—valued women's non-waged domestic labor and organized housewives as well as male and female wage-earners, to a great extent members shared Victorian gendered definitions of labor and productivity. Work and economic autonomy were manly; dependence was the condition of women, children, paupers, and the undeserving rich.

In the depression of the 1870s, the chronic threat of unemployment undermined labor's sense of itself as a class of manly producers, and prompted labor leaders to reevaluate their previously harsh judgment of the idle poor. Labor leaders redefined their concept of "the people" to include not only the noble worker and his family, but also the unemployed. Working-class Americans began to make distinctions between those ne'er-do-wells who would rather loaf than work, and those whose idleness resulted more from the structure of the economy than from personal inclination.[27] The very term "involuntary idleness" popularized in this period by the labor movement was a pointed refutation of the belief that whether one worked or not could be reduced to a matter of will. Yet while "involuntary idleness" emphasized the unwilling nature of honest workers' unemployment, the term also served to reinforce labor's contempt for those who were allegedly out of work by their own volition. Paradoxically, this formulation of unemployment, which had the potential to broaden the composition and concerns of the labor movement, also served implicitly to reinforce the notion of class as a marker of morality and character put forth by advocates of scientific charity—and ostensibly repudiated by labor movement activists.

Even as labor leaders insisted on the structural origins of unemployment, late Victorian working men and their families could still experience unemployment as a personal problem that struck at the core of the gender identities of working men and the women they had pledged to support.[28] The provider role was critical to the maintenance of male authority in the family. In their own households, the authority of husbands and fathers was potentially challenged as women and children became breadwinners. Although the importance placed on the family wage paid to a male provider underscored the economic subordination of all working-class women, married women at a keen disadvantage in the labor market could also resent having to assume the burden of a family's financial support, especially if the wages they earned threatened the morale of an unemployed husband.

Most working-class wives appear to have shared their husbands' commitment to a family wage.[29] In Philadelphia, white native-born and immigrant working-class families routinely dealt with structural under- and unemployment and seasonal fluctuations in the availability of work by sending children into the labor force as secondary breadwinners. Responding to the dearth of light industrial opportunities for their children and the availability of domestic service positions for black women, African American families in Philadelphia typically sent mothers rather than children into the labor force as supplementary wage earners. In the context of chronic structural under- and unemployment and household economies that were dependent on various combinations of adult wage-earning, child labor, domestic labor, keeping boarders, doing piecework and outwork—and, in the worst of times or for the poorest of households, pawning, mutual aid, charitable assistance, and scavenging—the family wage that would enable an adult male breadwinner to provide for the entire family was a significant if frequently unrealized goal.

As they contested mainstream social welfare rhetoric, labor leaders criticized the expansive definition of "pauperism" relied on by charity reformers and the mainstream press and defended the virtue of the poor against attacks by those who argued that the poor were poor because they were unwilling to work. As labor leader William Sylvis declared, "Let it be remembered that a large proportion of these poor people, called "paupers" by newspapers and officials, are honest working men and women, the profit of whose toil goes to make up the fortunes—the millions—of the few whose costly equipage jostle the starving mechanic in the same street."[30] Articles in the labor press began to identify with the plight of those workers who were "involuntarily idle," in contrast with the "idle rich, who they declared "paupers upon the producers of wealth." In the Philadelphia *Tocsin*, a labor organ of the Knights of Labor in the mid-1880s, union printer and labor columnist Frank Waters contrasted the honest producer to the monopolist and inquired, "what did monopoly, or money alone, ever produce (excepting a legion of widows, orphans, felons, and paupers)?"[31]

Yet as labor activists argued over who fit into the category "pauper" they revealed an ambivalence toward the casual poor that betrayed their own anxiety about downward mobility. While they expanded the notion of the people to include the poor, at other times they held the dependent poor in as much contempt as they held the rich. Waters predicted in an article mockingly titled "Appropriate Philanthropy" that "At the judgment seat rich paupers and poor paupers will receive their just dues, for the only distinction there is between the two grades of pauperism—the poor ask for what they want, and the rich take it without asking."[32]

After the 1870s, the image of the unmanned tramp was juxtaposed with the celebration of the honest mechanic, as the labor press began to use the tramp to characterize the plight of the adult male worker. By virtue of his joblessness, the tramp was placed outside of all that the Gilded Age labor movement professed to hold dear: home, hearth, family, and the satisfaction of a job well done. Even his reputation as a law-abiding citizen was under attack, as vagrancy laws both newly enacted and newly enforced made it virtually a crime for the unemployed to take to the roads in pursuit of work.[33]

Labor advocates opposed vagrancy acts as a clear assault on the mobility of labor—as indeed, they were, like similar laws passed in the Reconstruction and post-Reconstruction South to control the mobility of recently freed African Americans.[34] For skilled artisans, geographic mobility had long been an accustomed way to regulate supply and demand and to learn about wages and working in other regions of the country. Workers recognized all too well that any attack on labor mobility made "a prisoner in his own city or town of every mechanic who should become needy" and undermined their ability to demand higher wages.[35] Vagrancy laws were "the first step to enable the employers of labor to say to a man 'You must take the wages we offer you; if you don't, we will discharge you, and if you dare to go away you will be arrested as a tramp and sent to prison to work there for 40 cents a day.'"[36]

Workers considered the state's willingness to jail tramps as another manifestation of its collusion with capital, on a par with the use of state and federal troops to suppress strikes and labor unrest. The labor press argued that capitalists, the charities, state legislatures and the courts colluded to force men into prisons to work as convict labor. In 1879 the *Trades* told its readers how "Capital wants every penitentory [sic] filled, then enlarged, then crowded with men turned into prison laborers to turn out from manufacturers, to drive honest labor down—down to death."[37] A year later the journal reiterated, "Ward charitable organizations, under the cloak of charity, are the claws of the capitalistic devil fish which draw disemployed labor into the net which leads to prisons. . . . Capital fills prisons with machinery, passes laws which make men criminals, use the courts as drag nets to draw them in, and then fill the markets with forty cents a day products of labor, which takes the bread out of the mouths of those who have escaped the drag net."[38]

Labor activists and journalists also objected to the vagrancy acts because they broke down distinctions between members of the working class and common criminals. Although "society . . . made the tramps," vagrancy acts put workers in jail with criminals, even though "nine-tenths of [the workers were] more honest than the thieving rascals who passed the law."[39] Labor leaders claimed that the lack of provisions for laborers seeking work led the unemployed to commit crimes, so that they might benefit from the food and shelter supplied free in state prisons. In January 1877, the Philadelphia *Public Ledger* noted a telling event: a homeless man who had been refused shelter at the police station house broke the window of a saloon at Crown and Race Streets to provoke arrest. Incidents such as this were not uncommon—that same year, 2,209 people committed themselves voluntarily to Philadelphia's House of Correction.[40] The assertion that upright citizens were forced to break the law so that they could receive in jails the care that they were denied in their own homes was simultaneously a forceful critique of the social welfare system and an appeal to both the middle-class conscience and the desire for law and order.

Countering the mainstream perception of "married vagabonds" as lazy men unwilling to provide for their families, the labor press charged that the below-subsistence level wages paid by capital to labor made it impossible for men to support their wives and children. Low wages and male unemployment forced women from the home and children from school to earn wages; in turn, the employment of women and children at lower wages than those paid to male workers and the substitution of child and female workers for male labor undercut the ability of workingmen to provide for their families.[41] Consequently, it was capitalist avarice rather than the irre-sponsibility of working-class men that was to blame for the destruction of working-class family life and the exploitation of women and children. Arguing that the employment of women and children to do men's work impeded the "further progress of civilization" and its characteristic strict differentiation by sex, John Kirchner, a radical German immigrant cigar-maker, insisted, "Where a man's labor exists he should be employed to do it, and not take the woman and the child and make the man a thief and a tramp."[42]

Labor leaders advocated a variety of strategies to solve the problem of male unemployment, ranging from the restriction of women and children from the labor force to the adoption of a "living wage" and the eight-hour day.[43] By the mid-1880s, the call for the eight-hour day had gained strength and momentum to become one of the chief demands which united orga-nized labor. Workers asserted that shorter hours would spread the work that was available among more wage-earners and would allow members of the working class more time in which to educate themselves for active citi-zenship. The eight-hour day was also promoted as a vital first step in the establishment of a cooperative commonwealth in which all would benefit equally from the fruits of their labor.[44] Finally, the eight-hour day was also recognized as a way to end the tramping problem and to reconstitute the working-class family around a male provider.

"Fallen Women": Prostitution and Woman's Right to (Refrain from) Labor

Just as the tramp represented the fears of scientific charity reformers and labor activists about labor and masculinity, so the prostitute symbolized doubts about the ability of working-class women to fulfill the ideals of true womanhood. If the tramping question revolved around competing depic-tions of working-class men, by the 1870s the prostitute had become the shadow image of laboring women. Charity reformers, woman's rights advocates, and male and female labor activists all claimed the right to repre-sent women, and to define the meaning of women's wage labor and its rela-tionship to virtue and prostitution. Late Victorian reformers drew on and expanded upon a rich preexisting set of popular images about fallen women and institutional practices for their reform, but transformed them to serve their own rhetorical ends.

From the mid-1830s when religious women in the rural and small towns of the Northeast first joined with evangelical Protestant ministers in their anti-prostitution crusade through the years of the Civil War and beyond, female moral reformers used the prostitute as a symbol of male exploitation of women.[45] Although they also emphasized the importance of women's low wages and poor working conditions as factors that heightened women's vulnerability, moral reformers' rhetoric of seduction and betrayal focused attention on the control of male behavior and the imposition of a single standard of sexual morality, rather than on the transformation of all women's social and economic circumstances.[46] Throughout the nineteenth century evangelical moral reformers ran rescue homes, hired missionaries to preach to prostitutes, opened supervised boarding homes for working women, and organized working girls' clubs and Travelers' Aid societies as protective measures for working women.[47] Moreover, the theoretical contribution of evangelical moral reformers—the gendered analysis of the origins of prostitution, with its central narrative of seduction and betrayal—was popularized through novels and by the philanthropic efforts of other reformers throughout the century.

As the true woman's inverse or fallen sister, the prostitute represented the sexual and economic vulnerability of all women. Throughout the nineteenth century, however, sexual immorality was also believed to be the province of working-class, African American, and immigrant women. Thus the prostitute also symbolized class and racial anxieties about working-class, immigrant, and African American unruliness and social disorder and the contrasting purity of middle-class white women.

Ideally, "true women" did not participate in the labor force but devoted themselves instead to cultivating a moral environment in which to nurture children. In theory, market activity threatened women's morality; exposure to the vicissitudes of wage-work threatened the definition of women as self-less moral agents rather than calculating economic ones. The true woman who performed private labors of love stood in marked contrast to the prostitute's public sexual knowledge and economic agency.

The elaboration of a code of middle-class manliness that highlighted manly independence and self-control was also central to the development of Victorian separate spheres and the ongoing process of class differentiation. While innate purity was a definitive womanly characteristic, even respectable Victorian men had to struggle heroically with their immoral desires for alcohol, sex, and other vices. This very willingness to struggle to

control their passions and conquer their own sinful natures rendered middle-class men manly. For men, the ability to control one's passions was central to both independence and the ability to exercise legitimate authority
over those in their care.[48]

The ideologies of "true womanhood" and the "self-made man" each
worked to mark differences between men and women as innate.[49] Yet this
construction of "natural" and "universal" male and female traits was
defined in opposition to working-class, ethnic, and racialized African American men and women, whose manliness and womanliness could never be
assumed but was always open to investigation.[50] Independence and purity
were racialized as well as gendered concepts in Victorian culture and were
central to the white working class's continual project of racial differentiation. Indeed, as historian David Roediger has suggested, in the antebellum
era white native-born and Irish immigrant male workers defined themselves as manly workers in opposition to dependent African Americans as
well as to women; Irish workers claimed the prerogatives of whiteness, even
as they fought against allegations that the Irish were a race apart, lazy, sensual, and simian.[51]

In the last third of the nineteenth century, the popularization of social
Darwinism, which attempted to apply evolutionary theory to social relations, provided new material with which to rework the importance of sexual difference and its relationship to race and class. As women's social status
came to be used as a measure for each society's position in the evolutionary
hierarchy, the presence of immigrant, working-class, and African American
women in the workforce began to be perceived as an indication of these
groups' lower rank in human society. Wage-working ethnic and racialized
women were believed to be "primitive" and morally suspect because of
their presence as economic agents in the labor force and also because of
their alleged licentiousness.[52] And if nonwhite, ethnic, and laboring women
were born to their lower position on the evolutionary scale, other women
reverted back to the more primitive state of savagery when they fell from
grace. For such women, womanhood was not innate, but had to be taught.

Despite the overrepresentation of women and children among the ranks
of the poor, late nineteenth-century mainstream social welfare reformers
viewed poverty chiefly as the problem of male paupers and vagrants.[53]
Hence they tended to highlight pauperism and vagrancy as their major concerns, and to treat prostitution and female poverty as the unfortunate side
effects of male pauperism. Thus the prostitute's plight served primarily as a

way for social theorists to discuss the aberrant phenomenon of women without natural—that is male—protection and control.

Nonetheless, because instituting domesticity was at the heart of attempts to create order in the homes of the poor, female charity workers, like evangelical moral reformers, also assumed the project of retraining working-class and immigrant women in womanly domesticity and "right living." In this sense, their definition of "unnatural" or "fallen" womanhood was more expansive than that of other reformers who focused on extramarital sexuality alone, and their efforts to reconstitute working-class families by means of male breadwinning and female housekeeping involved them in protracted contests over both the meaning of motherhood and its historically and class-specific practices.[54]

Even more than female charity reformers, it was woman's rights activists who transformed the discussion about prostitution. As the postwar woman's movement and Reform Darwinist challenges to the orthodox liberalism that fueled charity reform developed simultaneously, an influential group of reformers drew on both reform currents and the new social sciences to formulate a new approach to prostitution that incorporated aspects of each political outlook.

Woman's Rights Activists and Woman's Right to Labor

At mid-century, a small group of woman's rights activists who fused notions of women's special nature and their shared humanity with men had insisted on women's social and political equality and their right to higher wages for women's work.[55] Just as antebellum moral reformers gendered the language of virtue and vice, woman's rights activists formulated a gendered analysis of the economy. While earlier moral reformers had identified the conditions of women's work as one source of prostitution, they had highlighted cruel seducers rather than adverse social and economic structures; at mid-century and throughout the Gilded Age, woman's rights reformers expanded the focus on women's work as a primary cause of prostitution. These reformers developed a critique of women's limited training and ability to achieve economic independence if necessary, because of the dual labor market that confined women to "a few overcrowded avenues of labor " which paid below-subsistence level wages.[56]

As woman's rights advocates investigated the conditions of women's work, they began to demand "untrammeled access to all fields of labor" and higher wages for women's work. In *Woman's Right to Labor* (1860) Caroline Dall asserted that the low wages of women's work and the limited nature of women's employment compelled women to "vicious courses for their daily bread."[57]

Postwar efforts to aid wage-earning women also grew out of the developing movement for woman's rights. For woman's rights advocates, the prostitute served more generally as a symbol of women's economic dependence on men—dependence shared by middle-class women too, not only because of limited avenues for female wage-earning, but because of nineteenth-century legal codes that hindered married women's ability to control property and claim their own wages.[58]

A close reading of "The Case of Rose Haggerty, " in Helen Campbell's *Prisoners of Poverty* (1887), a book devoted to sketches of women workers, provides an opportunity to analyze the themes present in the social-scientifically informed woman's rights narrative of prostitution.[59] Campbell devoted one of the earliest chapters of *Prisoners of Poverty* to the subject of prostitution, thereby recognizing prostitution as an occupation and the prostitute as a woman worker. The story confronts the major question posed by reformers: can a working girl remain respectable, given women's poor position in the labor market?

In "The Case of Rose Haggerty" Campbell argues that prostitution is a consequence of the overcrowding of poorly trained women into a few overfilled, low-paid "women's" occupations. She establishes the problem of the woman worker as the problem of all women, for any woman is vulnerable to having to earn her own living or support children on her own and may be forced to choose between suicide, starvation, or the wages of sin. At the same time, Campbell's "case study" also paints a portrait of the chaos and disorganization she believed characterized the family life of the immigrant poor.

"The Case of Rose Haggerty" is the allegedly "true" story of a decent working-class girl, the eldest daughter born to kind but intemperate Irish immigrant parents. A longshoreman, Rose's father drinks from inclination when he is between jobs; her mother drinks from despair when there's no fire in the stove or food on the table to feed her numerous children. Plucky and optimistic, Rose refuses "to be killed by semi-starvation or foul smells, or dirt or any nature whatsoever." She also retains a purity of character, which serves to isolate Rose from her immoral surroundings, making her a worthy heroine with whom Campbell's middle-class readers can sympathize. When she is seven, her father puts Rose in charge of the family budget, telling her, "you look out an' get any money you'll find in me pockets, an' keep the children straight, an' all the saints'll see you through the job."[60] Picking the pockets of the male breadwinner so the money can be spent on food rather than alcohol is, of course, the job of the wife of a drinking man, but Rose's mother can't be trusted: Rose also learns to hide the family's clothing and furniture so her mother can't pawn them when she's on a drinking spree. After her parents die, Rose is forced to become father/provider as well as mother to her younger siblings. Lacking the skills to become either a domestic servant or do "family sewing" as a seamstress in a private home, Rose works briefly in a bag factory and then acquires a sewing machine so she can work at home while overseeing the children.

An orphaned daughter struggling to support a household of young children, Rose exemplifies the problems of both single daughters and widowed or deserted wives and mothers. Wages fall during an economic downturn that coincides with the bitter cold of winter: the hungry children huddle under a quilt, watching Rose as she stitches at her sewing machine. "Put the children in an asylum, and then you can marry Mike Rooney and be comfortable enough," well-wishers advise Rose, but she replies, "I've mothered 'em so far, and I'll see 'em through." If I can't do it by honest work, there's one way left that's sure, an' I'll try that." After being cheated by a male foreman who docks her wages because of a few skipped stitches, Rose turns to the river, contemplating suicide. Just at the point where she is faced with either starvation or suicide, Rose is saved—or lost.[61]

"'Easy now,'" a male voice says. "You're breakin' your heart for trouble, an' here I am in the nick o' time. Come with me an' you'll have no more of it, for my pocket's full to-night, an' that's more'n it'll be in the mornin' if you don't take me in tow." This request—pick my pocket and take me in tow—is one Rose has heard before, from her father. Rose takes the sailor's arm and walks away; Campbell tells the reader, "She took his money when morning came." Rose rationalizes "it might be dishonor, but it was certainly food and warmth for the children." The sailor offers to marry Rose, but she refuses, saying "No man alive'll ever marry me after this night." Unwilling to relinquish her economic independence to a drinking man, Rose chooses the "prosperous" trade "in which wages never fail." Relying on the inaccurate

Victorian reform convention that prostitutes die young, Campbell ends her narrative of Rose's fall with the following challenge to the reader. "It's not a long life we live," Rose says quietly. "My kind die early. . . . But let God Almighty judge who's to blame most—I that was driven, or them that drove me to the pass I'm in."[62]

Campbell both echoes and challenges conventional Victorian views of prostitution—for Rose is not a passive victim but "chooses" prostitution as the lesser of two evils—as she uses the story of Rose Haggerty's downfall to highlight the perils prostitution holds for all women. Thus the prostitute—a marginal outcast figure and the most extreme example of the "fallen woman"—also serves as a symbol of the economic vulnerability of all women in a wage economy.

Although woman's rights advocates viewed the problem of financial dependency as a vulnerability potentially shared by all women, Campbell's portrait of Rose Haggerty is also nativist and class-specific. Although she portrays Rose's father sympathetically, noting that his drinking binges often followed periods of involuntary unemployment, Campbell sees prostitution at least partially related to the moral inadequacy and inability of poor immigrant parents to support their children, thus linking prostitution to the discourses of tramping and child neglect.

Like other middle-class reformers, Campbell is fascinated by the working-class daughter's assumption of early responsibility and the role reversal in the Haggerty family. Rose ultimately turns to prostitution *as* a dutiful daughter, fulfilling her obligations to her parents' otherwise unprotected children. By the end of the story Rose has become a fallen woman because of her altruistic struggle to put other's needs before her own; she is simultaneously both pure and degraded, selfless and mercenary, the antithesis of true womanhood and its incarnation.

The perception that low wages drove women to prostitution bolstered the woman's rights case for equal wages and wider fields of work. At the same time it placed a great deal of the blame for prostitution on male employers and poor providers. Female virtue was pitted against the capitalist marketplace controlled by men. In their consideration of the position of women in the labor force, many female reformers came the closest they would to forming either a critique of capitalist social relations or an alliance with the labor movement.[63] In the last quarter of the nineteenth century, woman's rights advocates and labor leaders began to highlight the need for decent wages and protective associations for workingwomen; some even conceded that working women might organize their own trade unions.

"Capital Will Not Be Slow to Unsex Her"

Like evangelicals and woman's rights advocates, male labor reformers also portrayed virtuous widowed and single working-class women forced to choose between the cruel alternatives of prostitution, suicide, or starvation. Although their sentimental images of poor working women overlapped, woman's rights and labor analyses differed in emphasis. For woman's rights advocates the prostitute embodied the economic vulnerability of all women, rich and poor; their analysis highlighted gender but left class position fluid. In contrast, male labor reformers used the issue of prostitution rhetorically to address the potential victimization of the entire working class.

Although ostensibly about women's relationship to paid labor and the relationship of wage-earning to true womanhood, the treatment of prostitution in the labor press also highlighted concerns about threats to working-class manliness.[64] For male labor leaders, the image of the working girl seduced by an aristocratic rake or forced to sell her honor as a victim of monopoly also told a story of what happened when men were no longer able to protect, provide for, and control wives and daughters. Just as the tramp evoked the threat of danger to working-class manhood—and the waif underscored laboring people's inability to protect and control their children—so prostitution highlighted the inability of laboring men to provide for their families. The question of the respectability of paid work for women, then, had a great deal to do with anxieties about the masculinity of laboring men.[65]

Paternalistic images were used to demonstrate the need for a family wage that would allow men to support their wives and children, but they were also used to rally workingmen to the cause of the formation of women's unions in an era when many in the labor movement believed that women workers undercut male wages and should be removed from the labor force. A minority of male labor leaders, recognizing the pressing need to organize women workers, realized that their participation would strengthen the labor movement as a whole as much as it would protect women workers.

Foreshadowing the commitment of the Knights of Labor to the organization of women workers, in the 1860s William Sylvis advocated the protection of the rights of female labor out of "motives of humanity" as well as "policy." He told workingmen, "Rest assured, gentlemen, we cannot go forward without marching hand in hand with woman. If we leave her behind, capital will not be slow to unsex her, and place her in many of those channels of labor now occupied by us. She must have the same inducements, and derive equal benefit from the reform we are striving to accomplish, to make ourselves secure."[66]

The Philadelphia *Tocsin* turned the usual deployment of paternalistic images of passive women on its head in the 1880s, when it advocated female enfranchisement and organization as the best strategies for the protection of this "helpless class of much neglected sufferers." The union printer and labor columnist Frank Waters reminded male readers that the labor movement was a "family" organized to protect the daughters and sisters of the working class when he noted, "The prospective future of a daughter or a sister is as of much importance to a father or a brother as his own personal welfare. . . . Those working women who are now so justly complaining are somebodies [sic] daughters or sisters."[67] Waters assured his readers that no man would want his own daughter or sister to become a prostitute, yet "when we are no more, who can say that mine or yours will not be among the future victims of vicissitudes, and perhaps shame, that thousands of their sex are lamenting today." If women workers were the victims of economic and sexual exploitation, Waters reasoned, then the organization of women into labor unions was preventive rescue work.

Waters also attempted to expose connections between the wealthy employers who exploited female labor and then financed philanthropic ventures to rescue "fallen" women.[68] He argued that the organization of women workers would be more than simply a "valuable addition to the labor movement"; it would also "lessen in future the need of public and private expenditure for odious charities and reformatories, the occupants of which, by right, ought to be maintained exclusively by those who have been instrumental in making them paupers." Urging union men to assist women in forming labor unions, trade assemblies, and protective associations so that working-class women would not end up in reformatories, Waters proclaimed, "By guarding the interests of feminine operatives now you may be indirectly shielding among the rescued working girls of future posterity your own flesh and blood."[69]

Labor's True Women Defend Their Honor: Working Girls Toiling for
Duty and Love

If for male labor leaders the prostitute ultimately represented the erosion of
the position of the male worker, organized female workers realized that
they were implicated directly in discussions of the respectability of working
women. Despite the emphasis on the conditions of women's work rather
than the innate immorality of laboring women, in practice the belief that all
women workers were at risk (whether because of the conditions under
which they toiled or the very fact of economic agency) translated easily into
the expansive notion that the virtue of all working women was suspect.
Confronted simultaneously by the representation of the prostitute as the
most victimized of all wage-earning women *and* of the working woman as a
prostitute who earned easy money without toiling at all, late nineteenth-
century working women were forced to assert their integrity. In the Gilded
Age labor movement, wage-earning women claimed the right to speak for
themselves and challenged dominant middle-class, woman's rights, and
male labor movement representations of working women as potential prostitutes. Insisting that their labor "for duty and love" defined them as "true
women," Philadelphia's working women denied that work inevitably sullied women and robbed them of their respectability.

   Like the dominant Victorian culture, the late nineteenth-century labor
movement romanticized "hearth and home" and woman's role as "queen of
the household."[70] Indeed, the Knights of Labor valued the culture of domesticity so highly that they used it as the standard by which the "public"
world should be judged. As historian Susan Levine has argued, both men
and women in the Knights of Labor "used the language of domesticity to
criticize the competitive capitalist system that they saw encroaching on
workers' traditional rights, dignity, and comforts."[71] Drawing on the
rhetoric of Victorian domesticity, they demanded shorter hours, higher
wages, and an end to child labor. Although they treasured domesticity, the
KOL welcomed women into the world of labor reform as workers and as
supporters of the movement's vision and activities. Relying on a broad
definition of the "producing class" the KOL recognized women's unpaid
domestic labor as valuable and women as producers. In the 1880s, housewives joined domestic workers, servants, and housekeepers and organized
in local assemblies. Single, widowed, and married women were encouraged
to join the Knights of Labor as wage-earners, as the wives of laboring men,

as the mothers of future workers, and as the sisters of working women whose honor was jeopardized by low wages and harassment by employers.[72]

The Knights of Labor also wanted to "infuse the public world" with women's moral character.[73] As activists in the KOL, both housewives and wage-earning women asserted their strength and commitment to equal roles for women in the labor movement and the rest of society. At the same time, both men and women in the labor movement were unsure of the role that women, and particularly married women, would play in the labor force once the "good time coming" had arrived; they hoped that in the cooperative commonwealth married women would be able to refrain from wage labor. Indeed, although the official policies of the Knights of Labor welcomed women into the organization, some male members remained uncomfortable working and organizing alongside women.[74] The uneasiness of some Knights about women's participation in the labor force can be read as a simultaneous defense of male "rights" to a family wage, a full-time homemaker and the manliness accorded good providers, and married women's "right" to remain in the domestic sphere, however expanded to encompass a vibrant working-class social, cultural and political life. It also had much to do with the belief that wage work as then constituted exploited and potentially tarnished womanhood.

An examination of late nineteenth-century labor rhetoric reveals tensions within the labor movement over representations of working women and the extent to which working women were vulnerable to victimization by virtue of their very presence in the labor force. This is especially apparent when we contrast labor rhetoric produced by men and women workers. Because the national labor movement was internally divided over the desirability of women's wage work, labor rhetoric fashioned by women workers in the 1880s necessarily countered not only the dominant Victorian representation of working women as economic agents on the road to moral ruin, but also the paternalistic tendency in the male-dominated labor movement to represent women as victims in need of male protection. In the 1880s working women in the KOL formulated a distinctive view regarding the respectability of paid work for women.[75] Although it did not directly address the issue of prostitution, the women's labor discourse attacked the central theme inherent in discussions of prostitution: the respectability of paid work for women and the integrity of all working class women, whether they earned wages or not.

Rather than emphasizing the vulnerability and victimization of working women, as both woman's rights advocates and male labor reformers did, female labor movement activists in Philadelphia and elsewhere asserted that women could work for wages and still maintain their respectability. In 1885 at the height of the eight-month-long carpet weavers' strike in Kensington, the textile district of Philadelphia populated chiefly by Irish and German immigrants and their children, A. M. Sheridan composed the "Song of the Carpet Weavers."[76] Highlighting the insensitivity of those "ladies proud and fair" who thoughtlessly trod on the beautiful floral carpets woven by the strikers, Sheridan asked:

> How many ladies proud and fair,
> Will tread o'er our carpets woven with care?
> With never a thought for the pale working girl,
> Whose youth is blighted with weary toil.

Paralleling those male workers who asserted that their manliness was rooted in the dignity of labor, Sheridan emphasized the superiority of those female carpet weavers active in the Knights of Labor to the "ladies by fortune and fashion spoiled" and insisted that working women, rather than the fashionable ladies who stepped over the carpets they wove, were the "true women that God had designed." Sheridan asserted:

> Ladies by fortune and fashion spoiled,
> But not our superiors, nay, the world
> Holds not the one who is above
> The working girl toiling for duty and love.[77]

Unlike male craftworkers whose manliness was an integral aspect of the dignity of labor, however, Sheridan defined the womanly superiority of working women not so much by the skilled nature of their work than by the reasons they toiled: for duty and for love. Male workers who earned wages to provide for their families might also toil for duty and love; however, while manly men were good providers, masculinity at the workplace was linked to the performance of skilled labor.[78] In contrast, Sheridan rhetorically positioned women carpet weavers as dutiful family members, whose wage work was defined in moral rather than economic terms or in relation to skill. Thus, Sheridan's defense of working women's honor simultaneously challenged and relied on the dominant ideology of domesticity.

Gilded Age women labor activists recognized that those who depicted women's work outside the home as the slippery slope that led to prostitution refuted not only women's right to productive labor, but also subjected working women's moral reputation to calumny. They defended the morality of women workers and argued that although they might be harmed by dangerous working conditions, women were not inevitably degraded by wage labor.

While they welcomed male cooperation at the workplace and in their labor struggles, they valued women's collective action above male protection and paternalism. In the "Song of the Carpet Weaver" Sheridan asserted that working women were truer women than any others on earth. Yet by redefining the meaning of their work as a labor of love performed for family members, she underscored the dominant ideology of domesticity even as she transformed it. This understanding of young women's wage labor was congruent with the experiences of those female textile workers who lived in households where family members pooled economic resources; it evaded addressing the familial and economic circumstances of that minority of women workers, whether widowed, deserted, or never married, who lived outside of families and supported themselves independently or created households with other working women. The redefinition of women's work as a labor of love also, of course, ignored the considerable contention between parents and their wage-earning children over the allocation of finances within the family economy.[79]

Waifs: Child Destroyers, Child Redeemers

The presence of poor and neglected children on the streets of major cities was unmistakable in the 1870s. In Philadelphia, homeless women and children wandered the main thoroughfares, begging. Children peddled their wares outside the department stores of the city's new commercial district where fashionable women shopped. Organ grinders, juvenile musicians, sellers of crockery and cough drops, and hawkers of songs all crowded the streets of the Philadelphia downtown. Within easy walking distance of the city's center were the squalid slums which housed Philadelphia's "degraded classes." Here small messenger boys ran errands for the inmates of brothels, while young girls were hired to clean the rooms. Children played in the streets, where "little mothers" of seven and eight minded siblings a few years younger.

Children served as a particularly potent symbol of exploitation and of reformers' hopes for the future of the republic throughout the Gilded Age. Labor and charity and child protection reformers all drew upon the same cultural images of children as powerful agents of destruction as well as redemption. Labor reformers considered poor children "ripe for entry into the path of crime" because the evils of child labor in factories and parental overwork prevented fathers and mothers from properly supervising and educating their children.[80] For the upper-middle-class reformers of the Society to Protect Children from Cruelty, however, the potential of children for evil was already being realized on city streets, and the families that sheltered poor children were as much part of the problem as part of the solution. Many reformers viewed working-class parenting as only one step away from neglect.[81]

Child Protection: To Place a "Shield Between the Hard Hand, and Its Helpless Victim"

Drawing on the popular image of the child redeemer, child protection reformers argued that working-class children were crucial participants in the struggle to prevent the development of a permanent underclass that would pass poverty, dependence, and vice from one generation to the next.[82] In their view, child-saving—rescuing children from their "unnatural" parents as well as from the milieu in which they lived—was tantamount to saving the republic.

Mid-century reformers had first explored the possibilities inherent in child-saving when the influx of impoverished Irish and German immigrants in the 1840s and 1850s had evoked the alarming specter of an urban proletariat festering in the slums of the nation's Eastern seaboard. By the postwar years, the visibility of urban poverty, coupled with widespread labor unrest, prompted reformers to renew their efforts to reform working-class family life.

Of course, poverty is not synonymous with cruelty and child neglect. To talk about "cruelty to children" is at the same time to define a norm of appropriate parenting. Among prosperous Americans, patterns of childrearing had changed significantly over the course of the nineteenth century. Most Americans no longer believed that children were miniature adults whose wills had to be broken. In the first half of the nineteenth century, the

sentimentalization of Calvinism and the influence of romanticism each contributed to the perception of childhood as a time of innocence, while the
belief in republican motherhood newly highlighted the significance of the
mother's role in childrearing. Maternal love and the need for children to
internalize values replaced the earlier emphasis on the submission to
parental authority and the use of corporal punishment.

Moreover, as self-restraint became central to evangelical Protestant constructions of manhood, it became unmanly for a father or a husband to give
way to his passions and beat his wife or children. Although even the SPCC
made distinctions between excessive beating and corporal punishment that
was warranted and applied "with no undue severity," ideally parents as
well as children were to internalize and practice self-control.[83]

Child welfare reformers who scrutinized the family life of the poor did so
in relation to new attitudes toward children and an intensified concern with
the social problems of the city. Childsavers were concerned with specific
incidents of violence, but they also expanded the concept of cruelty to
include the issue of child neglect, which encompassed the moral as well as
physical environment in which children were reared.

In the 1870s, reformers across the nation created organizations similar to
the Children's Aid Society, founded in New York City in the 1850s, and the
Pennsylvania Society to Protect Children from Cruelty (SPCC). Members of
Philadelphia's reform community had already organized orphanages and
institutions for dependent children, but no such organization had dared
intervene in the private arena of family relations or judge parental treatment
of children. As the SPCC Annual Reports noted, "It has been reserved very
much to this organization, as a specialty, to step in and place a 'shield
between the hard hand, and its helpless victim,' and put the offender, when
the circumstances warrant such a procedure, within the custody of the
proper officers of the law."[84]

Child welfare reformers argued that child welfare work was not only
humanitarian, but also politically expedient and economically efficient.
Charles Loring Brace summed up the mainstream reform outlook succinctly
when he told readers of his classic childsaving manifesto, *The Dangerous
Classes of New York and Twenty Years of Work Among Them* (1872), "The
cheapest and most efficacious way of dealing with the 'dangerous class' of
large cities, is not to punish them, but to prevent their growth. . . . The class
of a large city most dangerous to its property, its morals and its political life,
are the ignorant, destitute, untrained and abandoned youth: the outcast

street children grown up to be voters, to be the implements of demagogues, the 'feeders' of the criminals, and the sources of domestic outbreaks and violations of law."[85]

As child welfare reformers grew familiar with the living conditions of working-class families, they were forced to confront the dramatic contrast in the nature of childhood for middle-class children and children of the laboring poor. In the last decades of the nineteenth century, the period of semidependency between childhood and adulthood—later to be dubbed adolescence—was lengthening for those children of middle-class backgrounds whose families could afford to prolong their period of schooling before work or marriage. Working-class children, in contrast, were expected to contribute to the family economy by the time they entered their early teens. And children of extremely destitute families contributed cash and goods as soon as they were old enough to hawk newspapers, peddle oranges, and scour the railroad tracks and the streets for coal or chips for fuel.[86]

The obvious contrast in the experience of childhood for working- and middle-class children might have enabled reformers to conceptualize childhood as a social as much as a natural category. Child welfare reformers, however, were more likely to focus on the "unnatural" behavior of parents who encouraged a precocious independence in their offspring. The belief that parents and children had reversed roles in working-class families and the related perception that parents were neglecting their responsibilities toward their children was a dominant refrain in reform tracts and novels.

For childsavers, the issues of child labor and child neglect fused in their consideration of children's participation in the "street trades"—any income that could be gained in the street, from sweeping sidewalks, blackening boots, and running errands, to the hawking of produce, flowers, newspapers or other items, to the performance of acrobatic stunts or musical acts. In Philadelphia, the SPCC devoted a major portion of its resources to the suppression of the street trades. Addressing readers of its first Annual Report, the SPCC explained:

An important part of our work consists in pressing upon a portion of the community (who seem to have very inadequate and erroneous views of the parental relation), the real needs and positive rights of little children. It has been appalling, at times, to notice with what cruel indifference some parents will permit their very young children to wander, half-clothed, through the streets, begging or stealing. At night they find their way home; if successful upon their foraging expedition, they are suffered to share in what they have brought in; if not, they are often driven, with threats and curses, again into the streets, to remain until a late hour of the night.[87]

The belief that the street trades served as a conduit to channel boys into thievery and girls into prostitution was widespread among reformers. SPCC reformers noted, "The experience of the Society and the records of the courts show that children employed to beg and peddle on the street invariably end by stealing; the girls soon become prostitutes, and the boys professional thieves." And in 1880, the SPCC reported that they had collaborated with the Philadelphia police in the arrest of seven girls between the ages of nine and fifteen, who "infest the neighborhood of Second and Walnut Streets." The girls were accused of corrupting the "public morals . . . under the guise of selling matches and oranges"; they were all sent to the House of Refuge.[88]

Child welfare reformers opposed to children's participation in the street trades were disturbed by the failure of working-class parents to protect their vulnerable children from the lure of the street. But they were most perturbed by what they perceived of as the willingness of working-class parents to actually exploit their children in order to gain money. In its most extreme form, this view underlay the controversy in the 1880s over child life insurance, when opponents of life insurance for infants and children suggested that working-class parents might actually be tempted to let their sick children die in order to collect the burial insurance.[89] To their credit, although the Pennsylvania SPCC agreed to help other reformers convinced of the need to investigate children's burial insurance, like the Philadelphia Society to Organize Charity they stressed that most working-class parents loved their children too much to kill them for money. Like most child welfare reformers they felt that the need to prevent greedy parents from profiting from their children's labor rather than their death was a far more compelling concern.

This interpretation of children's begging, peddling, and scavenging fit neatly into prevalent beliefs about pauperism. Reminding its donors not to encourage child peddlers, the SPCC reported that investigations revealed that "in nearly every case" the parents of young street traders were "sufficiently able-bodied and strong, to secure for themselves and [their] children a living without depending on the mendicancy of their little ones." Moreover, they concluded, the only result from this mendicancy which

"Fortunes of a Street Waif, Stage One," from Charles L. Brace, *The Dangerous Classes of New York, and Twenty Years' Work Among Them* (1872). Like childsavers across the nation, reformers active in the Pennsylvania SPCC believed that children's work and play in the streets ultimately led boys into thievery and girls into prostitution.

"Fortunes of a Street Waif, Stage Two."

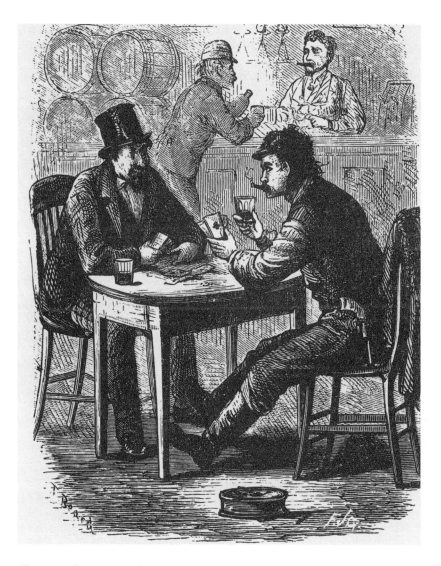

"Fortunes of a Street Waif, Stage Three."

"Fortunes of a Street Waif, Stage Four."

part of its campaign to convince parents that young children were people with rights—including the right to parental financial support—and not parental property.

The SPCC also favored child labor legislation that would regulate the employment of children in industrial manufacturing.[92] In 1885 a tour of Pennsylvania's mining districts convinced the SPCC to advocate stricter laws that would "extend to all manufacturing industries in which young children are employed."[93] They also supported the appointment of inspectors "to ferret out the willful violations of this humane law." Although the SPCC declared that children were at the mercy of both "heartless parents" and "rapacious employers," the society blamed the "insatiable longing of parents" for their children's earnings for rendering the existing child labor laws a "practical nullity."[94] Overall, the SPCC was more effective and far more widely recognized for its efforts to suppress children's participation in the street trades rather than child labor in Philadelphia's factories.[95]

The SPCC's commitment to the right of labor and capital to contract freely also limited its investigation into the alleged misdeeds of Philadelphia's employers. A complaint against Wanamaker's Department Store on behalf of its female workers highlights the ambiguity and the ultimate limitations of the SPCC stance against child labor. In July 1880, an anonymous letter writer who claimed to be an employee appealed to the society to stop the "refined torture" meted out to employees at Wanamaker's Department Store, where female employees were working "with thermometer ranging from 100–110 degrees." The SPCC refused to comply with this request. Case records noted "as those employed in this establishment are paid for services rendered, optional for them to remain, and at perfect liberty to leave at anytime. The Sec. [Secretary] decided that it was not a case properly coming under the care of this Society.[96]

Child Laborers: Exploited by Parents or Employers?

Like the issue of child neglect, the issue of child labor might have united labor leaders and child welfare reformers, since both groups condemned the need for children to work "in mills and factories at a premature age."[97] In Philadelphia in the 1890s, organized labor joined with reformers from organizations such as the SPCC, the Women's Christian Temperance Union, the Charity Organization Society, and the Public Education Association in support of protective labor legislation for children.[98]

If child welfare and labor reform opposition to child labor was mutual, however, their analyses of the phenomenon and their focus on different forms of child labor betrayed a striking difference that was at the heart of the labor question itself. The disagreement over the way to regulate child labor paralleled the debate over the distinctive definitions of labor and property that were formulated by orthodox liberal economic theorists and labor leaders in the 1870s and 1880s. Liberal economic theorists saw labor as a commodity that was bought and sold in the market according to the "natural" economic laws of supply and demand; they held that the only property involved in manufacturing was the capital invested by the owner and that workers' "ownership" of their labor did not translate into worker control of the manufacturing process. The liberal definitions of property and labor made it easier to justify the exclusion of workers' demands for control over the conditions of work and other aspects of production.

In contrast, labor theorists had traditionally seen labor as a form of inalienable property owned by the worker that should not be commodified. Labor leaders had asserted that labor was a form of property that only the wage-earner had the right to control, and had argued that capitalists who believed that labor was a commodity to be bought and sold like any other dehumanized their workers and so turned them into "slaves." By the 1870s, many labor movement leaders reluctantly accepted the idea of labor as a commodity, as long as there was "a clear delineation between that part of the workman's day which might be purchased for wages and that which remained inalienably his own."[99] It was this attempt to insist on "eight hours for work, eight hours for rest, and eight hours for what we will" that formed the backbone of the labor movement's critique of "wage-slavery" and its commitment to the eight-hour movement.

As they criticized the conditions in which children labored, reformers of both perspectives likened children either to a form of neglected parental property or to exploited commodities. Child welfare and charity reformers argued that ruthless parents treated their children like property; they forced their own children into factories and onto the streets while they remained home at leisure. Although many in the Philadelphia labor movement were opposed to both the fact of child labor and the exploitative conditions under which children toiled, working-class parents commonly considered children's labor and wages to be the property of their parents and relied on the necessary income children's labor provided. Many parents opposed protective labor legislation for children precisely because they were dependent on children's wages. Even those labor activists who supported protective labor legislation might nonetheless believe the wages a son or daughter earned in the mills or at domestic service belonged to their parents. Hence their critiques of child labor highlighted greedy employers rather than selfish parents.

Like child welfare reformers, labor leaders emphasized the need for working-class children to receive a proper education; they too pointed to the dire social consequences of child neglect. They focused, however, on the social conditions that led to "involuntary child neglect" rather than on the immorality and greediness of poor parents. Labor activists never failed to situate their discussions of child neglect within the context of the movement for the shorter working day. When they advocated shorter hours, one of the primary themes they returned to was the male worker's need for more time to devote to the upbringing of his children. When the Blair Committee of the United States Senate convened in 1883 to hear testimony on the relation of capital to labor, individuals and a wide variety of reform groups emphasized the impact of overwork and long hours on working-class family life. Excerpts from a letter read aloud at the hearings capture organized labor's appeal:

That the laborers of the country are dissatisfied, unhappy, and discontented must be apparent to all from the frequent strikes, the labor organizations, and constant agitation that is going on in relation to their interests. . . . My belief is that . . . they are overworked and underpaid. . . . This overtaxing of the physical powers of the mother at home and the father at his daily toil is apt to lay one or both into early graves, filling our orphan and half-orphan asylums with children whose parents have literally been worked to death.[100]

Labor leader William Sylvis had used the same reasoning over a decade earlier when he noted that men forced to work ten hours could "scarcely obtain a sight" of their children except on the Sabbath. Even more unfortunate were those families in which the mother too was "compelled to toil at some occupation independent of household duties." Deprived of protection and guidance from their hardworking parents, children in these households were "left to the evil associations and surroundings which train them in habits of vice and crime." Sylvis reiterated the cost of a ten-hour working day for the entire society when he reflected, "Could the inmates of the houses of refuge, houses of correction, and other institutions for the punishment of youthful offenders speak, they might trace their wanderings from the path of rectitude to involuntary neglect."[101]

Labor leaders claimed that capitalist avarice subverted natural family relations and "condemned children yet unborn to the brothel and the penitentiary."[102] Thus it was not working-class behavior but the relation of capital to labor that was in profound opposition to natural law. In the mid-1880s the *Tocsin* criticized the stewards of wealth who bequeathed on their deathbed "a remnant of the millions you have ground out of the half-starved families of your down-trodden workmen to the overpaid officials of certain charitable officials" and argued that labor activism rather than upper-class philanthropy was necessary to overturn the existing state of affairs.

A little more than a year after the *Tocsin* appealed to working men to rescue their sisters and daughters from low wages before they became the objects of rescue missions among the city's prostitutes, it charged "The Cruelty"—as the SPCC was often called—with "wanton neglect" of the city's child laborers.[103] In September 1886 the *Tocsin* claimed that Philadelphia's employers violated the state's labor laws with impunity. A manufacturer caught employing children in his mill risked only a nominal fifty dollar fine and the unlikely possibility of a prison sentence. Chiding the "working men of the commonwealth" for not fighting more forcefully for a tougher child labor law, the *Tocsin* reminded them that the SPCC could not be counted on to defend the interests of their children.

The inadequacy of child labor law and the apparent unwillingness of the SPCC to confront local employers directly became clear to the *Tocsin* when a young girl, Lizzie de Paul, was killed at work in Smyth's mill in 1886. The *Tocsin* noted, "When the Central Labor Union of this City undertook the prosecution of the owner of the mill at 19th and Pine Sts., the Committee waited upon the officers of the Society and solicited their co-operation in the suit, but to this day, although over a year has elapsed, not one word of encouragement has been received."[104] Although Smyth had been held for Court by the Magistrate, no action had been taken in the case. Terming the "so-called society" "not much better than a fraud," the *Tocsin* urged the SPCC "to join in the agitation for a more stringent law and heavier penalty for its violation" and pointed to the "exclusiveness" of the SPCC to explain the organization's "wanton neglect."[105] Noting that the SPCC's existence depended heavily on the financial contributions of many of Philadelphia's wealthy and charitably disposed citizens, the *Tocsin* proposed that the Society's financial dependence made political independence unlikely and hindered its ability to deal impartially and effectively with the problem of child labor. With one blow the *Tocsin* parodied both the SPCC's efforts to protect working-class children by investigating their families instead of their employers and the traditional republican fear that workers' financial dependence rendered them incapable of effective citizenship and independent political thought.[106]

Creating the Normative Family

To a great extent, mainstream social welfare reformers and labor activists shared a similar view of what the working-class family should be like, even as they used those norms to authorize very different political and social agendas. Through the process of problematizing the working-class family, then, both mainstream social welfare and oppositional labor reformers ultimately established the normative working-class family. The meaning of this norm was dependent nonetheless on the political context in which it was articulated: in labor rhetoric, the idealized family was used as the basis to launch a critique of capitalist social relations, while in social welfare rhetoric the family was to be the foundation of them. Yet the effect of both competing political discourses was to create a naturalized familial norm, even as they each chronicled its perilous instability.

Simultaneously, social welfare and labor reformers repudiated the notion of a coherent family life among the most destitute of the laboring poor: their portrait of men as (potential) tramps, women as (potential) prostitutes, and children as waifs testified not only to the reformers' own inability to recognize the kin and other social relations of the poor as constituting viable family life, but to their belief in the instability—even the impossibility—of family life among the "degraded" poor. Because tramps, prostitutes, and street children were all defined by their exclusion from family life, the discourses on tramping, prostitution, and street children all worked to establish the argument that for the most "degraded" of Philadelphians, family life was nonexistent.

Charity, child protection, and labor reformers competed for the authority to represent the laboring poor, to establish the content and meaning of working-class family norms and any departure from them. Each group also relied on a paternalistic familial metaphor to justify its claim to represent the victimized and/or threatening casual poor. Child welfare and charity reformers worked to expand the state's authority over individual families, by elaborating and relying on the practice of *parens patriae*, which justified state intervention in cases where parental involvement or care was deemed harmful or inadequate. Labor leaders' claim to represent the entire "family of labor" worked to create the illusion of an identity of interests within working-class families and among the working class as a whole. This hid the extent to which African Americans, southern and eastern European and Asian immigrants, women, the unskilled and the very poor, were typically marginalized or even misrepresented in labor reform discourse and in the American labor movement in the late nineteenth century.

As labor activists created an oppositional political culture, they skillfully mobilized dominant discourses in subversive ways: they demanded that Americans recognize who were the true paupers and unmanly dependents, the genuine child exploiters, the actual seducers of honest working women. Yet because it was founded on a repudiation of the "dangerous class, " even the oppositional discourse of the labor movement marginalized the "roughest" of the laboring poor.

Despite its claims to represent the entire working class and the laboring poor, the white male labor movement did not speak for the entire "family of labor." In the last decades of the nineteenth century, labor activists took a variety of stances regarding the role of the unemployed, women, African Americans, convicts, and Southern and Eastern European and Chinese immigrants in relation to the labor movement. Their images of prostitutes, street children, and tramps offered a powerful critique of American social relations, yet also revealed a significant ambivalence toward the role of women, the unskilled, and the unemployed in the labor movement. In the 1870s, the rhetorical defense of prostitutes and tramps became part of the political culture of labor journalists and trade unionists. Yet their uneasiness led labor leaders to differentiate "honest workers" from these members of the "degraded poor" even as they defended them as victims of exploitation and unemployment. Labor's negative identification with the victims of monopoly embodied two conflicting impulses: the desire to reclaim the republican legacy rightfully left to all of the members of the disinherited working class, and the determination to resist incorporation into the "residuum" of petty criminals, unmanly dependents, prostitutes, and street children who represented the death of the republic. This ambivalence toward a variety of groups—the unskilled, women workers, African Americans, immigrants from countries outside Western Europe, prostitutes, the unemployed—shaped the boundaries of the national labor movement and the issues it addressed, as well as the texture of social relations in working-class neighborhoods where roughness and respectability were acted out.

Respectability—and the defense of a particular idealized vision of the family—was an important organizing principle of the late Victorian labor movement, but it was nonetheless divisive. If gender and family issues caused tension between mainstream social welfare reformers and labor activists, they were also contested within the city's heterogeneous working class.

Chapter 2

Informing the "Cruelty"

Laboring Communities and Reform
Intervention

IN JANUARY 1877, Philadelphians turned their attention to the dramatic murder trial of Morris Springfield.[1] Although Springfield had been charged with murdering his sister, he had reason to expect sympathetic treatment from the city's residents, the press, and the judge. Alice had been a known prostitute; she had escaped while serving a second term in the House of Correction. While her death had been violent, Victorian Philadelphians were not surprised when fallen women came to no good end. On the other hand, her brother Morris was known as a kind and industrious workingman who was good to his mother, had had a "tender regard" for his sister, and had been allegedly undone by the failure of his repeated efforts to redeem her.

Throughout the trial, the defense employed such vivid and contrasting images of the dissolute prostitute and the respectable workingman that the murder victim almost seemed to be posthumously on trial for destroying her brother. Alice had left home about six years earlier to lead an "improper life" and had resisted all efforts by her brothers and sister to save her. Magistrate McClintock testified that on two occasions when Alice had appeared dirty, homeless, and under the influence of liquor he had committed her to the House of Correction for vagrancy. Her brother Morris had also had Alice committed to the House of Correction "not for punishment, but for reformation" but to no avail. A Springfield sister and her husband had taken Alice to the country in hopes of redeeming her, but Alice had "soon wearied of country life and returned to the city." After her return, Alice "looked so bad" that her sister no longer cared to acknowledge her as a relative. Her brother Thomas had found Alice living in a "low" house at Eighth and St. Mary Streets "frequented by colored men" and had informed her that Morris would pay her board in the House of the Good Shepherd, a Catholic reform institution for young women. When Alice refused this offer, Thomas had threatened her with another stint in the House of Correction.

Undaunted, "she replied that she had been there before and had escaped without any trouble, and that the place could not hold her."[2]

In assigning cultural meaning to Alice's murder, the defense attorney crafted a tale meant to save his client based on the premise that the defense of respectability could explain—if not justify—the murder of a sister-turned-prostitute. Respectability was both a family and a neighborhood responsibility.[3] Alice's notorious behavior had caused the entire Springfield family "grief, anxiety, and shame." Morris Springfield had been particularly disturbed by the taunts and jeers of neighbors, who had hooted at him in the streets to express their public disapproval of his sister's occupation. Indeed, the defense attorney insisted that Alice's misconduct had so under-mined his client's constitution that Morris "no longer knew what he was doing" the night he murdered his sister.[4]

The presentation of the case in the press and in court reveals how the images in political discourse and popular culture of the industrious work-ingman and the prostitute resonated in the city's laboring families and neighborhoods and were central to the self-representations of working-class people. As they testified, witnesses depicted Alice and her brother Morris in terms of categories embedded in the social experiences of daily life in work-ing-class neighborhoods. Such categories were also part of a broader effort by reformers and reputable working-class Philadelphians to create and fix social distinctions between members of the city's poorer classes that nonetheless remained dynamic and potentially unstable.

Victorian culture contained several related yet distinct standards of deco-rum for working-class men, women, and children: that voiced by Philadel-phia's charity reformers, who claimed to differentiate between the worthy and unworthy poor but whose belief in class as a moral marker made all of the poor potentially suspect; and the multiple and competing standards of residents of the city's working class communities. Gilded Age working-class respectability drew on aspects of republicanism, religious values favoring temperance, hard work, and sexual propriety, and an ongoing dia-logue with middle-class standards of domesticity, manliness, and womanly decorum. Like charity reformers, laboring people based social distinctions in working-class communities on attitudes toward drink, work, sexuality, domestic violence, and brawling. For the latter, however, financial success was not always a critical ingredient of respectability, nor a marker of moral character. Working-class people elaborated notions of "respectability" and "roughness" in terms of domestic and neighborhood concerns as well as workplace issues of skill and occupation; respectability evolved more from a repudiation of both the "idle rich" and the "degraded poor" rather than an attempt to imitate middle-class behavior.[5]

For white male workers in the late nineteenth-century labor movement, respectability was also part of a politicized construction of domesticity and of white working-class manhood.[6] Historians have begun to discuss the extent to which white workers coded "manliness" as white in the nineteenth century, but have yet to explore ways in which racialized notions of manliness and respectability variously created or transcended distinctions between white and African American laboring men and male workers of different ethnic backgrounds. With the exception of several labor associations composed entirely of African Americans, Philadelphia's trade unions generally excluded blacks from membership.[7] It is likely that, for the minority of African American laboring men able to secure relatively desirable positions on the railroads or in other skilled sectors of the labor force, respectability was synonymous with black working-class manhood.

If class conflict inflected white working-class domesticity with what Michael Denning has called "class accents" or class-specific meanings, in post-Reconstruction African American communities these class distinctions were complicated by racial politics as well. For aspiring members of the emergent black middle class, respectability was self-consciously at the heart of racial "uplift" and was perceived by its adherents as a significant emancipatory discourse. To achieve "the dual goals of racial self-help and respect from white America" late nineteenth-century African American middle-class men and women advocated temperance, hard work, piety, and sexual purity.[8] While the politics of respectability revealed class tensions between middle-class blacks and the laboring poor, it also signified differences of social status within the black working class itself, among whom as an ideology of racial pride and self-help it had many adherents.

Elaborated in very different contexts, then, working- and middle-class African American and white respectability carried distinctive cultural and political meanings, despite the apparent similarity in values. White working-class respectability was a dialogue between the white middle and working classes and within the working class as well as within individuals; for both whites and African Americans, working-class respectability was also part of a dialogue about the meanings of whiteness and blackness.[9]

In contrast to their respectable neighbors, rougher white and African American Philadelphians drew on the rowdier aspects of working-class culture which were increasingly repudiated by members of their own class over the course of the nineteenth century. In rougher neighborhoods, men and women alike drank and caroused on street corners and in grog shops and brothels. They gambled in policy houses and openly "ran the growler," as the custom of buying kettles of beer from local groceries or taverns was called. These Philadelphians tended to labor intermittently, and their work frequently tied into local networks of commercial vice.

The city's neighborhoods offered a parallel arena to the labor movement where those who could not distinguish themselves from the "degraded poor" by virtue of their craft autonomy could exercise another, different set of status distinctions.[10] Although it is not clear to what extent notions of respectability varied across ethnicities, native whites and African Americans and Irish, German, Jewish, and Italian immigrants all monitored the boundaries of approved and illicit behavior within their communities. Roughness and respectability, then, could divide men and women within each racial and ethnic group, even while the defense of respectability united men and women of diverse ethnic and religious backgrounds in the organized labor movement.

Even while the columns of the city's labor press were featuring prostitutes, beggars, and tramps as the unfortunate victims of monopoly, the rhetorical identification of the labor movement with the "rough" working class was probably accompanied by sharpening distinctions of respectability within working-class neighborhoods. It is doubtful that the labor movement's political analysis of the plight of the "rough" casual poor extended into actual neighborhood relations. The labor movement appealed to those Philadelphia workers who perceived working-class organization into trade unions as one way to avoid the descent into the ranks of the casual poor and petty criminal class.

Moreover, for some family and community members, recourse to reform intervention became part of the process of making these distinctions. In Philadelphia neighborhoods, laboring men and women negotiated—in both senses of the word—competing discourses of manhood, womanhood, and childhood through their recourse to, collaboration with, and repudiation of reform intervention. Reform intervention in laboring class neighborhoods can be understood as a set of practices through which the cultural categories of roughness and respectability and the social identities of both working-class residents and SPCC reformers were variously created, transformed, or reaffirmed.

The distinction between "public" and "private" conduct was blurred in Philadelphia's neighborhoods where residents were as committed to the

supervision of others' conduct as were moral reformers. Reform intervention relied on the complicity of a segment of the working class in the shared
policing of transgressions. Although reformers from the Society to Protect
Children from Cruelty worked closely with the police and magistrate
courts, they relied on the local community for evidence in their investigations.

In close-knit urban neighborhoods the correction of unruly children, abusive husbands, and neglectful mothers was considered a collective responsibility. Working-class family life was not marked by the intense privacy
which characterized Victorian middle-class domesticity. In Gilded Age
working-class communities, women were the moral guardians of the street
as well as the home.[11] Female neighborhood networks were central in
enforcing what one historian has termed a "domestically based neighborhood justice."[12] Neighbors used observation, gossip, threats to "inform the
Cruelty," and actual appeals to the SPCC to define proper family roles, set
standards of family and community behavior, establish their own
respectability, and elaborate social distinctions within the city's working
class.

Although many working-class men and women initiated complaints and
appeals to the SPCC, or else testified on behalf of neighbors under investigation, others who scorned the mores of the respectable working-class community and the dominant culture alike thwarted the agents' investigations
and repudiated their attempt to stake a claim in the elaboration of working-
class social norms. In rough neighborhoods, women's networks protected
friends, neighbors, and family members from the visits of the police and the
SPCC.

The varied responses of the city's residents to the presence of the SPCC
agents and the controversy surrounding the intervention of the SPCC in
working-class neighborhoods point to clear social divisions in Philadelphi-
a's working-class communities. The SPCC was simultaneously perceived as
a resource for troubled families and an organization inextricably bound up
with the police, magistrate courts, and the state. When agents intervened
without an invitation, family members could express fear, resentment,
indignation, and fierce dislike. Still other Philadelphians brought false
charges against relatives, tenants, debtors, or other enemies, well aware of
the power of an SPCC investigation to wreak havoc on a family's reputation
and destroy access to a grocer's or landlord's credit.

Cultural and social distinctions in working-class communities, then, were continually reworked as Philadelphians variously aided investigators, sought out reform intervention, or repudiated the activities of SPCC agents. Reform intervention was complicated and varied, with multiple consequences and meanings in laboring neighborhoods. As they worked with the SPCC, or alternately, by their collective efforts to thwart SPCC agents' investigations, both respectable and rough laboring Philadelphians created alternative discourses of "the family" and expressed complicated, tenuous relationships with the authority and resources of the state and quasi-public social service agencies.

Working-Class Neighborhoods in the "City of Homes"

Throughout the nineteenth century, the movement of native-born whites from rural to urban areas, the migration north by freed people and their children, and successive waves of European immigration continually transformed the city's neighborhoods. In contrast to New York with its scarce land and many-storied tenements, Philadelphia expanded horizontally. In the 1880s prosperous Episcopalian, Presbyterian, and Quaker Philadelphians began to leave the Society Hill area for the fashionable homes of Rittenhouse Square, or for comfortable large houses in the northern and western suburbs that were now within easy reach thanks to the expansion of the Pennsylvania Railroad lines.[13] As impoverished Russian Jewish immigrants settled in the neighborhood around South and Fourth Streets, more prosperous German Jewish families began to move into the area north of Market Street. Other middle-class residents moved into the homes vacated by the wealthy or built smaller houses in the northern and western sections of the city. And Philadelphia's Protestant and Catholic working class lived in the small row houses which lined the narrow streets of the city, in block after block of brick and stone.

Late nineteenth-century Philadelphia was known as the "City of Homes" because of the high rate of homeownership achieved by its residents.[14] Although Philadelphia did not have a tenement house problem comparable to that of New York, the city's pattern of development bred its own housing problems. Behind the neat rows of houses that made Philadelphia famous, the city's poor lived in back-alley shacks, decrepit buildings originally built as one-family houses that now housed several families, and one-room shanties in the older sections of the city. Built on subdivided lots and back yards, these houses remained invisible from the street.[15]

Kater Street. Photograph courtesy of Urban Archives, Temple University, Philadelphia. In the 1880s and 1890s, Italian and Russian Jewish immigrants resided in the eastern districts of the city that were bordered by the Delaware River.

Late nineteenth-century Philadelphia neighborhoods were characterized by ethnic diversity rather than by the differentiation and racial segregation that defined twentieth-century American cities. Certainly particular ethnic groups concentrated in certain parts of the city. For instance, many Philadelphians of German background lived in the northeast section of the city, and by 1880, skilled Irish immigrants and their descendants began to dominate southwest Philadelphia. Most of the city's neighborhoods, however, were shaped more by distinctive economic bases than by ethnicity.[16] Because of the need to live within close proximity to work, neighbors were more likely to share the same industrial affiliation than the same ethnic background. Although ethnic enclaves could develop when members of the same ethnic group worked in industries located in the same area of the city, for the most part immigrant groups did not live in "ethnic ghettos."

In contrast, race rather than industrial affiliation determined the residence patterns of the city's African American citizens.[17] With the exception of domestic servants who lived with their employers, discriminatory housing policies limited African Americans to distinct sections of the city. Recent migrants from the rural South found homes in the upper Fifth and lower Seventh Ward, places of extreme destitution. By 1900 the infusion of poor Russian immigrants had pushed African Americans from the Fifth Ward to the Seventh and Thirtieth Wards. Because blacks were a minority even in those wards with the highest percentage of African American residents, however, African Americans and whites lived in close proximity in the poorer areas of the city and came into contact daily.

Philadelphia had "decent" working-class neighborhoods such as the Kensington textile district, but it also had its share of slums notorious for their high rates of crime, disease, and infant mortality. Here the poorest of the city's Irish and African American residents made their homes. Beginning in the 1880s, immigrant Italian and Russian Jewish families also began to crowd into the eastern districts of the city bordered by the Delaware River. Along with their African American neighbors, they lived in neighborhoods where manufacturing establishments, stores, homes, and places of commercial vice were all located on the same streets. Many families lived in the notorious South Street corridor or Alaska district, chosen as the site of the University Settlement in 1893 precisely because of its "low" reputation.[18] A housing reformer described this area in the 1880s as "inhabited by the very lowest and most desperate characters, both white and black, a locality through which no sane, sober, respectable man or woman would ever think of passing, where licentiousness reigned supreme."[19]

As they mapped roughness and respectability geographically, Philadelphia's late Victorian reformers drew on the conventions of an earlier genre of urban exposés that shaped how Americans "read" cities and their inhabitants. These conventions were still fresh in 1848 when George G. "Gaslight" Foster published "Philadelphia in Slices" in the *New York Tribune*.[20] Foster depicted the city as a social, moral, and geographic entity divided by the oppositions of light and shadow, high and low, wealth and poverty, virtue and vice. His description of the wretched physical conditions in poor neighborhoods highlighted the environmental factors that contributed to the "social misery" of the poor. Foster's reliance on racial and ethnic stereotypes and his conflation of filth, disease, and the contagion of immorality nonetheless succeeded in implicating laboring people—particularly the city's free black community—in their own "degradation."[21]

Although late Victorian white urban reformers continued to rely on the conventions of the "secrets of the city" genre with its series of oppositions, its ethnographic characterization of immigrants and African Americans as dangerous "other," and its conflation of filth, disease, crime, and immorality, they also drew on new Social Darwinist concepts of racial hierarchy to map out the city's social terrain. Reformers used racial as well as moral categories to delineate the character of the city's neighborhoods. By the 1880s, the American working class was composed chiefly of immigrants, the native-born children of immigrants, and African Americans.[22] In an era of Social Darwinism and racially conceived nativism, racial categories and discourse shaped perceptions of Irish and Eastern and Southern European immigrants and their children as well as of African Americans. In the post-Reconstruction decades, African Americans' continuing experience of all forms of racial discrimination made their situation unique. In theory, however, African Americans and immigrant ethnic whites were seen as members of "races" located at the lower end of the evolutionary scale. If the Irish and Italian "races" were ranked higher on the evolutionary scale than the African American, they were still all allegedly characterized by their indolent sensuality and lack of work discipline. Social Darwinist views attributed both their class position and poverty to either hereditary or individual ineptitude in the struggle for the survival of the fittest.[23] Simultaneously, racial discourse framed reformers' perceptions of themselves as representatives of more evolved races, and their role in the transformation of poor African American and ethnic neighborhoods. In the early years of the SPCC, native-born board members employed as agents ex-police officers with Northern European immigrant backgrounds, who themselves frequently commented on the racial and ethnic composition of the neighborhoods they visited, reserving particular condemnation for locales where "blacks and whites" associated "promiscuously."[24]

White reformers and SPCC agents mistakenly portrayed the poorest neighborhoods not only as places where men, women, and children of all ages and races mingled "promiscuously," but where the moral standards were uniformly low. In part the perception among white reformers of widespread depravity in slum neighborhoods such as the South Street corridor arose out of an inability to grasp social distinctions more readily apparent to poor immigrant and African American residents, whose geographical mappings and social understandings of roughness and respectability were more nuanced. Even if they had no choice but to live among dance halls and low lodging houses, those who lived in notorious neighborhoods could still cling to the social distinctions of reputation and respectability which were pervasive in the "better" working-class districts. As a character in Harriet Beecher Stowe's novel *We and Our Neighbors* (1875) asserted, "with them a good name is more nearly an only treasure."[25]

In contrast to white reformers, African American reformers and investigators purposely highlighted "moral" and social distinctions within the poorest neighborhoods to undermine the use of poverty as an unambiguous moral marker. These reformers also used competing claims within black neighborhoods of roughness and respectability, the street and the church, to argue for the existence of a class of "better" Negros, hemmed in by racial discrimination in the labor and housing markets. In a pointed response to both Social Darwinist arguments about the innate racial inferiority of African Americans and claims that black morality had deteriorated since the demise of the "benevolent school" of slavery, W. E. B. Du Bois emphasized the significance of critical social distinctions among Philadelphia's black population. In *The Philadelphia Negro* (1899), he commented, "Investigators are often surprised in the worst districts [of Philadelphia] to see red-handed criminals and good-hearted, hard-working honest people living side by side in apparent harmony." Du Bois underscored the inability of "well-meaning" whites to comprehend the distinction between roughness and respectability in Philadelphia's African American communities, noting, "Well-meaning people continually . . . regale the thugs and whore-mongers and gamblers of Seventh and Lombard streets with congratulations on what the Negroes have done in a quarter century, and pity for their disabilities; and they scold the caterers of Addison street for the pickpockets and paupers of the race. . . . Nothing more exasperates the better class of Negroes than this tendency to ignore utterly their existence."[26]

Sharing to some extent the sensibility of white reformers who conflated sanitary and moral considerations and who distinguished between the worthy and unworthy poor, African American reformer Anna Julia Cooper nonetheless targeted racism rather than innate immorality as a prime factor in determining the squalid living conditions of urban blacks. In *A Voice from the South* (1892) she argued that segregated housing and the consequent overcrowding of urban African Americans into the poorest neighborhoods caused high infant mortality rates among urban blacks and forced respectable African Americans to live surrounded by filth and immorality.[27] Like Du Bois, Cooper argued that racist attitudes and practices obscured the existence of significant social and moral distinctions among blacks.

Cooper and Du Bois insisted that "hard-working, honest people" could be found in the most notorious neighborhoods in order to demonstrate the existence of a "better class" of blacks and refute claims to innate black immorality. Their goal was also to convince whites that the consequences of racism—unsanitary, overcrowded housing, low wages, blunted aspirations, and under- and unemployment—were deleterious to the morale and the morality of urban blacks, and therefore dangerous to the entire society. Du Bois argued, "Certainly a great amount of crime can be without doubt traced to the discrimination against Negro boys and girls in the matter of employment. . . . The social environment of excuse, listless despair, careless indulgence and lack of inspiration to work is the growing force that turns black boys and girls into gamblers, prostitutes, and rascals."[28]

Although he portrayed the poorest neighborhoods as more morally homogeneous than Du Bois and Cooper, George Gunton, an immigrant weaver and labor activist from Lancashire, England, also emphasized the detrimental environmental impact of low wages and poor housing on working-class morality. In 1887 Gunton argued that there were distinct differences within the American working class in regard to attitudes toward intemperance and domestic violence, and that these differences could be traced to the material conditions of particular neighborhoods. He claimed that in the better working-class districts neighbors were less willing to tolerate episodes of drunkenness and violence and would ostracize a man who drank habitually or was arrested for disturbing the peace or abusing his family. Indeed, in the 1880s the Knights of Labor declared desertion, drunkenness, and wife-beating grounds for expulsion.[29] Gunton's argument implicitly worked two ways: improvements in wages, housing, and sanitation could lay the groundwork for working-class self-improvement, but if left unchecked, deteriorating conditions could create drunkenness, violence, crime, and immorality.

Public Families

In Philadelphia's crowded working-class neighborhoods, many of the activities of daily life occurred on the stoops, in the yards, and in the streets. Much of women's domestic labor took place in the company of or within earshot of neighbors. Women and older children, especially daughters, hung up laundry, ran errands, and minded babies out of doors. They purchased fruits and vegetables from hucksters who hawked their wares throughout the city's poorer streets and alleys. Other work performed for cash within the neighborhood also brought women together in public and in their homes. Women who took in laundry and sewing carried bundles of clothing to and fro; working mothers who boarded babies met with their caretakers; midwives visited new and expectant mothers; and women who ran speakeasies or small grocery stores in their front rooms saw a steady stream of customers buying household goods, playing "policy," and "running the growler." With so little privacy, neighbors had ample opportunities to scrutinize and comment on one another's behavior.

Working-class families were "public" not only because living conditions made privacy difficult and ethnic and class traditions of mutual aid and communal social life made it unlikely, but because some members of the community were willing to involve local law enforcement agencies and quasi-public "private" organizations like the Society to Organize Charity and the Society to Protect Children from Cruelty in their neighbors' domestic affairs. At the same time that their access to material resources, ties to state power, and social standing gave charity and moral reformers the power to scrutinize the domestic arrangements of the poor, poverty and its exigencies deprived laboring people of privacy, subjecting their living conditions, household finances, sleeping arrangements, and family relations to investigation.[30] Despite the prerogatives of class, reformers were dependent on relatives and neighbors for much of their information. SPCC agents relied heavily on neighbors' keen powers of observation and readiness to pass judgment as they collected evidence about defendants' patterns of child care, cleanliness, drinking, spending, and sociability.

The intense public scrutiny that marked working-class life also had a kindlier side: neighbors and even passing strangers were quick to intervene when they discovered neglected, hungry, or otherwise mistreated children. As historians have noted, mutual aid and stern judgments, helpfulness and intrusiveness frequently went hand in hand.[31] Proximity to relatives and neighbors provided a considerable amount of mutual aid to distressed families and supported the weaker members of families—wives and children— in their struggles against abusive partners or harsh and neglectful parents. Yet neighbors' willingness to intervene in domestic conflicts also strictly cir-

Facing. Children playing on South Street. Photograph courtesy of the Philadelphia Jewish Archives Center. In the neighborhoods of the laboring poor, the street was a place of work and leisure for men, women, and children.

of those around them is apparent in the following accounts. One wintry day in 1896, an Irish woman named Mary C. returned home from work to find a strange woman in her house. The woman had been passing Mary's house when she saw a little barefoot boy on the front steps crying, clad only in a nightgown and an old coat. Entering a stranger's home, the woman found a younger child in the same condition inside. Angered to find a stranger in her own home chiding her for her neglect, Mary grew abusive. Undaunted, the woman sent clothing for the children, but also told a friend who then notified the SPCC.[33]

In another instance Margaret B. was visiting a woman when the screams of a child and the sound of blows in the house next door prompted her to enter Emma J.'s home, where she found two intoxicated women and a child who bore the marks of physical abuse and neglect. Removing the child from the house, she "paid a colored woman one dollar for cleaning and washing it" before bringing the child to the Sixth District Station House; police then notified the SPCC. Further investigation revealed that the "sufferer"—fourteen-month-old Lizzie W.—was boarded with the "defendant" while Lizzie's mother, Mattie, served a sentence in the House of Correction for her presence in a "disreputable house."[34]

Neighbors were particularly quick to come to the rescue if they believed children were suffering physical abuse. As he sat in his yard one evening in June 1880, William R. heard the cries of a child. Leaning over his fence to investigate, he discovered a woman striking a nine-year-old boy with a piece of board. When William R. remonstrated with the woman, she scolded him for his inquisitiveness, but he reported the case to the SPCC the next morning.[35] Although his neighbor chided him for his interference, William R. had acted in accordance with popular custom that recognized the community's role in protecting children.

Although explicit physical abuse attracted even the attention of passersby who were uninvolved in the daily life of the block, neighbors were more likely than outsiders to notice chronic forms of neglect as well as violence. They notified the SPCC when children were left unsupervised for too long or too often, or were chronically underfed and poorly clothed. The care and close attention of neighbors often testified to parental neglect. Needy children left to fend for themselves were simultaneously nobody's children and everybody's children; they were left to the supervision of all of the mothers on the street. Such children were the beneficiaries of a tradition of mutual aid in poor communities.

But there were limits to neighbors' tolerance and ability to provide non-reciprocal services. If local mutual aid continued for a prolonged period, or if neighbors' standards of childrearing had been violated, a mother's excessive reliance on her neighbors' willingness to assume her family responsibilities would become a case for the SPCC. Many of the anonymous letters mailed to the SPCC appear to have been sent from neighbors whose concern for mistreated local children was matched by their belief that a neighbors' expectations of mutual aid had become a nuisance.[36]

In 1887 the SPCC received an anonymous tip that Thomas C. and his wife Catherine of Kater Street in South Philadelphia neglected their four children, James, Maggie, Annie, and Amanda. The letter writer claimed that the children, who ranged in age from two to eight years, ran "the street from morning till night with scarcely any clothes." SPCC agents who questioned neighbors learned that while both parents were hardworking—Thomas was a bricklayer and Catherine worked in a mill—they went to work each day without arranging for the children's meals or supervision, and the neighbors were compelled to feed the children or see them go hungry.[37]

Another anonymous complaint informed the SPCC that Annie S. neglected her orphaned eight-year-old sister and her own four-year-old son and was not a fit person to care for the children. Annie left the children alone in the house all day when she went to work (possibly to clean or do laundry) in various houses of ill-fame; the children were left to wander the streets or visit the houses where Annie worked. SPCC records noted of another woman whose neighbors reported that her children had begged from them for a year and they had grown tired of it, "She (Dfdt) belongs to a family who has [sic] been noted as 'beats' for years and she is fully able to keep up the reputation."[38]

In another instance neighbors' offers of assistance clearly backfired. When the residents of a street observed their neighbor disposing of all his furniture as soon as his wife died, they thought that he was pawning his possessions to raise money for the burial expenses. The neighbors took up a collection to prevent the disgrace of a pauper burial, but the husband "departed for parts unknown," leaving his wife's corpse lying on the floor and the children unattended. His daughter Eliza was informally adopted by a neighboring family, but when the man was discovered at work in another part of the city several years later, the neighbors attempted to recover the expenses for her keep.[39]

Working-class Philadelphians made ready use of the SPCC when they discovered obvious instances of abuse or urgent neglect, but their turn to the SPCC to mediate conflicts among family members or neighbors was usually a last resort after they had interceded many times. Case records reveal that agents came across children who had been fed, clothed, and sheltered for weeks or months by local families. These cases testify not only to the extent of mutual aid among neighbors and relatives despite limited resources, but also the likely desire to avoid contact with an agency whose actions they could not control.

For some Philadelphians, the appeal to an upper-middle-class moral reform agency such as the SPCC involved an element of ethnic, racial, or class betrayal. Yet for those defending the reputation of their families and neighborhoods, the failure of respectability signaled by the misbehavior of others could likewise be interpreted as a form of personal and class and/or "racial" betrayal.

The process of "informing the Cruelty" defined both "complainants" and "defendants" within the neighborhood and at the SPCC office. Although agents weighed the reputation of the "complainant" as well as that of the "defendant" to establish the veracity of the charges, by filing a complaint one asserted one's own respectability while casting doubt on another's. This was so not only because of the specific charges, but because the very process of rendering neighbors clients of a reform organization stigmatized those whom the "complainant" wished to either chastise or help. While charity workers frequently demanded that the poor prove themselves worthy by establishing their respectability before receiving aid, becoming a client of a charitable or reform agency could establish one's *loss* of respectability among working-class people.

Parents often sent children rather than older family members to stand on soup lines to avoid the embarrassment of receiving "relief." For destitute, deserted wives and mothers sent to the almshouse, the stigma of institutionalization was acute. The horror of pauper burials was widely shared across ethnic boundaries, and many parents feared the institutionalization of orphans and half-orphans—no matter how desperate they might have been for the aid. In a society that valued independence and frequently defined it in economic terms, and in which the dominant culture equated poverty with laziness and immorality, the public labeling of oneself as a dependent involved tremendous humiliation and loss of face.[40] How much greater, then, must have been the loss of respectability and reputation involved when parents were charged with child abuse, neglect, and cruelty.

The "Cruelty" had an impact even on those families it never contacted directly. Neighbors warned abusive or neglectful parents that they would notify the SPCC to frighten the guilty parties into changing their behavior. Two women who were said to be strangers in one neighborhood appeared at a small store run by a woman with a reputation for sexual misconduct and rapped at the window, warning the proprietor of their intention to "inform the Society" if she did not stop whipping her child. Neighbors told agents investigating another case that the complaint brought against one mother was untrue since "she does not whip the child at all. as she is afraid of this Society." In 1880 a distraught woman appeared at the SPCC office carrying a letter that was purportedly a warning from the SPCC about her ill-treatment of her children. The SPCC had never sent the letter, but the Secretary informed the woman that since no one would trouble to send such a letter without just cause, she had better make sure to take good care of her children.[41]

Like incidents of outright cruelty, suspicions of improper mothering galvanized working-class women's appeals to the SPCC. One woman sought out the SPCC because an acquaintance of hers had been drinking heavily, forcing her son and daughter to scavenge food from gutters and garbage barrels. The defendant's next door neighbor confirmed this story and declared that her neighbor was "a disgrace to her sex." In another instance, five matrons who lived on Agate Street in Kensington testified to the ill effects of intemperance on the children of a local family which the neighbors took turns feeding. One witness testified that she had been alarmed when she overheard the loud cries of the eight-month-old baby suddenly "sink into a muffled noise." Racing into the house, she found the drunken mother had rolled over onto the baby and was inadvertently smothering it. Another witness had entered the same house on another occasion to discover the baby perched atop a steep flight of stairs. By the time neighbors invited agents to investigate, every household possession had been pawned for rum and the house was so dirty that the agent "lit a cigar to kill the smell." When the parents were sent to the House of Refuge for three months, the magistrate assigned custody of the children to the SPCC, who allowed the children "to remain with the friends who had for some time past cared for them."[42]

Because sexual propriety was an important marker of respectability in working-class neighborhoods, neighbors' complaints to the SPCC also focused on sexual misconduct. At one end of a continuum were appeals motivated by a desire to protect a young woman thought to be in danger of "ruin." At the other end were clear cases of prostitution, where neighbors appealed to the SPCC to put an end to the drunken carousals, fighting, and singing that punctuated their sleep and taught their children an unwelcome lesson about the profitability of immorality.[43]

When the mother of an adolescent girl appeared unwilling to correct her daughter or protect her from exposure to the immoral conduct of others, neighborhood women might demonstrate their concern and their own commitment to respectability by notifying the SPCC. In 1901 the SPCC received an anonymous complaint about Sarah, the "very pretty" thirteen-year-old daughter of a "Hebrew" woman with a newsstand at a busy corner in the center of the city. The complainant suggested that Sarah was from all appearances "very fond of men." She had been seen doing "some very improper things," had been out late at night, and had been observed in possession of "quite a sum of money." In spite of a these signs of imminent ruin, the correspondent complained that Sarah's mother "shuts her eyes" and "abuses people who tell her about the girl." When questioned Sarah claimed that she had done nothing wrong and had been visiting her friend Ida when observed out at night. She declared she was glad a law had been passed to prohibit girls her age from selling newspapers, since she would much prefer to work in one of the department stores or in the music store where she was currently employed. Sarah's defense reveals a clear understanding that her shift from selling newspapers—a street trade that reformers and respectable parents considered a precursor to prostitution—to work in the retail sector, typically filled by native-born rather than immigrant young women—implied a significant gain in status and respectability.[44]

Proper but poor Philadelphians who lived near houses of ill-fame worked hand-in-hand with the SPCC to prohibit the presence of young girls in houses of prostitution. The SPCC emphasized that "the breaking up of such establishments properly belongs to the police department of the city" and commented that "it forms no part of the duty of this Society to wage war against such, except in those cases where girls who are minors are inmates of such dens of infamy." Nonetheless in the early 1880s, the SPCC lobbied successfully for the legal right to remove minors "whether they are the children of the occupants or not." While annual reports claimed much popular sympathy for their efforts to return "fallen" adolescent girls to their families or place them in suitable reformatories, the law making it illegal to harbor a minor in a house of ill-fame made any children found during a police raid vulnerable to seizure, whether they were the children of prostitutes or of their landlords or domestic servants.[45]

Prostitutes themselves appear to have been divided in their views regarding the suitability of the brothel as a place to raise young children and for young girls to work. As the SPCC's aggressive policy of removing children from brothels became known, some prostitutes began to board their children in nearby households where they could oversee the children's welfare without risking SPCC intervention. Another mother arrested by the SPCC surrendered the custody of her seven-year-old daughter to the Society, although case records indicated she "[professed] some attachment for her daughter." In 1896 agents removed a seven-year-old Jewish boy from Reuben and Fannie L.'s "fast" house; the United Hebrew Charities placed the boy with foster parents who promised to send him to "Public and Religious School." Some houses of prostitution also refused to board adolescent girls who were clearly minors.[46]

In 1893, the SPCC received a letter informing agents that a fourteen-year-old girl had been seen in Mazie W.'s house of ill-fame on Noble Street in Northern Liberties. Mazie admitted to agents that she "kept a bad house" and stated that Carrie, the girl in question, had been hired two weeks earlier to help with the housework in the afternoons. Carrie's parents lived in the rear of the house; her mother claimed that the family was very poor and needed Carrie's wages to maintain her three younger siblings. For the SPCC, as for the original complainant, Carrie's work in the brothel was problematic, casting doubt on her reputation while indicting her parents' childrearing practices. To her parents, however, Carrie was neither a bad girl nor an exploited child but a dutiful daughter. Unmoved by this explanation, the SPCC informed the family that if Carrie continued her housework in the brothel she would be removed by the Society and her parents would be arrested.[47]

In other cases neighbors were motivated by sheer outrage at sexual behavior of adult women that was in obvious violation of respectable mores. In 1896 Hester D. called at the SPCC office to inform authorities of the notorious behavior of her next-door neighbor, Susannah J. Witnesses told the agents that "there were drunken carousals there almost continuously." Neighbors claimed that they had observed Susannah in her yard "in an entirely nude condition, with a number of men," and that she had been "seen in the water closet in almost the same condition" with a man, and that they had been "seen on the floor together."[48] However scandalized Susannah's neighbors may have been, they had completed a thorough investigation themselves before notifying the SPCC.

Such detail characterized many cases of this type, suggesting the use of neighborhood gossip to delineate the boundaries of acceptable and inappropriate behavior. Although the target of one investigation was brought to the attention of the SPCC by an anonymous letter, agents found seven women and three men eager to testify about a neighboring woman's drunkenness, sexual misbehavior, and neglect of her children. Neighbors informed the agents that while the husband had steady work at good wages as a painter, he had no control over his family and spent all of his leisure in taverns, "perhaps through disgust at the negligence of his wife in regard to his children and home comforts." Without a "protector" the children had suffered woefully, running the streets "wild in a dirty, filthy condition and hungry." While the neighbors fed the children, their mother allowed "the young lads in the neighborhood" to "take liberties with her" in her house. In a similar case, neighbors characterized a German woman with the telling comment that when hucksters came to her house they did not receive cash for their vegetables, "her lewdness satisfying their demands."[49]

Finally, neighbors intervened in cases of incest, that most "private" of offenses. Middle-class social observers commonly described crowded working-class homes as breeding grounds for incest, because they both considered working-class men sensual and lacking self-control and also believed that environmental factors contributed to working-class immorality. Henry Boies, a member of the Pennsylvania Board of Public Charities, argued that "the huddling of whole families . . . into one room, in which to live and sleep in the midst of the uncleanness of beastly poverty and the indiscriminate cohabitation of the sexes" involved "the greatest temptation to intemperance, licentiousness, and crime."[50]

In mainstream reform thought, incest served as a metaphor for family disintegration among the poor. Significantly, some Catholic and radical critiques of childsaving relied on the same metaphor but encoded it with new meaning. Inverting the notion of immigrant working-class households as breeding grounds for incest, they argued that childsavers destroyed families and inadvertently facilitated incestuous relations among the poor. In the 1850s, the Children's Aid Society of New York began to ship the orphans and half-orphans of the children of the laboring poor to homes in the West, in the belief that a rural upbringing would provide a strong foundation for a moral and productive future. Fearful that Catholic children would be raised in Protestant homes, Catholic critics of the "orphan trains" argued that reformers' reliance on family separation made it possible for brothers and sisters separated and sent out West to marry each other unwittingly. In the early 1890s Alice Rhine of the Socialist Labor Party echoed these charges. In this way, critics of Protestant childsavers sensationalized the practice of removing children from their families by identifying incest with reformers rather than with the targets of investigations.[51]

Incest did occur in the crowded homes of the city's poorer families, as it no doubt also occurred in the homes of more prosperous families under less scrutiny. But when incidents of incest became well known, working-class men and women responded with anger and indignation. In 1880 public opinion in Frankford, a northeastern district of the city, was "incensed" over claims that a father and daughter were living as man and wife. Rumors also surfaced of an attempted "outrage" on the thirteen-year-old child of this union, who had "been heard to protest against her bondage."[52] Witnesses testified that the unusual union was "common talk around Frankford" and that public outrage had earlier driven the defendants out of another neighborhood.

The agent throughly documented the housing conditions he observed, drawing connections between filth, overcrowding, family disorganization, and incest. He noted that the defendants occupied a two-story frame house with two rooms on each floor. The stove was in the lower level of the house, which was used as a kitchen, dining room, and sorting room for rags, iron, and bones. One of the top rooms was rented by a boarder. The other room served as a bedroom for the man, woman, and her five daughters, who all occupied one bed. During the trial the woman alleged that she had had two previous husbands. The first had been hanged "for some crime not stated"; the second "mysteriously disappeared"; and "now she has her father as a husband, but he winds up in jail." Although she "conveniently went into a spasm" when asked about her relations with her father, the abused daughter described her own ill-treatment. With her testimony, the man was convicted and sentenced to a year of hard labor and solitary confinement at the Eastern Penitentiary and a $150 fine. The children were committed to the care of the SPCC and placed in a local orphanage.[53]

Whose Family? Whose Standards?

The same scrutiny and interest in each other's household affairs that formed the basis for testimony of violence or neglect could also provide evidence of good character. Philadelphia working-class residents insisted on their right to define the meaning of family relations when they defended their neighbors against reformers' charges. For example, neighbors came to the defense of a recently widowed man under investigation in 1879 for failing to provide properly for his five children. Speculating that a resident who had since left the neighborhood had mailed the anonymous complaint, neighbors convinced the agent that, "The man is a sober industrious man. his [late] wife is spoken of as being every inch a lady. and the neighbors say that on her account they would not see the children suffer in any way, but they know the man is struggling manfully to keep his family together, and he should receive praise instead of censure." Similarly, her neighbors on Leithgow Street spoke well of Annie S., charged by a policeman with sending her thirteen-year-old daughter Lottie out to beg. They informed agents she was a "hard-working woman" who "works hard at the wash-tub, and trys [sic] to make a living for her children." Annie admitted that she sent Lottie out at times when they were in want, but said that she made money scrubbing steps rather than begging. One neighbor described the subject of another investigation for neglect as a "sober, hardworking woman" who "would make any sacrifice for her children." In another instance, six neighbors and two policemen sided with a mother accused of alleged cruelty, claiming she was a "hard working, sober, industrious woman who tries to do what is right" and that her sons were "scamps who need correction which she applies with no undue severity."[54]

The character testimonials offered by neighbors indicate that respectable working-class standards of manliness and maternal care centered around hard work, sobriety, and solicitude for children, coupled with a willingness to rely on both physical "correction" and children's labor. Of course, men and women who sought to defend others against SPCC allegations would be likely to couch their defense in terms meant to appeal to the values of the SPCC agents. But the tone of the remarks and the frequency with which phrases reappear indicate that many residents themselves subscribed to values of thrift, sobriety, hard work, and domesticity. The appeal of these values, which were also those prescribed by child welfare reformers and charity visitors, implies neither the imposition of genteel norms of domesticity nor working-class emulation of the Victorian middle class, but a complex negotiation of meaning within and between classes. If neighbors' statements sound like a sentimental defense of the worthy poor that drew on imagery similar to that of reformers, the context in which their judgments were formed and spoken lent their words a different meaning. A good mother by working-class standards might be forced by misfortune to take in the wash of a "low" lodging house or send her children peddling. If these disreputable practices lowered a family's social status—and they did—they did not always destroy a woman's reputation as a mother. Nor did they necessarily warrant providing information to agents who might take steps to remove the children. When neighbors insisted on a mother's love and sacrifices for her children or a father's dedication to supporting his family, their defense bespoke first-hand knowledge of the difficult circumstances of raising children in the city's poorer wards. They were not identifying their neighbors as good providers or "true women" by middle-class standards of parenting and domesticity. Instead, they were defending the conduct and reputation of those accused of wrongdoing by representatives of another class and way of life who were less familiar with the intimate details of raising children in poverty.

Even when they were committed to values similar to those of upper-middle-class reformers, the distinctions they made between respectable and disreputable behavior drew less from upper-middle-class assessments of the worthy poor than from the specific class experiences of laboring families. In some instances, the content of what it meant to be a good mother or a good provider differed for SPCC reformers and the laboring people they interrogated. In other cases, what would at first glance appear to be similar definitions of good motherhood or fatherhood instead took on very different, politically charged meaning because of the different social position of the speakers articulating codes of domesticity.[55] Rather than internalizing the values of upper-middle-class charity and child welfare reformers, then, laboring people's commitment to working-class respectability was motivated by different concerns, arose in a different context, and ultimately carried different meanings.

In one sense each SPCC investigation was a dramatic event, an attempt to determine if a defendant was a decent or dangerous mother, a good provider or a neglectful father, to establish the falsity or truth of charges with a clear and certain answer. Yet investigations were by nature dynamic: in their effort to fix social categories and label defendants, complainants and SPCC investigators opened every aspect of the neighborhood to scrutiny and inadvertently provided a forum for the discussion and clarification of working-class values. This process could be costly for families: an investigation could destroy one's reputation or threaten one's sense of self and identity as a good mother, housekeeper, or provider. For the more fortunate, an investigation could reaffirm a family's honor and reputation and clarify its social standing on the street.

"As Soon as Agents Go in the Neighborhood a Crowd Collects Which Shouts of an Investigation"

While some working-class residents of Philadelphia considered the SPCC an aid in promoting neighborhood respectability, others shunned it, as they did the police and other representatives of the law. In 1892 the SPCC noted, "The reformer will ever be considered an as intruding enemy by those whose vicious plans he seeks to circumvent. In proportion as one earns the approbation of the wise and virtuous in the community, he is apt to draw upon himself the hate and ill-will of the vicious and evil-doer." This distrust of the SPCC was reflected in its popular nickname, "the Cruelty." Opposition to the SPCC was also evident in the refusal of many citizens to testify against neighbors. SPCC case records are replete with cases in which no evidence could be gleaned from the community. In other cases, the knowledge that an SPCC agent was venturing into the vicinity would prompt the residents to take collective action to prevent an investigation. Drawing on an effective intelligence network among the poor, men, women, and children would cry out the warning "Investigation! Investigation!" whenever an SPCC agent drew near.[56]

Although there were many reasons for residents of the city's rougher neighborhoods to wish to escape the scrutiny of the SPCC, at stake was its right to intrude into the streets and homes of the city's families. In late nineteenth-century cities, gangs of boys and young men often patrolled the streets, claiming well-marked territory as their own and discouraging intruders, whether toughs from other neighborhoods, representatives of the law, or other outsiders. In Philadelphia's poorer African American, Irish Catholic, German, Italian and Jewish neighborhoods, racial, religious, and ethnic resentments and/or language barriers contributed to the pervasive distrust of outsiders.[57]

Class hostility and antagonism for those moral reformers who sought to close the brothels and speakeasies and transform the character of the city's "low" neighborhoods also shaped such responses. For instance, in 1880 philanthropists funded by Theodore Starr razed several "miserable, filthy shanties" in the Alaska district and evicted the "lewd white women" who lived there in an attempt to replace the neighborhood's "vicious and law-less" inhabitants with "respectable and industrious" residents. During the time the model housing was being erected, "groups of men and women would often gather about it, and, after using the most loathesome language, would laugh boisterously and declare openly that 'none of you tony crowd could drive them out by building tony houses in St. Mary Street.'" Similarly, preachers, "friendly visitors," and SPCC agents faced taunts, ridicule, and other forms of intimidation when they entered the city's rougher neighbor-hoods.[58] In the case of the SPCC, neighborhood hostility was motivated by the recognition that an SPCC agent's visit could provoke a number of unpleasant and potentially serious consequences, ranging from loss of repu-tation to a term in the House of Correction and the removal of one's chil-dren.

Many of the survival strategies of the chronic poor—begging, scavenging, pawning clothes and household goods, participating in the street trades, petty theft, and casual prostitution—by definition constituted child abuse to SPCC agents, rendering poor families vulnerable to unsolicited interven-tion. Although the SPCC claimed to investigate suspected Philadelphians in all walks of life, making no distinction "between the rich and poor and between those who live in larger houses and those who live in courts and alleys," the poorest families were least able to provide an appropriate mate-rial and moral environment for their children. In this sense the SPCC was indeed a class-biased society that proposed to attack and "root out" the domestic habits of the chronic poor. Class conflict was embedded in the actual practice of reform intervention and in the vision of family life that formed the ideological basis for philanthropic activities.[59] Reformers' con-cerns were shaped in the context of fears of political upheaval, labor un-rest, and the social and political threat posed by the growth of a property-less working class chiefly composed of immigrants, their native-born chil-dren, and African Americans. Moreover, despite the willingness of some working-class neighbors to cooperate with SPCC agents in instances of com-pelling need, reformers' definitions of abuse, proper parenting, and the nature of family life were frequently class-bound. Legislation advocated by groups such as the SPCC, regulating begging and children's work in the street trades, was widely perceived as an attack on the family economy of the poor.

Over the course of the nineteenth century, parental custody rights evolved from a property right in children to a trust dependent upon the fulfillment of parental responsibilities. As the SPCC and similar organizations across the nation took a larger role in defining parental responsibilities, families least able to approximate this ideal—whether because of poverty, the death of the primary breadwinner, or the nature or location of the mother's or children's employment—became vulnerable to the placement of children in other homes or institutions. For instance, in 1877 the SPCC arrested Mamie H. on a charge of vagrancy in order to gain custody of her three- or four-year-old daughter. Agents claimed Mamie was "to be seen frequently in the squares sitting around plying her trade [as] a prostitute." Mamie was released but "warned to stop her evil course." Within two weeks, she had been placed in the House of Correction; four days later, she was "again on the street begging in any direction to have this child restored." Meanwhile her daughter had been placed in another home and given a new name. In November 1878 another "shocking instance of cruel neglect and starvation" also resulted in the mother's arrest in order to place her daughter in an institution. A "colored infant," eighteen-month-old E.O., was routinely left "in a bath-room, without food or fire, for hours" until she had "wasted to a mere skeleton." When questioned, her "unnatural mother" claimed she could not afford to pay for childcare during the hours she was at work. The case was dismissed when the mother, arrested for cruelty and neglect, agreed to "assign the child to the care of the Society." The SPCC placed the daughter in the Colored Shelter and took credit for saving her life.[60] Clearly, for laboring people as well as for upper-middle-class reformers, the decision to leave an eighteen-month-old child alone, cold and hungry, was perceived as a lapse of good mothering, a lapse that for reformers justified terminating maternal custody. Yet other cases of apparent maternal neglect or cruelty were not so clear cut. By the standards of the laboring poor, it was perhaps regrettable but nonetheless within the realm of acceptable mothering to leave a ten-year-old child in charge of the household, or to send an eleven- or twelve-year-old son or daughter on the streets to peddle.

Single mothers' keen awareness of the disparity between middle-class norms and more flexible standards of maternal care among the laboring poor could cause these mothers great consternation as they did the best they could against nearly insurmountable odds. On a winter day early in 1880, a worried mother who earned wages outside the home hastened to the SPCC office, stating that she had "overheard one of her next door neighbors say, during a drunken brawl . . . that they had intended trying to have her children taken away from her. and would use the SPCC to do so." Clearly cognizant of both middle-class cultural disapproval of mothers who left their children home alone and the power of the SPCC to remove children from homes they deemed unfit, Eliza B. told SPCC reformers that, although she had steady work at sewing, she had not gone to work that morning, "for she felt that she must come to the Soc. and make known her position." She admitted that she was gone all day, but claimed she left "plenty at home " for her children to eat and "they did not want for any food or clothing." Furthermore, she left the house key with her oldest son so they "might go in and out as they pleased," she never drank, and always returned home early.[61] As a mother who struggled to support her children, Eliza was acutely aware that her wage-work outside the home—undertaken as a maternal responsibility—in itself rendered her vulnerable to charges of child neglect.

More than any other activity of the SPCC, use of the controversial legal doctrine *parens patriae*—which permitted the state to remove children from parents deemed unfit—struck fear into Philadelphia's poorer families and neighborhoods and demonstrated the cost laboring families could pay for their poverty as well as their deviation from genteel norms. For many of the city's poorest residents, SPCC intrusion into the neighborhood evoked the possibility of family disruption.

By the late nineteenth century popular representations of the "Cruelty" and its practice of family disruption had assumed a central place in contemporary fiction about the laboring poor.[62] In *The Charity Girl*, Caroline Pemberton drew on her previous experience as a Philadelphia child welfare worker to provide an insider's critique of scientific charity and childsaving. Several years after the publication of *Your Little Brother James* (1896), Pemberton denounced her previous philanthropic activities to become a committed socialist. Her political transformation from well-meaning charity worker to fierce critic of organized philanthropy is amply reflected in *The Charity Girl*, published in installments in the *International Socialist Review* from March 1901 to January 1902. As an author of both fiction and the "fiction" of case records, Pemberton was familiar with both literary conventions and the cultural conventions that shaped the tales told in case records.[63] To criticize mainstream late nineteenth-century benevolence and make a case for social and political transformation, *The Charity Girl* reverses the case record formula. Such records typically first locate the defendants morally and geographically and then attempt to establish the plausibility of the charges against them. If the charges are "true," the record discusses the problem and ends by locating its etiology in individual immorality and its solution in action taken by the SPCC, other charitable or reform institutions, and the police. In contrast, *The Charity Girl* is based on the premise that the origin of family problems are social, that individuals are the innocent victims of environmental conditions, and that the actions of benevolent agencies are inadvertently harmful.

The first installment of *The Charity Girl* opens with the "capture" of the three McPherson children. Here Pemberton depicts the Society to Protect Children from Cruelty from the perspective of the children of the poor—as an agency that inflicts cruelty on those unfortunate enough to be the victims of poverty, parental unemployment, or inadvertent child neglect. Pemberton uses language cleverly to make her point: the McPherson children are not rescued but captured, and families are destroyed and orphans created when children are removed from their homes. Instead of orphaned children searching for homes, Pemberton depicts institutions clamoring hungrily for inmates. Throughout the novel, the McPherson children are victims rather than beneficiaries of philanthropy. One brother dies in the poorhouse after he contracts a contagious disease during a stint in an orphanage; another brother is taken from a reformatory and placed with strangers and never heard from again. Mattie McPherson is overworked and abused as a foster child, only to become an unwed mother while in the putative care of a series of child welfare and philanthropic organizations. While an inmate of "St. Agnes' Holy House," a fictional home for unwed mothers, Mattie is visited by a philanthropist from the Association for Sociological Research, an "influential organization, liberally supported by people of wealth and culture" which has a "Department of Waifs and Strays." Mattie's defense of her parents' "misuse" of her and her attack on scientific charity provide the means for Pemberton's critique of forced family separation and institutionalization.

"Martha [Mattie] this is the gentleman from the good society that has looked after you like a loving parent since you was took away by the 'Croolty' from your first parents that misused you so dreadful."

"They didn't misuse me," muttered the girl sullenly.

"They didn't? Not when they spent all their money on drink and gave you nothin' to eat and no clothes to put on your back?"

"That warn't misusin'," explained the Magdalen desperately. "Pappy was out o'work, and me mammy'd drink jes' to keep up her sperrits. I've been misused worse since I left 'em—abused more than they ever done. I'd go back right to-morrow if I knowed where they was."[64]

While Pemberton does not deny that the McPhersons failed to provide adequately for their children, she argues that poverty and unemployment rather than innate depravity led to their drunkenness and inadvertent child neglect. The solution, therefore, is the transformation of environmental conditions rather than family separation.

In the 1850s, attempts to break the cycle of dependency and "viciousness" had taken precedence over the preservation of poor families. Charles Loring Brace of the Children's Aid Society in New York City had advocated family separation as a positive strategy to prevent the growth of the dangerous class. But by the 1890s, charging that the SPCC and similar organizations were destroying the home rather than preserving it, critics within reform ranks themselves questioned if the tactic of separating family members and placing children in institutions served the ultimate aim of preserving the American family. By the turn of the century, child protection reformers disillusioned with institutional solutions called for the preservation of the family through casework if possible, and the placement of children in other families rather than in institutions if necessary. "Family-style" rather than large congregate institutions were to be a last resort. From its inception, the Pennsylvania SPCC had favored the placement of children in foster families over institutional care. In the early 1890s, however, the SPCC responded directly to criticisms aired at a national conference of charity reformers and reemphasized its commitment to preserve family life if at all possible, resorting to the removal of children in only the most serious of cases.[65]

While debates over the merits and disadvantages of family separation and institutionalization raged in social science and reform circles and became the basis for fictionalized treatments of the poor, active resistance to this practice united the residents in the city's "low" neighborhoods.[66] One of the most common responses to the visit of an SPCC agent was the withholding of information or the refusal to testify. Such noncompliance was not always a mark of hostility; it could reveal an unwillingness to lose a day's work by becoming involved in a court case; the dread of possible retaliations by the neighbor under investigation; or a simple language barrier. Agents who were unable to procure the desired information often believed that they had been foiled by the moral homogeneity they perceived in "low" neighborhoods. In case records they noted the difficulties encountered in Italian and Jewish neighborhoods where the residents claimed ignorance of English. Agents complained that other ethnic groups practiced a similar clannishness, refusing to testify against friends and foes alike. SPCC investigators reported that they could not gain any information in "localities occupied by colored people, who will not give any information about their neighbors." Nor was the task easier in neighborhoods where the residents were predominantly "poor Irish people." In other cases they noted that as the neighbors were "of the same class " as the defendants under investigation, no evidence could be obtained. When agents investigated a charge of drunkenness in June 1879 in a section of the city noted for its houses of prostitution they recorded their failure to procure evidence with the comment, "None of the neighbors will testify against this party, and no wonder for it is in the midst of infamy and degradation, the slums of Spafford, and Alaska streets congregate here."[67]

Sometimes neighbors refused to offer information to agents and then warned the subject of the investigation of the agent's visit. In such cases the agent might find on a return visit that the suspect had moved to a different community. While neighbors might pass on information in an effort to help one another, combining to repel an agent's visit could work to the advantage of all those who lived on the street. In communities where the local economy was based on commerce in sex and alcohol, neighbors' attitudes toward the saloons and brothels in their midst could be ambivalent. Seamstresses, laundresses, landlords, lodging-house and saloon keepers, and domestic servants might have extensive ties to local brothels; but they could also suffer the consequences of a police raid or an agent's visit. For instance, if a young child was found in a house of ill-repute, all the residents of the house could end up in jail. Similarly, a keen agent who came to investigate a case of cruelty in one household might also notice the children of another household out peddling, or a woman in another building "running the growler."[68]

The female networks that enabled respectable women to police their own neighborhoods through gossip and observation also enabled "rougher" women to protect their homes and families as they united to resist the potential loss of child custody. Women played a prominent role in the intelligence networks of the poor. When necessary, they relied on neighbors for shelter, protection, and defense against constables and SPCC agents. An agent whose inquiries had not been fruitful noted, "The women in the neighborhood are all of the lowest class and at once spoke for the defense of Defdts." When police returned with a warrant to arrest the couple under suspicion, they discovered they were too late; the defendants in the case had already left the vicinity. Case records for a similar incident noted "The woman had been informed that the Cruelty would be put on her, and she left home early this morning with her children. She being thoroughly frightened." Finding the house deserted, the agent left a card with the next-door neighbor, noting that he would prosecute unless the defendants called immediately at the SPCC office. Returning on another day, he discovered that the family had moved; the neighbors claimed ignorance of their whereabouts.[69]

In another case a woman under investigation for drunkenness and child neglect rallied her neighbors on Susquehanna Street in Kensington for support. The agent recorded, "She denied that she drank or neglected her children, but it was evident that she ran the growler not only for herself, but the neighbors. She was sober when agents saw her. She made a great noise and attracted the attention of the people in the neighborhood. No evidence could be obtained against Dfdts as the neighborhood is inhabited by the lowest white and colored people to be found."[70]

In another instance, neighbors distracted the SPCC agents, allowing the woman under suspicion to slip away unnoticed.

In still another incident, agents recounted how "As soon as it was known that Agents were in the neighborhood, a general alarm spread among the neighbors, and the corners were immediately filled—by all sorts of people, but none of them were willing to tell where Defdts were although some of them said they had seen the man and the woman a short time before. . . . Every person seemed interested in getting Defdts away."[71]

Notified by neighbors, the "woman defendant" removed her six- and eight-year-old daughters from school despite the protests of their teacher, and the family went into hiding. Agents soon learned that investigations and arrests were best conducted at night in order to catch sleeping families unaware. And in recognition that the removal of children was a volatile event, in 1881 the SPCC awarded Charles Smith ten dollars for "safely transferring a child to St. John's Orphan Asylum . . . at considerable risk of personal violence at the hands of an infuriated mother who endeavored to wrest her child from his custody."[72]

Potential Resource, Potential Foe

Significantly, the dislike among rougher working-class communities of out-side intervention on the part of police and reformers also coexisted with widespread popular use of the SPCC, police, and the courts to settle dis-putes among neighbors. Poor Philadelphians clearly believed in their right to make money any way that they were able or to send their children ped-dling regardless of the law. But as citizens they also believed in their right to seek legal backing to discipline an unruly child, prosecute the theft of a shawl stolen from a clothesline, or collect a debt unpaid.[73] Many Philadel-phians must have expected in at least some instances to find a crude form of justice at the hands of reformers and judges.

As they used the SPCC to mediate between quarreling neighbors and acrimonious family members, Philadelphians couched their appeals in terms that indicate a clear understanding of the SPCC's policies regarding begging, prostitution, street-selling, and drink, as well as a potent recogni-tion of reformers' power to remove children from custody. Malicious com-plaints of intemperance, abuse, or immorality often deliberately played on the imagery reformers themselves used in describing the lives of the "degraded poor." Attempts to manipulate the SPCC to punish others could serve as opportunities to mock the reformers' stance on the family as well.

Since intrusion into domestic affairs was bitterly resented, calling the police or taking a complaint to the SPCC or to court could be a most vindic-tive recourse. In some cases sheer malice could provoke a false complaint, as when a woman charged her sister with drunkenness and child abuse in an attempt to oust her from the house the two families shared. Discovering that a family squabble was behind the charges, the Secretary informed her that the family conflict was not a proper case for the Society. The SPCC dis-missed another case in which charges in an anonymous letter accused a woman of being a drunkard who neglected her infant. Case records noted, "A quarrel between two women, one wishing to use the Society as a cats-paw in order to revenge herself for an imaginary wrong."[74]

Although the SPCC did not exist to protect the rights of creditors, land-lords and grocers unable to collect debts pressed unfounded charges of drunkenness and neglect against tenants and customers. Even the hint of an SPCC investigation could send unruly or debt-ridden tenants packing, enabling a landlord to cut his losses. In 1880 Frederick R. called at the SPCC to state that his wife was not a drinking woman and was kind to his chil-dren, and that he was willing to confront the anonymous letter-writer who had issued a complaint of neglect and abuse. He told SPCC officials that he supposed that Mrs. L. of Cuthbert Street had penned the complaint because he owed her two dollars and eighty-seven cents for groceries. When his wife sent two dollars to settle their account, the grocer had refused them further credit since the payment was not in full.[75] In another case dismissed by the SPCC, a man stated that a certain family were "professional beggars," that the father was a drunkard and the mother a prostitute. During a conversation at the SPCC office, the man admitted that he was the rental agent for the house the defendants lived in and that his primary interest was in evicting the tenants rather than reforming their family life.

Even residents of the "demimonde" acted as informants as they sought revenge against those who had cheated or ill-treated them, calling attention to previously tolerated practices certain to provoke reform intervention once disclosed. In May 1896, Mamie C.—formerly known as Mary C. before she became an inmate of Sallie T.'s "bawdy" house—pressed charges against Sallie T. for harboring a minor (Sallie's six-year-old daughter) in a house of ill-fame. Sallie was arrested and brought to the Central Station and charged with keeping a bawdy house and selling liquor without a license. In court Mamie testified that she had met Sallie in Wanamaker's Department Store, where she had been employed until taking up residence in Sallie's brothel. Sallie had come to the store to sell corsets, claiming that she represented a New York house; case records noted "She (Dfdt) no doubt does this as a cloak to live an immoral life, which she does at home." Since Mamie was legally an adult and a "witting victim" in the words of the SPCC, all would have been well but for a quarrel between the two women. While living in the brothel, Mamie had become diseased and had left for treatment in the Hospital. Upon her release, she had gone to Sallie's house to claim her clothes, but Sallie refused to hand them over. In an act of revenge, Mamie informed the SPCC of six-year-old Henrietta's presence in the house.[76]

These are among the most conspicuous incidents in which Philadelphians tried to manipulate reformers' assumptions to achieve their own ends. The SPCC, however, was well aware of this tendency and insisted that its extensive investigations were necessary precisely to weed out false charges.

Negotiating Respectability in Laboring Communities

Late nineteenth-century working-class Philadelphians perceived the SPCC as a prying, intrusive group of meddlesome moral reformers but also as a somewhat effective ally of the respectable working class. Working-class residents' attempts to use the SPCC to achieve their own ends were an extension of informal means of shaping community behavior such as gossip, ostracism, and cat-calling and hooting in the streets. Over the years in annual reports, board minutes and fund-raising speeches, the SPCC reported a gradual if sometimes grudging acceptance of the SPCC in Philadelphia's families and neighborhoods. The reliance of respectable Philadelphians on the authority of the SPCC and the resources it controlled ultimately served to confer legitimacy on the organization's role in working-class families and neighborhoods. Conflict over the definition of the SPCC's mission persisted, however, among family members and in the city's poorer neighborhoods as well as between the SPCC and its "clients." Appeals to the SPCC were simultaneously encounters between and among social classes and men and women; they were complex interactions shaped by a variety of motivations and intentions, ranging from attempts to use the Society as a "cat's-paw," to efforts to enforce the claims of respectability among family members and neighbors.[77]

In the city's rougher wards, condemnation of the SPCC's intervention endured, along with opposition to the police force—and it should be recalled that consolidated municipal police forces had only arisen in the mid-nineteenth century. The pervasive hatred of the SPCC in Philadelphia's "low" neighborhoods in the Gilded Age is reminiscent of the antagonism displayed in earlier decades toward moral reformers in poor districts that historians have noted in Philadelphia and other cities. As an obvious refutation of the genteel mores of the middle class, the street culture of rough men and women demonstrated a strong sense of class identity that rivaled that of the respectable working class.

Yet the resistance to authority displayed by residents of tough neighborhoods did not rest on a sustained analysis of class relations like that informing the labor movement's disdain for moral reformers. Ironically, those who most strongly repudiated laws enforcing genteel family norms were the least interested in organizing politically as a class. As historian Kenneth Fones-Wolf notes, rougher Philadelphians actually served to fragment a working-class political presence in Philadelphia when they "helped Republican bosses 'mobilize the slum vote'" in exchange for keeping moral reformers out of their neighborhoods.[78]

Rough opposition to the police and the SPCC coexisted alongside attempts to use city services, from private charities and public relief, to the courts, police station houses, and the SPCC.[79] The same people who might find themselves on the wrong side of the law might also seek lodging in station houses or wayfarer's lodges, or even mail in a complaint to the SPCC. From this perspective, the SPCC was merely one more in a chain of services, although differentiated by its dreaded ability to remove children as victims of cruelty or neglect. Interactions with the SPCC initiated by laboring men and women differed from local sanctions in one crucial respect: the SPCC was not a neutral arena for working-class neighbors and families but an upper-middle-class organization connected with the police and court system. In its ability to imprison parents, remove children, and define a family's parenting as inadequate, the SPCC had substantial power. Although SPCC investigations provided opportunities to continually survey and redraw fluid boundaries between respectability and its transgression, they may have also heightened divisions between the respectable and disreputable poor as legal sanctions intensified the risk of deviance.[80]

Despite its considerable power to implement its vision through legal means, the SPCC provided a forum for women and children as well as men, African Americans and immigrants as well as native whites, the poor as well as the prosperous, to articulate standards of proper parenting and public and private behavior. As they responded to reform interventions—at times actively seeking out reformers, other times shunning them as intruders—the city's laboring men, women, and children articulated their own, frequently conflicting perspectives on appropriate standards of behavior. Just as the SPCC relied on the aid of a segment of the working class to police transgressions, so many of the city's laboring poor used complaints to the SPCC to establish their own values.

Both the norm of the respectable laboring family and its antithesis were constructed by negotiation between families and child welfare reformers, as well as within the working class. The SPCC was created partly in response to reformers' alarm at the disparity between the childrearing standards of the prosperous and the poor. But the readiness of laboring people to "inform the Cruelty" revealed dissension over domestic issues within laboring communities. The presence of the reformers in poor neighborhoods, the material and ideological resources they had at their disposal, and the positions they took on specific childrearing practices such as physical correction and children's labor in the street trades encouraged laboring people to continually renegotiate family and community norms. Throughout the late nineteenth century, this process was also underway in the households and families of Philadelphia's laboring poor.

Chapter 3

Dens of Inequities
Laboring Families and Reform Intervention

EARLY IN JULY 1878, an agent of the Pennsylvania Society to Protect Children from Cruelty (SPCC) visited a working-class district of Philadelphia to investigate charges of drunkenness and immorality lodged against a pair of sisters. The charges were serious, as were the potential consequences of the agent's visit. The women were alleged to associate with disreputable persons and visit houses of ill-fame, accompanied by their young children. Afterward, they were thought to squander the proceeds on rum. Although one of the women, Kate, had been separated from her husband for over ten months, it was rumored that she had recently borne a child.[1]

As a representative of the SPCC, the agent's task was to impress notions of proper parenting and morality upon the young mothers. If necessary, he would work with the police and courts to arrest and separate family members, sending the mothers to the House of Correction and placing their children in an institution or with relatives or neighbors.[2] The agent also possessed certain powers not officially delegated to him by the SPCC charter: his visit could injure a woman's reputation in the neighborhood and affect her credit status with the landlord and at the grocer's.

Although reform of working-class family life was at the heart of the SPCC investigations, a careful reading of the evidence for this case and others like it highlights both the significant role family members played in striving to shape reform intervention and the ways that laboring people themselves used and influenced representations of the poor as they did so.[3] Popular representations of the urban poor—of good providers and tramps; thrifty housewives and fallen women; dutiful daughters and "street arabs"— shaped working-class self-representations as well as representational strategies employed by working-class people in their interactions with reformers.[4]

The charge that Kate and Maggie were unfit mothers who lived off the proceeds of prostitution had in fact originated with their husbands, who urged the SPCC to remove the children from maternal custody. When questioned, the sisters admitted that they worked in a house of ill-fame, but stated in their defense that they merely did the women's laundry to support themselves and their children. Twelve-year-old Mary, the eldest daughter, accompanied her mother, but only to earn her fifty-cent contribution to the family economy by running errands for the lady of the house on Saturday nights. Mary was a dutiful daughter, not a bad girl on the road to ruin. Maggie alleged that her husband had done nothing for her since they were married, that he drank excessively and refused to work. In other words, he was lazy and a drunkard, rather than a good provider whose economic support of his wife and children earned him the right to direct family affairs. And Kate insisted that her husband had left her in August. She claimed the baby had been born the early part of May—that is, within nine months of her husband's departure. Furthermore, she testified that she was a deserted wife whose impending maternity had brought out the worst in her husband, who was "in the habit of leaving her when she got in that condition."[5]

The disagreement between the accused women and their husbands also points to intrafamilial tensions regarding social norms as much as conflict between upper- and upper-middle-class social reformers and their working-class clientele.[6] The two husbands' insistence that their wives' work in a brothel was improper suggests the possibility that certain values integral to middle-class domesticity were also part of working-class culture. Yet the wives' insistence that a good mother could take in the wash of the local brothel in order to feed her children if her husband did not provide financial support also suggests that working-class culture had its own distinctive, more flexible, ways of measuring maternal duty. Finally, the possibility that the men may have hoped to wield the SPCC's authority as a weapon against their wives in a quarrel that had nothing to do with childrearing standards must also be considered.

Were Kate and Maggie two decent hard-working mothers, deserted by drunken males and struggling to survive? Or did they personify the true woman's fallen sister, the unfit mother working in a brothel? As Kate, Maggie, and their husbands told tales to the SPCC agent, they engaged in power struggles over which representations would be central to the interpretation of the family quarrel and how their meanings would be interpreted. Using their knowledge of the dominant construction of true womanhood, the two men appealed to the SPCC for aid in disciplining their wives. As they defended themselves, their wives redefined respectable norms of good motherhood to encompass their work in a brothel, by playing on the working-class understanding that women's wage labor was acceptable if done to support their children. Even as they expanded the meaning of respectability almost beyond recognition in order to locate themselves within its contours, the women drew on notions of the normative family shared by the dominant Victorian culture and its respectable working-class counterpart, to label themselves as good mothers and their husbands as worthless unmanly brutes and poor providers.

As the case of Kate, Maggie, and their husbands demonstrates, reformers did not monopolize either the representation or labeling of experience.[7] Laboring people shared in the practice and the power of labeling and the cultural production of narratives about errant family members. Representations of tramps and good providers, fallen women and unnatural mothers, hard-working wives and mothers and dutiful daughters and waifs, were not imposed on laboring families; rather, working people were central to their creation. In their struggles with family members and reformers, working-class people were both producers and consumers of cultural narratives about the laboring poor—narratives that described problems and their origins and offered solutions.[8] As they spun tales, husbands, wives, and children tried to gain some power in material ways—to get child support, custody, aid from charitable organizations, or exert authority over spouses or children.

Poor Providers and Abusive Fathers, Unwilling Housekeepers, Unfaithful Wives, and Unnatural Mothers

The SPCC's case accounts of unruly women, abusive husbands, disobedient children, sex and drinking, curses and brawling all testify that family relations could be fraught with conflict. The parents and children who appear in the case records are not representative of all of Philadelphia's working-class families, for the problems that distressed them were unusually severe. But many families that never came to the attention of the SPCC were troubled by similar conflicts. Disputes over men's ability to provide for their families, housewives' management of the family budget, and children's economic and social autonomy were structured into daily life in an era in which necessity compelled family members to pool their resources in order to survive.

Domestic conflict between men and women and parents and children typically occurred either when shared cultural definitions of appropriate behavior were not fulfilled, or were being renegotiated. At other times all parties involved shared similar understandings of appropriate behavior, but disagreed over the actual extent of familial obligations or were simply unwilling to behave accordingly. Arbitrary explosions and disputes related to episodes of alcohol abuse are also documented in the records. Significantly, cases involving explicit physical violence between spouses or parents and children formed a minority of those handled by the SPCC.[9]

As family members appealed to the SPCC to police transgressions in their families, they frequently drew on widely-held notions of the respectable family shared to different effect by both the dominant Victorian culture and its working-class counterpart. There were important differences, though, in the way ideology shaped their understanding of family conflict. In their analyses of daughters gone bad, husbands' drunkenness and failure to provide, women's refusal to cook and clean, laboring and poor families tended not to draw on the politicized accounts of the labor movement but to highlight individual character flaws and irresponsibility. It is, after all, more difficult to maintain a political analysis of an individual's—and particularly a relative's—troubles at close range. Yet the stories laboring people told reformers in order to explain hopeless despair, depression and drinking binges, pawned bedclothes and empty pots and pans, ragged hungry children and dirty houses sometimes betrayed a more nuanced sense of causality that was distinct from reform analyses of poverty.

Philadelphia's men, women, and children used the SPCC to enforce gender-specific family obligations. Parents demanded obedience from both boys and girls, but expectations for sons and daughters were different. Boys were expected to obey their parents, to sleep at home rather than occasionally slipping away to sleep on the wharves, and to turn over some of their wages to their mother. Daughters were expected to contribute most if not all of their wages if they worked outside the home. If they did not earn regular wages, they performed household labor and became "little mothers" to their younger brothers and sisters. They were also expected to refrain from improper sexual encounters with men, and to avoid dance halls and places of ill-repute.

Working-class husbands and wives also had clearly defined expectations of one another, although unsteady work and low wages often hindered their fulfillment. Husbands were expected to be "good providers" who turned over most of their wages to their wives.[10] So firm was the equation of husbands and providers—despite the contribution of women and children to the family economy—that for some Philadelphians it was the provision of economic support, rather than a marriage license, that earned men the right to call themselves husbands. As one witness to a neighbor's matrimonial disputes claimed, "Dfdt was continually quarreling with her husband . . . and she frequently heard her tell her husband . . . that he had no business in the home as she received money from another man . . . to pay the rent."[11]

While a good husband might keep a certain amount of his earnings to spend on beer, a wife could complain if her husband spent too much money on alcohol or if he became intoxicated on a regular basis. Being a good husband also entailed being a good father: a man was expected to chastise disobedient children and take an interest in their welfare. But if he punished his children too severely or beat his wife, he would be considered abusive by his neighbors as well as his family.[12] Wives were expected to manage the family income, supervise young children, remain faithful to their husbands, and perform domestic labor within the household.

As historians Ellen Ross and Christine Stansell have argued, mothering and housekeeping are socially and historically specific practices; their tenets varied even within working-class neighborhoods.[13] In the poorest households, efficient housekeeping and appropriate mothering might include pawning and retrieving of household goods, relying on the rewards of children's labor in the street trades, and other practices that were anathema to SPCC reformers and "better" working-class families alike. Like husbands, wives might drink beer, although women's drunkenness was generally less tolerated than men's. Unlike African American families, who frequently depended on the wages of married women, most Irish and German families preferred to rely on the economic contributions of children rather than wives. White working-class women could also work regularly outside the home, however, if their husbands' wages were not enough to support the family, however, or if the children were too young to work. Like African American women, they could also take in lodgers or work as washerwomen. Hard-pressed by the high rents landlords demanded from blacks and the low wages paid to black men, many African-American wives and mothers also lived out for several days of the week, working as servants in other people's homes.[14]

In 1880, 27.1 percent of African American, 16.9 percent of Irish, 5.9 percent of German, and 14.3 percent of native white families in Philadelphia were headed by women.[15] In all ethnic groups, widowhood—rather than separation, divorce, and single motherhood combined—accounted for the greatest number of female-headed households. A consequence of irregular employment, poor housing and sanitation, and inadequate public health services, differential mortality rates for black men meant that many African American women were widowed in their thirties and forties and raised their children by themselves or with other women.[16]

Women who belonged to groups overrepresented among the city's chronic poor—African Americans, female heads of households, members of unskilled Irish families in the childbearing stage of the life cycle—were by definition excluded from genteel "true womanhood" but could aim for respectability as measured by distinctive working-class standards. Working-class mothers did not necessarily lose respectability if they had to work for wages. If done as a labor of love, mothers who sewed, cleaned, or washed to earn money to support their children could earn the approval as well as the pity of their neighbors. Wives were also expected to be thrifty managers of the family budget and to make sure that the children were clothed and fed. When necessary, women also assumed the responsibility for negotiating with the local charities as an extension of their duties as wives and mothers. In 1880, close to 15 percent of the city's population had some sort of interaction with Philadelphia's public and voluntary agencies, and this figure probably underestimates the extent of charitable contacts in the city, since families were likelier to need public or private "relief" at different points in the life cycle.[17]

Heartfelt complaints by spouses illuminate the expectations men and women might bring to marriage, as well as their clear understanding and deliberate, sometimes even instrumental reference to the tropes—the tramp, the drunken husband, the deserted wife, the fallen woman, the dangerous mother—reformers relied on as they assessed working-class men and women. Women were judged by their performance of domestic duties, husbands by their willingness and ability to provide for their families. During investigations, reformers read domestic details for clues to character that helped establish the veracity of a complaint or the legitimacy of a family's need. A well-scoured but empty pot could serve as shorthand for a sober, industrious, but destitute wife whose husband was a poor provider; a dirty room became code for a poor housewife and dangerous mother while a house devoid of furnishings signaled trips to the pawnshop to procure money for drink. Called to a case in which a couple's drunken quarrel resulted in the wife's death four days after Christmas in 1879, the SPCC agent noted all the domestic details that might reveal the story of this family's downfall: the dirty house and filthy mattress, the room devoid of all furnishings but "a table, trunk, and a very small stove on which was pot with a chicken in it, partly boiled, showing at least that the man had provided food."[18] A drunkard and a brute in prison for murdering the mother of his eighteen-month-old twins, still this husband had not failed as a provider.

Husbands who pressed charges against their wives at the SPCC office shared agents' concerns, claiming their wives were intemperate, neglected their children, engaged in sexual immorality, and refused to do housework. When an agent visited one husband at work because neighbors had brought his family to the attention of the Society, he seconded their complaints, stating that his wife's unwillingness to prepare meals, keep the fire lit, or to care for the children had caused considerable marital difficulties. Another husband who begged agents to give his wife a second chance to stop drinking later notified agents when his wife broke her temperance pledge.[19]

The ongoing struggle between the SPCC and working-class Philadelphians to define the organization's mission also affected the way people framed their complaints. Because the SPCC was concerned primarily with child abuse, agents were willing to intervene only in those cases in which a wife's misconduct hindered her maternal, as opposed to her wifely, responsibilities. For this reason husbands motivated by anger at a wife's sexual unfaithfulness, nagging, or disobedience sometimes disguised their complaints in the form of paternal concern. For instance, an African American man named Fred J. appeared at the SPCC office in the winter of 1887 and informed Agent Watson that his wife Delia was intemperate, neglected her child, and ran "around with a bad character, known as 'RailRoad' Bill." When agents duly investigated, however, they found no evidence of neglect. Contrary to Fred's claims, Delia was not a drunkard, a fallen woman, or a dangerous mother, but Fred's behavior was quite arguably akin to that of a tramp's. Agents learned that Fred had contributed nothing for the support of his wife and their two children since he had left home nearly two years earlier. When Fred returned, he found Delia living with another man. Fred, Delia, Bill, and the children were currently all living in one room, and Fred was "anxious to get the woman to leave [Bill] . . . and live with him again." For her part, Delia underscored the association between husbands and good providers, claiming that Fred was no longer her husband since he had not supported her and their children. She refused to live with him again and alleged "that when she did live with him, he ill-treated her and the children." After unraveling the conflicting statements of Fred and Delia, the agent determined, "As this seems to be a fight between the two men to get possession of the woman, no action can be taken at present."[20]

Clearly, disputes between husbands and wives were at the heart of many a case of alleged child neglect. In April 1877 Max F. called at the SPCC office to complain that his wife Tillie had left him two months before, taking their two-and-a-half-year-old child, Lottie. Presenting himself as a concerned father, Max depicted his wife as a dangerous mother. Although Max did not claim his wife was a prostitute, the portrait he painted of Tillie—a woman with a dependent child, a loose reputation, and no honest way of making a living—made it likely that she might be forced to exchange sex for money. Max claimed that Tillie's conduct was "censurable" (in the words of the agent) and that (in Max's words) she "goes with another man." Furthermore, Max believed that, as Tillie was entirely unable to support either herself or their child, their daughter was "suffering for want of food." There is no reason to doubt Max's concern for his daughter or his belief in his wife's dependence, for with a two-and-a-half-year-old daughter, Tillie would likely be hard-pressed to support herself and her child. Max was probably equally motivated, however, by the desire to punish his wife for her departure and his consequent humiliation. He told the SPCC agent and secretary that Tillie's conduct had come as a surprise. He had returned home one day to find Tillie had disappeared along with their possessions, leaving him "a dissolute home. without wife. child. or furniture."[21] Max was left a deserted spouse, a situation culturally reserved for dependent women victimized by brutish men.

When the agent investigated he learned that the charge of infidelity was unfounded and "that one side of a story is very good until the other side is heard." Neighbors all spoke "kindly and respectfully" of Tillie, who appeared to be "an industrious hard-working woman" quite "able to make a living for herself and her child." Max, however, was reputed to be a drunken and abusive husband. Tillie declared that she was perfectly willing to allow Max to see their daughter, but insisted that he must be sober when he did. Six months later the tables were turned, when Tillie lodged a complaint with the SPCC against her husband, who "greatly annoyed her by his drunken and disorderly behavior." The agent advised her to have him arrested and placed in the House of Correction.[22]

Because agents relied on the testimony of numerous witnesses, husbands were not always successful in their attempts to turn SPCC intervention to their own ends. But even an investigation that reaffirmed the propriety of a woman's mothering could harm her reputation in the neighborhood, because the notoriety that accompanied an agent's visit provided an opportunity for the circulation of scurrilous gossip.

The extent to which husbands knew how to formulate their original complaints when they appealed to agents also demonstrates that there was widespread awareness of the SPCC's standards of proper parenting, even when they were not adhered to. In 1896 Peter U. informed SPCC officials that his wife Emma had taken their two daughters to live in a house that was "the resort of black and white who run the growler. and that it was not a fit place for the children." Investigation revealed that after the couple had quarreled, Emma had left with the children and Peter had sold the household goods. The agent deemed both parents unworthy and was "unable to find which was the worse of the two." As disturbed by the proximity of whites and African Americans as he was by intemperance, the agent noted that Emma and the children were staying in the only white household on the street, and that "they were of the lowest class and associate blacks and whites promiscuously . . . and drink and carouse." The investigation caused a great stir in the neighborhood; Emma took advantage of the commotion to run away, while Peter seized possession of the children.[23]

Although working-class sociability violated the norms of the middle and upper middle class, SPCC reformers depended on it for evidence, and agents readily violated their own norms of privacy as they encouraged neighbors to talk. The residents of an entire street might be privy to intimate—if not secret—relations between husbands and wives. When a man called to notify the SPCC that he was no longer living with his wife, who neglected their child, pawned their clothing, and brought their child with her into saloons, the agent relied on the dense sociability of the couple's South Philadelphia neighborhood to ascertain the truth. One neighbor declared that the wife had never been seen intoxicated or in saloons, but that she did not have a high opinion of the wife's morality. The grocer said that she owed him twenty dollars for items bought on credit and that he considered her "a little 'gay'" (prostitutes were referred to as "gay" women), but he knew nothing more than that. The landlady and another woman defended the man's wife, however, stating that she did not drink and pawned clothing only to provide food for herself and her child. The witnesses informed the agent that the couple had gone to court, where the husband had been ordered to pay the woman five dollars a week. The SPCC dropped the case when it learned that the man was following his wife on the street and harassing her at every turn in an effort to secure a divorce.[24]

Wives elaborated on the trope of the good provider and its opposite, the tramp, as they turned to the SPCC for help in dealing with husbands who were abusive or failed to support the family financially. In the process, complainants opened themselves as well as their husbands to investigation, rendering their mothering, housekeeping, cleanliness, honesty, and decency vulnerable to scrutiny and judgment. As they criticized their spouses women relied on their status as respectable wives and good mothers to justify their claims against their husbands. Only by defiantly exposing their husbands' inadequacy could some wives successfully take on the maternal task of feeding and protecting their children. In the process, in the name of good motherhood, women could move from dependence to assertion.

Women's financial dependence on and vulnerability to men was a key element in the charity reform, woman's rights, male labor, and laboring women's stories of economic need. Wives' complaints to the SPCC about men who drank excessively or refused to turn their wages over to their wives, however, typically had more in common with the charity reform story of the tramp's willful idleness than with the under- and unemployment highlighted by the labor movement. In part this followed from the process of intervention, which both created and limited the ways that laboring people could articulate demands to particular agencies.[25] When husbands refused to earn or hand over wages, the SPCC's specific mandate forced women to press claims as mothers rather than wives. Moreover, economic neediness alone placed women and children under the rubric of the Charity Organization Society rather than the SPCC, who could address poverty only if redefined as child neglect. While the COS's insistence on recipients' worthiness encouraged women to present themselves and their families in the best light, the SPCC would only take action in cases of nonsupport if they found evidence of a father's abuse.

The notion of the good provider that equated being a husband with breadwinning—so central to the labor movement's demand for the family wage—also empowered women to press their claims against men who failed to support their families. The formulation of the husband as either a good or a poor provider—relied on by wives as well as the SPCC—individualized and personalized the problem of under- and unemployment and low wages, turning it into a story about the husband's inadequacy or unmanly disavowal of his responsibility to support his wife and children. In 1880 a wife brought her husband with her to the SPCC office, where she complained that her husband's wages could not support their fifteen children. Rejecting the woman's charge that her husband was a poor provider, SPCC reformers rewrote her tale as a story about working-class sensuality, the intemperance of German immigrants, and the various ways that money spent on alcohol interfered with family planning. The Secretary recorded:

This case is not one for the Society. it has its ludicrous side, the plntff and dfndt come together—the man in appearance was a quiet, good-natured sort of a fellow, the woman charged him with neglecting his family and not properly providing for them. She said he would every once in a while get full of beer, also that instead of earning $12 per week, he ought to be getting $20 per week—the man told her to get the situation for him and he would take it, also stated that his "frau" drank "as mucher more as he"—every week he gave her $11 50/100 of his earnings and very often the whole $12 00/100—the man said he knew he had a growing family which was likely to be increased—didn't know when it was to stop. he was doing the best he could for his family. Advised him not to drink any beer, and he would be able to have a little more money in case of further trouble. The woman said she didn't want him to stop his beer for she would not then get any. she wanted him to get a better situation or else make him increase his wages where he is now employed.[26]

In 1887 an anonymous letter called the attention of SPCC agents to Edwin and Margaret B. and their five children, aged one year to six years. The complaint stated that the children were begging on the street and that the father's whereabouts were unknown. Upon investigation the agent learned that Edwin B., now thought to be in West Philadelphia, had been drinking heavily and had not worked for nine months. He had left a week ago, saying he "would not return until he got work." Margaret B., who was characterized by the agent as a sober woman, needed immediate relief in order to care for her five children. Unlike many of the poor, she was willing to receive "indoor" or institutional relief, as long as she and her children were not separated. The Society arranged for a warrant for the husband's arrest for nonsupport. One week after the original complaint was filed, Edwin B.'s brother called at the Society office, perhaps motivated by the humiliation of the SPCC investigation, the imminent and stigmatizing institutionalization of his sister-in-law and his brother's children, and the desire to distance himself from his intemperate and unemployed brother. He stated that his brother was a "worthless fellow" who could get work if he wanted; their father had been helping him but had grown tired of doing so.[27]

Rather than following the labor movement tale of unemployment as the force that destroyed families—turning men into tramps, children into beggars, and wives into deserted women dependent on charity—and portraying his brother as a victim of unemployment, the man depicted his brother as worthless: he drank, did not support his family, and refused to get work. In this scenario, Edwin B.'s individual moral failure had pauperized his wife and children.

Unlike Edwin B.'s brother, many working people had more complicated understandings of the correlation between drinking and unemployment. By the 1890s, even Frances Willard of the Women's Christian Temperance Union had declared that poverty caused intemperance as much as intemperance generated poverty.[28] Yet this case highlights the underside of respectability and the tendency even among the laboring poor to characterize chronically unemployed people as worthless, especially if they drank.

Wives portrayed husbands as abusive fathers as well as poor providers. Here too they had to formulate complaints as mothers rather than as wives, but they were not always able to rely on the testimony of their children. In 1878 Mrs. Z. called at the SPCC office and stated that she was afraid to live with her husband, who had "pitched her out into the street." She was informed that "the Soc. was not for the purpose of protecting wives but children" and officials suggested that she return with witnesses to present a case about the abuse of her children. Although four other women were willing to testify in her defense, her son was not. When she returned to the SPCC office with her eldest son, "the Sec. [Secretary] requested the lad to come to him and tell him all about it." At this the boy replied "that he would not lie against his father and immediately ran downstairs. The woman was dumbfounded and left."[29]

Working-class women could draw on the Victorian convention of the working-class man as brute as they formulated complaints about their spouses. Whether used to refer to drunkards, wife-beaters, or child abusers, the term was reserved for all men who chose not or were unable to exercise control over their passions—whether sexual lust, desire for alcohol, or violent anger. Nonetheless, racial, ethnic and class as well as gender content were central to the image of the male brute. While innate characteristics allegedly rendered all men potentially passionate, sexual, and violent, respectable middle- and working-class men were supposed to exercise self-control, becoming "manly" through restraint of their natures.

Although temperance advocates used the term to refer to all men who abused their families by their addiction to alcohol, by the late nineteenth century the brute had become shorthand for immigrant and African American men. Indeed the newly developing disciplines of social science lent scientific credence to this popular view. As historian Elizabeth Fee has argued, social scientists viewed the middle-class Victorian family as the apex of civilization, the "end result of a long historical struggle against the crude desires of nature." In comparison, working class, immigrant, and African

American people were closer to nature than to civilization: their lives and domestic habits were seen as anthropological survivals of earlier stages of evolution.[30] In her account of the immigrant poor, *Darkness and Daylight,* reformer Helen Campbell concurred that brutes were frequently found in immigrant neighborhoods but were less well known among native-born Americans, claiming, "It is because New York is less an American city than almost any other in the United States that the need for the 'Society for the Prevention of Cruelty to Children' was so sore." [31]

Countering this image of working-class and black men as sexual, violent brutes, female African American anti-lynching activists and adherents of the Victorian labor movement's analysis of prostitution argued, respectively, that it was white and upper-class men who were the real brutes, because they preyed on the virtue of African American and white working-class women.[32] Although representational strategies of both the labor movement and the anti-lynching campaign involved identifying working-class and African American men as manly, as opposed to upper-class men or white men who were identified as brutes, individual women seeking protection from violent spouses targeted specific working-class men as violent and out of control.

Laboring women who sought to protect their children from abusive fathers demanded that they and their children be treated safely and decently. Ellen C. filed a complaint with the SPCC against her husband, John, charging that he "ill treated" their six-year-old daughter. The SPCC Secretary recorded that "He has treated the child badly since its infancy and did express the wish that it would die, and even said he wished he could get candy with poison to give it." Ellen wanted the SPCC to scare her husband with a warning, but refused to have him arrested. John's unmanly behavior was also evidenced by the fact that Ellen had assumed the provider role; she was supporting her husband as well as her child, who she placed in the Jane Kent Day Nursery.[33] As the Secretary recorded, "Although he pays the rent, he gives her but a dollar and a half a week while she earns from six to six and a half. . . . Agent advised her that an arrest would be the only effective means of teaching him that he would not be allowed to ill-treat the child. But she is afraid he will leave her as she expects to be out of work before long." [34]

SPCC agents aided and encouraged wives to obtain financial support from their husbands, but these efforts sometimes met with resistance from wives as well as husbands. While wives wielded the threat to call in "the

Society" as a weapon, they were often reluctant to follow the SPCC's advice to take their husbands to court to punish transgressions of husbandly responsibility.[35] This ambivalence stemmed not only from emotional unwillingness to follow through on charges against their husbands but also realistic appraisals that took into account the improbability of ever receiving financial support from husbands humiliated by a fine and a stint in jail. When Maggie O' C. appeared at the SPCC in 1879, she "made a most pitiable complaint about her husband's cruelty and neglect." But when agents informed her that they would arrest her husband if he were guilty as charged, Maggie grew indignant. She asserted with spirit that "she would not allow anything of the kind, he should not be put away" and declared that she wanted the Society to force him to support her, not to arrest him. Agents informed her that "the Guardians of the Poor, was the place she wanted to find."[36]

Deserted wives made choices; although frequently destitute they were not necessarily passive or dependent. Yet even assertive women willing to go to court discovered the problems involved in enforcing their claims for support. When a German woman named Gertie W. asked for aid in March 1896, she had already taken her husband to court the previous November. The judge had ordered Gertie's husband Jonathan to pay her three dollars a week. When Gertie insisted that this sum was not enough, the judge told her that "she should either take that or go back and live with her husband." The records noted "she did the latter, and since then he has not worked or contributed a penny towards her support, and he has not lived with her for some time." Because she could expect little support from her parents, she had gone to work in a mill. When Gertie appealed to the SPCC, the agent told her that "if she wanted support, it was her duty to prosecute her husband, as she was the only one who could do so," and offered legal assistance. She declined the offer, however, claiming she could not lose the time from work. In an accurate assessment of her predicament, Gertie pointed out the futility of arresting her husband for "if he [her husband] was sent to prison he could not support the children, and if she leave [sic] him go, he will not."[37]

Gertie could be cast as a deserted wife, victimized by a worthless husband, yet she was clearly resourceful and had her own outlook on the form intervention should take. Women's determination to define their own needs and strategies, coupled with a skeptical attitude about the feasibility of achieving their goals by arresting husbands for nonsupport, frustrated

SPCC agents who resented having their efforts to prosecute come to naught. Annie C. told agents that her husband was a wood turner, and could have had plenty of work but chose to drink and neglect his children instead, deserting Annie when she was "in the midst of confinement." After Annie informed her husband that "she would report him to the 'cruelty'" he had not come home, leaving her in destitute circumstances and unable to pay the rent. Witnesses who had been feeding the woman and her children for the last five weeks confirmed that they had seen the husband leave home with the last two blankets. Agents arranged for the arrest of Annie's husband, but were dismayed when she had little to say in court. The Secretary noted "while she admitted what she had told at this office and to Agent at her house was true, yet everything she said had to be literally dragged from her."[38] Although the SPCC provided much-needed assistance and encouragement for women who prosecuted husbands for abuse, their aid could not change the structural factors that enforced women's economic dependency on abusive husbands and fathers.

Dutiful Sons and Daughters or Apprentices in Tramping, Thievery, and Prostitution

Parents and children alike struggled to redefine their reciprocal obligations during the late nineteenth century. In the eighteenth and early nineteenth centuries, parent-child relations had been determined chiefly by the father's patriarchal control over the family's property and the labor power of its members. The economic independence of grown children was ordinarily linked to either the transmission of family property and/or craft skills. But by the late nineteenth century, particularly in cities, traditional patriarchal control over children's labor had greatly weakened, along with parental ability to replicate their children's class position through the transmission of property or traditional craft skills. Families of all class backgrounds were forced to develop new strategies to secure their children's futures.[39] At the same time that traditional patriarchal authority eroded in all classes, the ability of laboring men to provide for their wives and children without relying on the wages of other family members grew tenuous. It was in this space—between parental reliance on children's income or labor and the breakdown of parental and especially paternal power and authority—that struggles between parents and children emerged.[40]

The SPCC attempted to support the individual rights of children, while also working to restore the eroded power of parents. As Linda Gordon has noted, SPCCs all over the country "aimed as much to reinforce a failing parental/paternal authority as to limit it."[41] SPCC agents and parents worked closely together to assert authority over unruly sons and rebellious daughters, backed by police and the courts. At other times agents and parents differed in their assessments of what children should deserve and parents should demand. In instances where the assumptions of agents and parents conflicted, mothers and fathers who thought they were acting appropriately were perceived by agents as exploitative or neglectful. In these cases, agents could work with police to arrest parents if earnest discussions at the SPCC office did not bring about the desired transformation in parental outlook and behavior.

Reformers who promoted child labor legislation, compulsory schooling, and strict enforcement of prohibitions regulating children's participation in the street trades tried to impose on society a middle-class construction of childhood as a period of innocence, vulnerability, and parental protection.[42] Working-class parents and their children did not always take a similar stance in this contest between classes over the proper meaning of childhood. For many native-born children of immigrant parents, the process of Americanization coincided with the assertion of greater privileges.[43] With the intervention of reformers, sons' and daughters' demands for greater economic and personal autonomy were translated into disagreements between both generations and classes over the extent of parental responsibilities and children's obligations.

Cultural differences regarding parental supervision figured in SPCC cases concerning adolescents as well as young children. When Johanna G. moved to Pittsburgh, she left her fifteen-year-old daughter in Philadelphia where she was earning her living as a domestic servant. When her employers moved away and left the girl on her own, she readily found another situation as a servant in Katie McC.'s household, where she earned $1.50 per week. When her new mistress claimed she could afford to pay only $1 per week, the young domestic replied that she would not stay for that amount and left. At this point she came to the attention of the SPCC, who interviewed her old employer, her aunt, and her cousin. Although her former employer had found no fault with her, the SPCC placed her in the House of the Good Shepherd after officials learned of her mother's absence. When Johanna G. returned to the city three months later, she called at the SPCC office to remove her daughter from the reform institution, but "the Secretary declined to let her." The SPCC Secretary probably felt that no proper mother would have left a fifteen-year-old daughter to fend for herself in the city. Yet Johanna's behavior was not exceptional, and her daughter could have been portrayed as a self-reliant wage-earner as easily as a neglected child.[44] Working-class adolescents were expected to fend for themselves because parents could offer little financial assistance. Indeed parents who did not teach sons and daughters to take care of themselves at a young age were remiss in fulfilling their responsibilities to their children, especially since many children would witness the death of one or both parents before they reached adulthood. Johanna's daughter may have learned the lesson of self-sufficiency too well, for if she had been willing to work for low wages she might not have been sent to the House of the Good Shepherd.

Poor parents fully expected children either to contribute unpaid household labor or to earn money from a young age. Although it believed working-class adolescents should contribute to their own support, the SPCC considered parental reliance on young children's labor abusive, particularly if it involved exposure to strangers on the city streets or led children into saloons, low lodging houses, or theaters. By the late 1870s, the perception of children's labor as property owned by their parents was challenged by children and the SPCC alike.

Throughout the Gilded Age, agents actively searched out child street-sellers, beggars, musicians, and other performers in a campaign to remove children from streets and theaters. These efforts resulted in repeated clashes with working-class parents, who resented being told what to do and feared the loss of their children's income. SPCC agents visited twelve-year-old Hannah's parents after she was found playing her violin on Market Street. The agent noted that her mother was "a cripple and the father was feeble-minded"; "they appeared very anxious to know how they should get their living."[45] Undeterred, he informed them that "their condition did not warrant them in violating the law, or else all the others would be making the same complaint." When an agent investigated allegations that Anthony L. sent two boys and a girl on the streets with fiddles and a harp, he found the Italian residents of their South Philadelphia neighborhood very agitated over the SPCC's policies concerning street musicians. The Secretary noted, "This neighborhood is full of just such cases, and action of the Soc. is occasioning much consternation among them. Agent saw them reading the law which had been sent among them and gesticulating violently they appeard very much incensed, but talking in their native tongue, the Agt. could not understand them."[46]

Even young children were aware of the laws against peddling. For instance, a six-year-old boy who sold newspapers on Broad and Chestnut Streets after midnight ran away when an agent approached to question him.[47] Although children participated in the street trades with their parents' knowledge and frequently at their bidding, the opportunities the streets presented for pleasure and profit could lead to familial conflict. Parents as well as reformers feared that the street trades could incline boys toward a future of vagrancy and girls toward a life of prostitution. Both parents and SPCC agents maintained a vigilant watch for the warning signs of tramping and prostitution. In 1880 the SPCC recorded that two German American sisters, Lottie and Minnie U., were "spoken of as very nice girls, but the parents compel them to sell papers on the streets—it is a mere question of time how long they will keep their good name."[48]

Although SPCC agents and parents alike could agree on the need for supervision for young boys drawn to the independence of street life from an early age, their reasons often differed. Agents, policemen, and parents were concerned with boys who preferred the hand-to-mouth existence of street life, occasional vagrancy, and the companionship of other boys to the steadier routines of home life and pursuit of a trade. While the SPCC feared that street life, like the street trades, exposed children to immorality and led to a life of crime, parents looked with disfavor on their sons' propensity to roam the streets and sleep outdoors because such a life encouraged them to neglect their familial responsibilities.

Runaway boys were a common sight on Philadelphia's streets. Since they relied on petty theft and pillaging for their survival, such boys could be a nuisance for shopkeepers and the police. Officers informed SPCC agents when they found boys sleeping in boxes, on the wharves, or in station houses, and agents tried to place such boys under proper supervision.[49] When an orphaned boy whose aunt and uncle could not afford to support him any longer was discovered on the wharves searching for a place to sleep, SPCC agents arranged his job as a doorboy in a model lodging house and found a family willing to adopt him.[50] But the distinction between boys left to fend for themselves because parents could not or would not support them and boys drawn by the lure of the streets could be a fine one. Experienced agents found that in some cases it was a distinction not worth pursuing if a boy was judged in need of reform.

Just as the accusations of quarreling spouses were couched in terms likely to appeal to the SPCC, so youths apprehended by SPCC agents used tales of parental cruelty and exploitation in their own defense. When sons or daughters maintained that their parents forced them to peddle, they knew this charge would win sympathy from the SPCC. One newsboy questioned by SPCC agents claimed that if he did not take home fifty to sixty cents profit every night, he would be beaten. He stated that he had joined the "Newsboy's Home" in order to escape the claims of his father, but if his father met him on the street, he forced the boy to accompany him home. When the boy's father called at the SPCC office he told a somewhat different story. He declared that he did not want his son to be a bootblack or a newsboy, but wished him to learn a trade, but the boy preferred "an arab life."[51] Was the enterprising newsboy willful and impudent, escaping appropriate parental supervision, or an exploited child in danger of his mercenary father's wrath? Each tale was in its way plausible. Even as he disapproved of his son's participation in the street trades, preferring that the boy learn a skill, a father could reasonably expect a working son to hand over the money he earned, and he might beat him if the boy refused. One twelve-year-old boy came to the office of the SPCC to inform authorities that he was the main support of his entire family, was forced to steal potatoes at the wharf, and was beaten if he refused. Neighbors defended his parents, however, and claimed that the only basis for the disobedient boy's tales of cruelty was his desire to escape the "confinement of his home."[52]

Dissatisfied adolescents attempted to use the SPCC's position against children's work in the street trades and concern with parental exploitation of children to gain leverage in their families. Lena G., a fourteen-year-old German Jewish girl described in the case records as a "Jewess" and a "child of unusual smartness," called at the SPCC office to complain that her parents sent her to peddle with a basket. Lena claimed that if she did not bring home enough money her parents beat and cursed at her. While Lena elaborated on the theme of the exploitative parents, her mother and father characterized her as wayward and disobedient. After her parents relinquished custody, Lena "was placed temporarily in the Howard Home until a place could be found for her," preferably with her aunt in New Jersey. Shortly after Lena returned to her family and the troubles were renewed, despite her parents' promise to "keep her off the streets." Yet Lena remained unwilling to testify against her mother, and the case could go no further until a neighbor volunteered to testify before the magistrate and Lena's mother was arrested.[53]

In another dispute, between a daughter and her father and stepmother, that was allegedly over wages, eighteen-year-old Bella S. drew a portrait of her home life designed to appeal to the prejudices and assumptions of the SPCC. Bella claimed her father was an "idle, drunken, worthless fellow," that she was not allowed to keep a cent of her wages, even to buy clothing, that her parents had threatened to commit her to an institution if she did not turn over her wages, and that her parents and their nine children all slept in one room. Here was a portrait that confirmed the worst the SPCC knew about working-class family life, for Bella depicted exploitative parents who were raising their large family in a situation conducive to incest. When agents investigated they discovered Bella had lied: there were only five children in the family and the apartment contained two rooms. Only one of Bella's claims appeared to be accurate: Bella's family did indeed want her to be "put away."[54]

For sons and particularly for daughters, the struggle to control their own wages was an explicit reason to lodge a complaint with the SPCC against parents and guardians. Parents and children alike were aware that the possession of money provided youthful wage-earners some leverage within the family, as well as access to those city pleasures—such as fancy clothing and theater tickets—that could be purchased. The ways in which children handled their wages raised a number of controversial issues: did sons and daughters defer to parental authority or spend their own wages as they saw fit? Did they treat themselves as individuals, or did they put familial needs first and contribute their wages to pay for food and rent? Finally, were adolescent sons and daughters caught in the snares of "fast" commercial entertainments, spending—or wasting—their money in dance halls and saloons? As quarrels over the money children earned at work spilled into the SPCC office, parents walked a fine line to avoid both the charge of exploiting children by controlling their wages and that of neglecting adolescent children who had escaped their control.

For parents, sons' and daughters' insistence that their wages were their own could be interpreted as a premature claim to adult status and a selfish assertion of individualism. A son's determination to keep most of his wages could be perceived as testimony to his desire to assume the pleasures as well as the responsibilities of adulthood. In contrast, a daughter's insistence on the right to spend her wages as she pleased was understood by parents as an early sign of insubordination, a possible indicator of precocious sexuality, and a good predictor of future immorality. In 1887 sixteen-year-old Hannah N. took the uncle with whom she had lived since she was orphaned to court, because he took the money she earned and whipped her when she refused to comply with his wishes. Hannah claimed that although she had entered domestic service, her uncle still claimed a right to her wages. In court, her uncle testified that he only meant to "keep her from getting into the ways of this Country and being impertinent." Nonetheless, the SPCC took Hannah's side and issued her a letter of protection to keep her uncle from annoying her.[55] Hannah held several positions in domestic service, always notifying the SPCC when she moved; the following year she informed the SPCC that she had married a teacher and she and her husband were now boarding in a house in South Philadelphia.

Parents and guardians who believed in their right to their daughters' wages could appear at their daughters' workplaces or even resort to violence to assert their claims. Katie C. brought an adult woman to the SPCC office to witness her complaint that her father came to the mill where she worked to claim her wages. The thirteen-year-old stated that her father had contributed nothing for her support for the past three to four months, yet he wanted her to maintain him.[56] In July 1879 a seventeen-year-old girl came to the SPCC for assistance in handling her mother. She informed the agent that her mother pawned her clothing and took her wages, "not leaving her anything to provide herself with in way of necessaries." Furthermore, her mother had created a disturbance at the home where the girl was employed. She "came to the house and drew a knife on the child [and] hit her with a rolling pin" until she was finally expelled by the master of the house where the girl was in service.[57]

Often daughters were fighting for the right to retain a portion rather than all of their wages. When fifteen-year-old Eliza entered domestic service, her employer complained to the SPCC that Eliza's father came each Saturday to take her two dollars home with him. Eliza stated that she had not been allowed to keep more than six or eight dollars of her pay although she had worked for the past nine months or so. When Eliza requested permission to retain enough of her wages to buy a desperately needed pair of shoes, her father "cursed and swore." After investigation revealed that Eliza was truthful and had been a satisfactory servant while her widowed father lived "as man and wife" with a woman he was not married to, the SPCC decided in favor of Eliza, the dutiful daughter, rather than the exploitative and immoral father. The agent told her "to buy sufficient clothing for herself. and keep account of the money she spends. and if she has anything left give it to her father."[58]

Although SPCC agents believed that working adolescents should be able to retain some of their wages, they were suspicious of daughters who lived at home but refused to contribute to the family economy. When fourteen-year-old Mary Q. charged her father with felonious assault, the agents refused to believe her when they learned that she and her older sisters bore a "loose" reputation and spent their wages on clothes. Agents commented:

> This is a singular family. There are eight children and Mary . . . is the only one at work. Annie, Maggie, and Hannah bear the reputation of being of the loose kind, and they are running about with boys night and day. Mary has been in the House of [the] Good Shepherd, having been placed there by her father. . . . It would be wrong to depend entirely upon the story of Mary, as she is as bad as her oldest sisters. These girls refuse to do anything toward the support of the family, and when they are working and get their wages, they give fifty cents to their mother and keep the rest, saying they must have it for clothes.[59]

Like runaway daughters and girls who peddled on the streets, girls who chose pleasure over work and familial responsibilities were perceived by agents and relatives alike as taking the first step toward prostitution. If the SPCC supported respectable daughters' independence regarding wages, they converged with working-class parents in their desire to control adolescent female sexuality.

"Lewd and Incorrigible Daughters" on the Road to Ruin

Reformers intent on inculcating feminine propriety frequently formed alliances with determined parents bent on getting daughters to adhere to respectable working-class standards of feminine decorum. While mothers sometimes came to the defense of daughters whose alleged misconduct brought them to the attention of authorities, many parents sought out the SPCC for advice in dealing with their daughters' rebelliousness.[60] Nonetheless, even as reformers and parents joined together to police the behavior of adolescent girls and keep them from prostitution, their understanding of the nuances of respectability may have varied.

Sexual propriety could have different meanings to middle-class reformers and working-class parents and children. Even respectable working-class girls and young women had greater access to public space, dressed more colorfully, and frequented places of amusement that middle-class women considered disreputable—all without compromising their reputations.[61]

However rough they might appear by middle-class standards, their behavior adhered nonetheless to the distinct norms of respectable behavior for young women within working-class communities.

But working-class girls in anonymous public spaces were also constantly under suspicion. They were forced to distinguish themselves from rougher girls, but they could not demonstrate their respectability in the same ways that middle-class women did. Less sheltered than their more prosperous sisters, they frequently contended with situations unknown to middle-class women that might expose them to danger—from walking alone at night, to living in lodgings, to dealing with employers and the possibility of sexual harassment at their workplaces.[62]

In the late nineteenth century several cultural narratives were available for understanding young girls' turn to sexual immorality. These included the labor movement tales of the virtuous working girl seduced by an aristocratic rake and of the honest working girl forced to sell herself rather than starve, and the melodramatic seduction and betrayal story that told of female virtue and male vice and the unfairness of the double standard. Other narratives included the woman's movement's cautionary tale of the perils of women's economic dependence and the dearth of economic opportunities for self-supporting females; the African American critique of white sexual license and the rape and sexual harassment of virtuous black women; and the child welfare reform story of undisciplined pleasure-seeking girls, beyond parental protection and control.

Individual case records rarely addressed these overtly ideological narratives that highlighted class and racial conflict as well as gender inequality. Records included few if any claims about aristocratic seducers or women sullied by wage labor, forced into vice by low wages or the need to support orphaned siblings. Nor were records filled with sentimental tales of virtuous country girls come to the city in search of "honest employment" who found betrayal instead. Instead, they were peopled with another familiar stereotype: girls who started out—in the words of Helen Campbell—as "honest working girls who want dresses and fun" but whose pursuit of these delights inevitably put them on the road to ruin.[63] Stories of girls enticed by their love for finery, the lucrative wages of sin, or pleasure-seeking young men all show up in records of intervention into the lives of "bad girls."

The tale of adventurous "pleasure-seeking" girls in need of either rescue or incarceration formed the basis of parents' and other relatives' complaints to the SPCC. But although parents and child welfare reformers alike believed sexually active girls posed a danger to themselves and others, reformers and complainants frequently differed in their explanations of a daughter's fall. Parents typically highlighted their daughter's incorrigibility while reformers also faulted working-class childrearing.

Florence P.'s case tells a tale of inadequate parental supervision of a working-class girl tempted by the pleasures of the city, of girls' awareness of their sexuality as their "capital," of the SPCC's desire to remove her from temptation, and of the Society's belief in the redemptive nature of domestic service and rural life. In August 1893 an SPCC agent was called to the Eighth District Station House where thirteen-year-old Florence was being held, after having been handed over to the police by the proprietress of a lodging house at Eleventh and Callowhill Streets. Two days earlier, Florence and another girl had left their homes to attend the National Theatre. After the show, the girls had walked the streets for a while before seeking lodging for the night. The next day, Florence and her friend went to South Street, where they purchased two dresses for a dollar. When they returned to the lodging house, the proprietress hauled the two girls into the local station house. Perhaps she disapproved of their behavior; perhaps she wished to preserve the standing of her lodging house by avoiding charges of harboring minors in a house of ill-repute. When the SPCC agent visited the address Florence had given him, he discovered that she had left home Tuesday evening without any money. Convinced that if Florence was returned to her parents' supervision she was sure to become a prostitute, the agent persuaded Florence's father to assign her custody to the SPCC. The SPCC placed Florence as a domestic servant, hoping that a supervised position in rural surroundings would keep her from harm.[64]

Child welfare reformers and worried parents read details of their daughters' behavior for clues indicating their potential downfall; the notion that all "bad girls" were potential prostitutes justified intervention. Portents of future immorality included dislike of "honest" labor; general incorrigibility and "pleasure-seeking"; desire for "dresses and fun"; intemperance; presence in dance houses, theaters, low lodging houses or with men on the street and wharves; inadequate parental supervision; the example of a parent or older sister gone bad; and drunken or abusive parents or stepparents.[65]

Although respectable working-class Victorian families were reticent about sex and tried to guard their daughters' reputations, prostitutes were a visible presence in laboring neighborhoods. While mothers acted in the belief that ignorance was the best defense against too-early sex and reproduction and the best way to guard their daughters' reputations, prostitutes imparted the lesson that sex was a commodity that could pay comparatively well. As parents knew, most working-class girls entered prostitution less because of seduction and betrayal than because of the perceived lure of the profits of vice in comparison to the familiar reality of hard work and low pay, less from the desperate search for income described by labor reformers than from the love of finery, the search for pleasure, and the example held out to them by other women who viewed their sexuality as their capital. Other girls who had experienced sexual abuse at the hands or relatives, neighbors, or family acquaintances perhaps entered "the life" as a way of coming to terms with an overly sexualized sense of self. Prostitutes' outcast status and shameful reputations were held out as a cautionary tale for rebellious daughters, but the warning could sometimes backfire: in comparison to other women of their class, prostitutes who worked in the "better" establishments dressed and ate relatively well, had access to money, and were economically independent of individual men and of Victorian self-sacrifice.[66] And as Ellen Ross, Linda Gordon, Christine Stansell, and Judith Walkowitz have observed, working-class marriage revolved around a bargain between men and women—often fulfilled in the breach—in which women traded domestic labor and sex for economic support for themselves and their children.[67] This understanding also framed the legal definition of marriage as a contractual relationship in nineteenth-century America. Thus the exchange of sex and companionship for money, food, and gifts was an extension of typical male-female interactions.

From the earliest days of the Pennsylvania SPCC, case records attest to the intergenerational conflict between parents and daughters concerning sexual conduct and the ambiguous circumstances surrounding some exchanges of sex for cash. As an SPCC agent strolled down Sansom Street in the center city on one of the last days of 1876, his attention was drawn to a scene in an office: " a man standing with his person exposed and a little girl about twelve years of age handling him." The agent waited until the girl left the office and then "accused her of her doings." The girl "denied it at first, but upon threatening her with arrest she admitted the fact." She claimed that the man had offered her twenty-five cents for her participation and refused to let her leave until she complied. She begged the agent not to inform her mother, pleading "that she would kill her if she knew it." The agent decided not to prosecute, believing that "suspicion of [her] complicity would kill the case."[68] Clearly it is impossible to determine whether the girl was a willing partner, as the agent believed, or an unwilling participant, as she claimed. This and other cases highlight the range of contexts in which female sexual activity took place and complicate notions of agency, rebellion, and desire.[69]

Whether for cash or for pleasure, sexual activity was one of the few outlets of rebellion available to working-class girls.[70] For many adolescent daughters, sexual expression was a deliberate attempt to use "rough" behavior to shame family members who aspired to respectability. In these cases, sexual activity was neither a phase of courtship, accompanied by plans to marry in the immediate future, nor the expression of an alternative morality, despite the differences social commentators observed between permissible middle- and working-class forms of courtship.[71] Rather, such behavior was a deliberate attempt to flout the conventions of the neighborhood as well as those of the larger society.

It is difficult to distinguish with certainty between manifestations of "incorrigibility" and "wild" behavior and the emergence of a new form of working-class sociability and courtship that engendered a great deal of intergenerational conflict. In the late nineteenth century, the growth of commercialized leisure created new settings for young working men and women to meet and socialize. In pairs or in larger groups, "respectable" young women began to attend theaters, fairs, circuses, and dance and music halls—traditional settings for prostitutes to ply their trade.[72] This environment allowed some girls to test the limits of acceptable behavior, far from the watchful eyes of parents and neighbors.

Some young women appear to have traded sexual favors for meals, theater tickets, and a good time rather than cash. Their reliance on "treating" underscored the links between the commercialization of leisure in the late nineteenth century and women's unequal position in the labor market. As the practice of "treating" became the norm for social encounters between young urban working women and their "gentlemen friends," individual families and working-class communities renegotiated roughness and respectability.[73] Nonetheless, parents and reformers remained suspicious of young women's familiarity with men, and if such behavior continued for long it might attract the attention of disapproving parents as well as SPCC agents and police officers. In 1896, two fourteen-year-old girls were referred to the SPCC after it was discovered that they had accompanied two men to an assignation house. Earlier that day, they had attended the theater. After the show, they were picked up on the street by two men who treated the girls to oyster stew and offered to buy them beer. Although the girls insisted on drinking soda water instead of beer, they went freely to the assignation house.[74]

When seduction stories were recounted in the records, the "seducers" were typically not the wealthy cads and white employers of labor movement rhetoric and anti-lynching polemics but rather working-class "gentlemen friends." SPCC agents took testimony from a group of six girls between the ages of thirteen and fifteen who admitted to sleeping with men in a livery stable. After detailing that escapade, one of the girls also confessed that when the "Circus was at Broad and Dauphin Sts. she visited that vicinity" with her friend Ida. It was there that they met "gentlemen friends," who after some conversation took the girls to a hotel known as the "Punch Bowl." The girls were introduced to "a number of disreputable females" and "induced to drink Port wine to the extent of twenty glasses or more." The girl under investigation claimed that she was—in the words of the SPCC Secretary—"induced" to have intercourse while intoxicated.[75]

Parents and adult siblings who appealed to the SPCC for help displayed concern for the family's reputation as well as for their daughters' and sisters' welfare. In the summer of 1878, two brothers were "very much distressed" when their seventeen-year-old sister was "enticed away by a man who repairs clocks, and placed in a house of prostitution on Bainbridge Street." The brothers had the girl arrested and sent to the House of Correction for three months, but after her release she returned to the house of ill-fame. To her brothers' great shame, their sister was "determined to remain where she is" and claimed that "if she is taken away [from the brothel] she will return to it."[76]

In another instance, a brother and married sister requested the aid of the SPCC in handling their orphaned fifteen-year-old sister Katie, who had immigrated to the United States some seven months earlier. Katie "admitted . . . that she had been ruined" at the wharves by a man who was employed in the vicinity of New Market Street and Fairmount Avenue. She had since gone to live in a beer saloon that doubled as a boarding house, which her brother and sister felt was improper. When the SPCC placed her as a servant in a home in West Philadelphia, Katie went reluctantly. Her dislike of steady labor—a portender of immorality—quickly became apparent. A day later her mistress returned her to the SPCC, claiming Katie was unwilling to work. With her sister's permission, the SPCC placed Katie in the House of Refuge.[77]

Parents could contact the SPCC on their own or act in response to the police or SPCC agents. When police picked up fourteen-year-old Sophia B. on the street around midnight looking for lodging, her "industrious" but poor German parents were quite willing to see her placed in the House of the Good Shepherd. When an African American woman named Cornelia T. saw her runaway daughter Stella in a dancehouse at the corner of Sixth Street and Harmony Court, she swore out a warrant for the fourteen-year-old's arrest and had her committed to the House of Refuge. The families of Theresa Mc. and Margaret Mc. had their daughters committed to the House of the Good Shepherd when they discovered them having "illicit intercourse"; Theresa claimed she had done so "of her own free will" and had "gone with other men" as well.[78]

The extent to which parents and guardians initiated complaints and attempted to place daughters in the House of Refuge, House of the Good Shepherd, and Magdalen Asylum supports revisionist historical interpretations that have stressed the role of parents as well as that of the state in committing "wayward" children. Threats to commit a rebellious daughter to an institution scared more than one girl; at least one daughter ran away from home after her mother threatened to send her to the House of Refuge for keeping bad company.[79] The knowledge that other girls in the neighborhood had been sent to reform institutions served as a warning to girls who were never incarcerated.

While Irish Catholic parents may have considered the House of the Good Shepherd particularly appropriate for their daughters because it was run by nuns, non-Catholic parents also used the institution to reform wayward daughters. Jacob R., a Jewish tailor in the vicinity of Sixth and South Streets whose wife was in the Philadelphia Hospital, asked the SPCC to place his sixteen-year-old daughter Rachel in St. Joseph's Protectory when she was found entering a "low" lodging house with Morris K. Earlier Rachel's older sister had been placed in the House of the Good Shepherd with her father's consent. Clearly, this Jewish parent preferred to see his daughters in the city's Catholic reform institutions than in the brothels of their Jewish immigrant neighborhood.[80]

The metaphor of moral contagion—which conflated issues of disease, sanitation, and morality—shaped institutional practices: reformers attempted to sift good but unprotected girls from "vicious" girls seeking admission to the Homeless Girls' Lodging-Houses in New York City and expelled inmates who were "filled with disease" from rescue homes.[81] Parents, too, used the metaphor of contagion to refer to the influence of bad companions and older siblings with tarnished reputations. At age seventeen Mattie, an "inmate of the various low dens of infamy in Middle Alley and Bay Street," already had a reputation as a "notorious street-walker." When she began efforts to persuade her two younger sisters to "follow the same kind of life," her father appealed to the SPCC. He was relieved when she was committed to the House of Correction for six months, beyond the reach of her sisters. Minnie F. had her daughter arrested when she left her position as a servant to accompany another girl to a well-known house of prostitution, "where she at once entered on a life of shame."[82]

Parents who sought the aid of legal authorities probably hoped to frighten their daughters into obedience. Indeed, many girls who dabbled in occasional prostitution were able to make a safe transition to marriage and respectability after intervention. Their ability to do so testified to the flexibility of working-class respectability and contradicted the literary convention that death inevitably followed a turn to prostitution. At sixteen, Harriet G. accompanied a young man to a house of ill-fame in Middle Alley, where she remained for two days before coming to the attention of the police and the SPCC. After her removal from the house, Harriet appeared quite contrite and professed an earnest desire to change. Sometime later, she visited the office of the SPCC to report that she had "married a very respectable man," the mate of a large vessel.[83] Her desire to prove she had reformed and done well by marrying a respectable man indicates that at least some young women internalized the standards of respectable domesticity they had temporarily repudiated.

In several cases, girls given the choice of remaining in the House of the Good Shepherd or the House of Refuge or returning to the custody of their parents chose to stay in the institution. In these situations, daughters' claims that they turned to prostitution because of abuse or neglect appear convincing. As Linda Gordon points out in her study of the Massachusetts Society to Protect Children from Cruelty, childsavers were aware of a connection, subsequently rediscovered by contemporary scholars of sexual abuse, between "incestuous molestation in childhood and subsequent sexual misbehavior."[84]

Protection from Lewd and Incorrigible Adults: Practices Too Terrible to Name

The SPCC also received requests for help from daughters whose mothers or guardians were involved in prostitution, although these incidents were unusual. Fifteen-year-old Ellen appeared at the SPCC office in 1878 to inform agents that her guardian, Jennie R., had been "of late keeping an assignation house." The investigator noted that the house was "not directly a house of ill-fame, yet prostitutes gather there and take men away with them." On one visit he "found (2) women playing Bagatelle and willing to drink with anybody." Ellen "was obliged to keep tally." Several days later he returned with police officers to raid the house. He recounted with traces of satisfaction, "There was a scene of confusion at the station house hearing great was their consternation when they found that they had been fooling with agents of the Soc."[85] When Ellen requested help in finding a position, she was placed with a photographer on Chestnut Street.

In February 1877 the SPCC received a letter from an attorney stating that Mary D. kept a house of ill fame on Hope Street, where she lived with her two daughters. The elder, a twelve-year-old Irish American girl named Catherine, was very anxious to remove herself and her ten-year-old sister Bridget from maternal custody so they would no longer be continually obliged to witness "disgraceful scenes." The SPCC wrote to the attorney, explaining they were waiting for a law that related to such cases to pass the state legislature. Unwilling to wait, the resourceful Catherine appeared at the SPCC office two weeks later, seeking "official" approval to live with the woman who was sheltering her.[86]

Adolescent girls also appealed to the SPCC for help in dealing with cases of sexual abuse by family members. In 1879, a mother accompanied her daughter Dora to the SPCC to press charges against Dora's father for "attempted incest." The agent brought Dora to the Central Station house where he obtained a warrant for the arrest of her father, who was committed in default of $1,200 bail. Several days later Dora called again at the SPCC office, this time stating that her mother wished her to withdraw her complaint and had threatened to drown herself if Dora did not comply. The SPCC refused to drop the charge, saying it was now in the hands of the Society.

Like other cases initiated by family members, Dora's appeal highlights the complexity of intervention: SPCC aid and legal activity on behalf of one family member could be contested by another while resulting in the incarceration of a third. Moreover, SPCC officials could be invited to intervene more readily than they could be convinced to desist. This case also highlights the difficulties inherent in being a dutiful daughter in a troubled household: was it better to defiantly break the silence and accuse her father of attempted incest, or did a good girl have to hold her tongue and guard the family secret?[87]

Despite the proliferation of categories of sexual deviance and desire, late Victorian reformers and laboring people alike shared a limited vocabulary with which to talk about incest and rape and therefore articulate the unspeakable.[88] Their discussion drew on and transformed already available categories—the brute, the dutiful daughter, the bad girl—and much less frequently, on the cultural narrative of seduction and betrayal.

When reformers told stories about incest, their narratives were about the inability of immigrant and poor men to control their sexual appetites, especially when drunk. As Linda Gordon has noted, however, sexual abuse of female relatives was calculated and sometimes occurred over long periods of time; it was not the result of a single, drunken episode when a father, stepfather, or uncle lost control.[89] Nonetheless, because of their strong preference for working-class temperance and their belief in the evils of drink, alcohol often figured prominently in reformers' narratives of sexual abuse. Abusive men may have also acted on the cultural belief that alcohol served to release passions otherwise bottled up, therefore absolving themselves from responsibility for their actions. SPCC narratives also prominently featured the role of reformers in the rescue of otherwise unprotected girls.

Although reformers blamed abusive men rather than the girls the men violated, their plans to rehabilitate girls who had experienced a premature brush with sexuality were similar to the reform scenario associated with "bad girls," unwed mothers, and other fallen women: inculcating domesticity and appropriate models of family life. Reformers' plans for abused "defendants" often included removing them from their home environments and placing them as domestic servants in proper rural families far removed from the evil influences of city streets.

Although its annual reports included veiled references to those "practices" whose "terrible nature must forever remain—from the very foulness of the crimes—a part of the unwritten history of the Society's work," the SPCC pioneered efforts to work with youthful victims of sexual abuse.[90] Like other upper- and upper-middle-class social welfare reformers, the SPCC emphasized the significance of class, but agents and members also realized that incest was a crime committed by men against girls.[91]

By the early twentieth century, social workers would label any sexually experienced girl, no matter how unwilling, a "sex delinquent."[92] In the last decades of the nineteenth century, however, SPCC reformers did not necessarily regard young women with a history of sexual abuse as bad girls, although they did believe they were at risk for future sexual immorality and in need of careful supervision. This relatively nonjudgmental stance was related to reformers' attitudes about uncontrolled male sexuality: SPCC agents were wont to describe sexually active women and even prostitutes as "victims" of male sexuality. Their perception of male sexuality as aggressive also enabled them to believe girls' tales of mistreatment.[93] Like advocates of temperance and women's rights, the SPCC supported local efforts to appoint police matrons to deal with abused girls and women who had to spend time in police stations for whatever reason.[94] Although their analysis of male violence incorporated notions of female vulnerability to male power, however, the SPCC insisted on the limited extent of their mandate; they referred abused women to police authorities and refused to handle cases of wife-beating.

Evidence suggests that stepdaughters and eldest daughters in households where the mother was sick or dead were particularly at risk of sexual abuse by male relatives. In her study of the Massachusetts SPCC, Linda Gordon found that "22 percent of incest episodes happened in male-headed single-parent households, while such households constituted only 3.6 percent of the total sample."[95] Where eldest daughters acted as surrogate mothers, they might also be forced into the role of surrogate wives. In such cases, the support of the SPCC could be particularly valuable.

In 1880, a twelve-year-old girl called for help at the SPCC office. Nellie stated that her mother had died a little over two years before. Within four months her father had married a "worthless 'woman of the town'" who deserted him five weeks before Nellie's appearance at the SPCC. Nellie had since taken on the tasks of housekeeper and mother to her ten-year-old sister. Records noted that "about 5 AM yesterday her father attempted to commit an outrage upon her." Nellie was given a letter of protection against her father, who was requested to visit the SPCC office. Subsequently, her sister was placed elsewhere and the SPCC found Nellie a position as a servant.[96]

Gordon has argued that father-daughter incest is particularly painful because of the dilemma it presents for daughters who have been socialized to be both sexually "pure" and obedient.[97] Dutiful daughterhood could trap girls who were otherwise isolated or unprotected, often because their mothers were absent, ill, or themselves the victim of violence. Yet in the paradoxical injunction to be both good daughters and bad girls, some girls found the authority they needed to confront their abusers. Other daughters protected themselves from domestic sexual abuse by claiming the identity of "bad girl" and taking to the streets.[98]

In 1887 Annie appeared at the SPCC office for protection from the sexual abuse of the stepfather who had raised her singlehandedly since she was five. SPCC records recount the case in excruciating detail: "On June 1st he (defdt) told her to come upstairs to his room which she did he then pushed her on the bed and said he wanted to examine her and see if she had been with a man she told him he should not, and began to cry, and said she would scream. out of the window, he said he would kill her if she did. he then forced her down. and looked at her person. and said she was never with a man. and that he would be the first one."[99]

During this ordeal, which must have lasted several hours, Annie was sent to purchase whiskey and sweet-oil for use as lubrication, and was threatened with a revolver when she resisted. She testified that during the act he informed her that she was not his child, but if she had been "he would have lost his arm before he would have done what he did to her." Annie may have attempted to reason with him by emphasizing her need to remain chaste in order to remain marriageable (although we have seen that women did not necessarily enter marriage lacking prior sexual experience): her stepfather counseled Annie "if she ever got married to set the time when she was sick" [menstruating] "so that her condition would not be seen by her husband." He also tried to convince Annie to blame her rape on another man who had "tried to take liberties with her." Later the same night he tried to have sex with her again, but had to send her out to buy some oyster stew to fortify him since he "was too drunk to do anything."[100]

Forcing Annie to acquiesce like an obedient daughter, her stepfather simultaneously underscored the importance of virginity and the illicit nature of father/daughter sexual relations. The SPCC's aid was clearly critical: they helped Annie press charges and continued to aid her throughout the case. Eventually, Annie's stepfather was sentenced to nine years in the Eastern Penitentiary, and the SPCC found her a position in the country to lessen the probability that sexual abuse would lead Annie to turn to prostitution.[101] Annie must have appreciated the SPCC's help, for she kept in touch for four years, notifying the agency when she changed situations.

While the tale of seduction and betrayal did not enable daughters to talk to reformers about incest, in some instances it did allow young women to bring up the subject of rape.[102] In 1893, a fifteen-year-old runaway named Flora, six months pregnant, was brought to the SPCC office after she sought lodging in a police station house. She claimed her name was Mary, that her father had died of consumption three months earlier, and that her mother had died two weeks after her father, leaving her to seek shelter with a married woman in their New Jersey town. Flora claimed the woman had turned her away the day before with a small sum of money and the advice to seek employment in Philadelphia. After her rendition of this tale, she confessed her real name and told agents her parents were living in Chestnut Hill, an outlying district of Philadelphia. Flora had been boarding with her aunt in a section of the city more conveniently located to her job in a mill. About six months earlier she had been "feloniously assaulted" by a man she did not know and had not seen since. When her aunt informed her that she was pregnant, the distressed young woman had run away, afraid her parents might find out. The SPCC arranged a reconciliation between Flora and her concerned parents, who arrived to take her home.[103]

The cultural convention of the country girl drawn to the city to seek her fortune or hide her disgrace would have been familiar to SPCC agents and board members as well as to working class men and women. It is not clear if the SPCC knew right away that Flora was pregnant; the police would have brought a homeless, unemployed, and unchaperoned fifteen-year-old to the SPCC office, pregnant or not. Flora's rendition of her tale might have forced officials to talk about her pregnancy while explaining her status as a single girl expecting a baby. It is also possible that Flora's sexual experience was consensual, but that rape by a stranger was a more acceptable way to explain her pregnancy. The cultural narrative of the outcast girl gone to the big city to make her way in the world that Flora employed to keep her own story secret served to bridge the gap between what could not and what had to be said.

Laboring Families and Family Politics

As they shaped cultural narratives of the urban poor, laboring people also shaped reform intervention in their families and neighborhoods. For many Philadelphians, the SPCC served as a potential resource to resolve dilemmas ranging from economic privation to physical abuse. By problematizing the working class family, SPCC reformers inadvertently opened up the possibility that family members with the least power could use the SPCC to gain advantage. Husbands and fathers called in the SPCC to shore up their eroding authority over wives and children; women and children tried to engage agents' sympathies and channel SPCC resources to fulfill their own needs and desires. Sometimes as a calculated strategy, sometimes un-self-consciously, clients or "defendants" used reform terminology and popular representations of the poor provided the narrative means to construct a case likely to sound plausible to those deciding on a course of action.

Working-class Philadelphians had a history of using the courts to reconcile family and neighborhood disputes long before the SPCC was founded.
Appeals to the SPCC were therefore part of a larger pattern of working-class
manipulation of the legal system and of relying on institutions such as
orphanages and reform schools to board unruly children or those they
could no longer support.[104]

Criticizing an earlier perception of the family as a hierarchy in which
fathers had property rights over their children and to some extent their
wives, the SPCC recognized that husbands, wives, and children might each
have individual interests in apparent conflict with the collective well-being
of the entire family. The Society was particularly important for women and
children who sought help in dealing with desertion, nonsupport, and child
abuse. Widespread awareness of the activities of the SPCC served to change
public perceptions of the acceptability of physical abuse of children, while
access to the SPCC offered some recourse to victims. Ultimately, though, the
ability of women and children to remove themselves from abusive families
was limited by their social and economic inequality within the larger society. For wives, the threat to call in the "Cruelty" could encourage a husband
to desert; court testimony against an abusive husband that resulted in a
prison term could rob the family of critical economic support. For children,
removal from their families of origin might mean placement in an orphanage, the House of Refuge, or with other families where they were likely to
be treated as servants. Intervention was a calculated risk: it opened possibilities but also occurred in the context of inequality—both within individual
families and between reformers and clients. And intervention worked dif-
ferently, with different consequences, for individual family members. For
parents who sought to institutionalize rebellious daughters, intervention
may have achieved the desired results; their daughters probably felt differ-
ently.

Case records revealed the manipulation of shared cultural images—if not
identical meanings—by men, women, and children under investigation
who sought to challenge reform interventions. Strategies for self-defense
varied. Some people responded by admitting the factual nature of the
charges but redefining their meaning. Others used equally charged cultural
images to accuse their accusers. An analysis of SPCC records reveals neither
the simple manipulation of reformers' categories nor the internalization of
the dominant culture—but rather people working through culture to
express their own agency.

Representations of deserted wives, tramps and brutes, rebellious street urchins and rowdy girls, good providers and housewives, and dutiful daughters, potentially worked to empower some people even as they targeted others for reform intervention. The language of good motherhood and dutiful daughterhood enabled women to shape claims for better treatment, even as it could be used to constrain women's activities. As a good mother, a woman could demand aid for hungry children, economic support from an absent spouse, or protection from an abusive father. Claiming the identity of a dutiful daughter, an adolescent wage-earner could appeal to the SPCC to keep some of her pay—but not without labeling her parents as exploitative.

A dutiful daughter—as incest cases make all too clear—did not have the same power as a male brute or a drunken father, but she could use the SPCC to gain more. Still, for every girl or woman empowered by the identity of the dutiful daughter or the good mother, another could be deemed a bad girl or an unfit mother, risking institutionalization or loss of custody. Similarly, a wife whose husband beat her and her children might have the legal power to testify as a witness in order to have him incarcerated, but she might lack the economic power to support herself and her children should her husband go to jail.

Family members appealed to the SPCC to enforce their expectations of appropriate gender-specific behavior, but they could use the SPCC to achieve more power in their families only if their aspirations matched those of the SPCC. The common interests of parents and SPCC agents were particularly apparent in the desire to enforce parental control over rebellious sons and sexually active daughters.

Ironically, as family members joined with the SPCC in efforts to negotiate proper family roles, they helped establish and renew commitment to a type of family that was unachievable in practice for many laboring men, women, and children—and undesired by others. As charity, child welfare, and labor reformers and other respectable Philadelphians worked to shore up the normative family, they declared other kinds of families illegitimate. Chapters four and five consider the efforts of laboring communities and reformers to stigmatize single motherhood and add the figures of the "unwed" and "unnatural" mother to our characterizations of fallen women.

Chapter 4
Illegitimate Mothers, Redemptive Maternity

IN 1893 ALICE HAMILTON took a moment's rest from her busy rounds as a medical student to reflect on her experiences treating an unmarried mother in an Ann Arbor hospital. In a letter to her cousin Agnes, she recounted:

Little Miss Jackson's baby came a week ago. . . . I didn't hear until the next morning that the baby was born dead. Then I went in to see her and she told me all about it and cried so because it hadn't lived long enough for her to hold even a minute. To all of us it seemed such a good thing that it should die, but of course she loved it. Yet she couldn't have kept it, for she is going to live with her brother and he would never take her if he knew of this. I asked her how she came to get into trouble and she began to cry again. Then she told me that she had not meant to be bad but they were to be married very soon, the house was all ready and she didn't think there would be any harm and then, just a little while after, he was killed in an accident. Poor little girl, she is only twenty now. Fanny says she is sorry the baby died, for she thinks it would be a restraint on her afterwards always, but I don't believe she will be bad again.[1]

Alice Hamilton's letter highlights several important themes that are vital to a consideration of unwed motherhood in late nineteenth-century America: the widespread conviction that unmarried mothers had been seduced under promise of marriage and then thwarted by circumstances or victimized by male betrayal; the perception that in most cases an unwed daughter's pregnancy posed a crisis of reputation for her entire family with devastating consequences for herself and her child; and finally, the fervent reform belief that a "fallen" woman could redeem herself by caring for her child.

In a society where most respectable late Victorian Americans of all social classes simultaneously romanticized the institution of motherhood and feared extramarital female sexuality, unwed mothers were located ambiguously at the cultural boundaries between calculating and dangerously sexual prostitutes and self-sacrificing asexual mothers.[2] Because it recognized both the transgressive nature of single women's maternity and the sanctified status accorded motherhood—if not individual mothers—the concept of redemptive maternity attempted to reconcile these tensions. In practice, however, reconciliation could never be perfectly realized, nor was it meant to be, for it highlighted the very cultural preoccupation—female extramarital sexuality—it was meant to obscure.

By according equal significance to both the sinfulness of women's extra-marital sexual experience and the potential for positive change, redemptive maternity forever stigmatized unwed mothers. Yet their commitment to the transformative power of motherhood led some late nineteenth-century evangelical Protestant women reformers to sanction attempts to keep unwed mothers and their children together—rather than denying aid because they were "unworthy" as punitive charity reformers did, or sepa-rating "fallen" women from their "innocent" children as other child welfare reformers had advocated.

Thus, recognizing the need for institutions to mediate the breakdown in family relations that often accompanied an unwed daughter's pregnancy, female reformers throughout the nation began to create homes for unwed mothers and their infants. Although these reformers built on over fifty years of charitable and religious reform activities, refuges for unwed mothers embodied a complex series of shifts in social policy and the intersection of two distinct avenues of reform: efforts to reform "fallen" women that emerged out of work with prostitutes, and Gilded Age campaigns to pre-vent infanticide and protect foundlings and neglected children. In the last two decades of the nineteenth century, reformers began to argue that the problems surrounding illegitimacy could be resolved only by focusing specifically on the social and economic problems of unmarried mothers.[3]

Like the representation of the prostitute—that other "fallen" woman—the image of the unwed and deserted mother was particularly charged for mid-dle-class and respectable working-class urban Americans. Female purity and male breadwinning were central to the construction of diverse racial, ethnic, and class identities, but single mothers were neither pure nor pro-vided for.[4] Instead, either as self-supporting mothers when the family wage was the ideal, or as women who were economically dependent yet lacked husbands to provide for them, single mothers directly challenged social norms regarding who could be sexually active, bear children, and head households. In myriad ways, single mothers and the illegitimate children they bore represented yet another variant of family breakdown.

"The Street Girl's End," from Charles L. Brace, *The Dangerous Classes of New York, and Twenty Years' Work Among Them* (1872). Reformers and authors of sentimental and sensational fiction depicted early death by suicide as a likely fate of fallen women.

In reform literature, in sentimental and sensational fiction, and in urban sketches that told the story of woman's virtue under siege, the unwed mother was usually portrayed in one of two ways: either she was forced to support herself and her child by prostitution, or else—so overcome by shame that she barely knew what she was doing—she threatened to kill either herself or her child in the madness that was thought to follow betrayal. George Foster embellished the cultural convention of the seduced and abandoned girl adrift in the wicked city in his lurid "guidebook" *Philadelphia in Slices* (1848). His readers clearly recognized his portrayal of the fallen women who strolled the streets of the metropolis, even if they had never visited the city's haunts of vice and crime. For Foster, the loss of a woman's chastity was but the first step down the path to total degradation. No longer bound by the dictates of true womanhood, a "fallen woman" might even prove capable of destroying the fruit of her sin, her own child:

The great source whence the ranks of prostitutes are replenished is young women from the country, who, seduced and in the way of becoming mothers, fly from home to the city to escape disgrace and infamy, and come to the city with anguish and desperation in their hearts. Either murdering their infants or abandoning them upon a doorstep, they are thenceforth ready for any course of crime that will procure them a living, or, if they still have struggling scruples, stern necessity soon overcomes them.[5]

Although Foster's guidebook was clearly of the sensational mid-Victorian genre contrasting rural innocence and urban wickedness, serious reformers echoed his perception of unwed mothers as poised at the brink of either infanticide or prostitution, if not both. In a lecture in 1871 that emphasized the correlation between illegitimacy and infant mortality, Philadelphia physician John Parry described the course open to an unwed mother in "Christian Philadelphia": "Clinging to her child, she may struggle on amidst poverty and distress until, to obtain daily bread for both, she yields once more to temptation and plunges for a whole life-time into the dark vortex of sin. . . . That these mothers should destroy their own offspring is not surprising."[6]

Although it vividly dramatized her social and economic plight, the image of the unwed mother forced to choose between prostitution or infanticide was flawed. While there was and still is a close if complicated correlation between illegitimacy and infant mortality (if not necessarily infanticide), the association between illegitimacy and prostitution was less clear. Most unwed mothers did not become prostitutes, nor did most women who became prostitutes do so as a result of bearing an illegitimate child.[7] Prostitution and illegitimacy appear to have been distinct social phenomena. In fact, women who frequented brothels were more likely to have access to knowledge about contraception and abortion than respectable young women who kept their trysts with their suitors secret until they were pregnant.[8] Nonetheless, in the decades following the Civil War, reformers seeking the origins of prostitution and infanticide began to focus on the predicament of unwed mothers.

Reformers reasoned that if left to her own limited resources, an unwed mother who was refused honest work might be forced to turn to prostitution. But if encouraged at this critical moment, an unwed mother could be transformed for life. As Harriet Beecher Stowe surmised in her novel *We and Our Neighbors* (1875), "Perhaps there is never a time when man or woman has a better chance, with suitable help, of building a good character than just after a humiliating fall which has taught the sinner his own weakness and given him a sad experience of the bitterness of sin."[9]

Reformers argued that with the birth of a first illegitimate child, an unwed mother could either embrace further sin and degradation and assume the "gay" life of a prostitute or seek redemption by cultivating her maternal spirit and returning to true womanhood. This belief that the power and sanctity of motherhood could restore even a "fallen" woman gave rise to homes for unwed mothers that began to proliferate in rural towns and metropolitan centers across America. In these years reformers and laboring people alike worked to clarify distinctions between hardened prostitutes and erring young women who, though unwed mothers, were still capable of returning to respectability.

Although illegitimacy was clearly perceived as a social problem in the dominant Victorian culture, historians still know little about the construction of illegitimacy in late nineteenth-century native-born white, African American, and immigrant working-class cultures. Women who bore children outside marriage had certainly faced difficulties throughout American history, but there is some evidence that illegitimacy posed greater social and economic problems for more working-class women in these years.[10] Historians have tentatively suggested that illegitimate births rose slightly in the 1880s and 1890s, after rising in the eighteenth century and then declining for much of the nineteenth century.[11] By the late nineteenth century, informal common-law marriage, separation, divorce, and remarriage were common among some segments of Philadelphia's working class, but scorned by others who considered such behavior disgraceful.[12] As the social distinctions between working-class roughness and respectability sharpened in the 1880s and 1890s, the significance of sexual respectability for working-class women grew. Meanwhile the expansion of commercialized leisure afforded native-born women and the daughters of German, Irish, and Jewish immigrants new arenas for heterosocial recreation in the form of dance halls, amusement parks, and fairs.[13]

While some young Gilded Age working-class women like Miss Jackson continued to place their faith in promises of marriage, the irregular nature of employment for working-class men made such promises harder to fulfill.[14] For working-class men and women, then, Gilded Age courtship presented a paradox: expanded opportunities for sexual experimentation coexisted with a heightened sense of the consequences of an unwanted pregnancy. Throughout the eighteenth and nineteenth centuries, single and married women relied on abortifacients to induce early abortions, but such drugs were not always either safe or effective. Although many women continued their use or else sought what case records referred to as "criminal operations" after the criminalization of abortion in the second half of the nineteenth century, by the 1890s such a pregnancy had become more difficult to terminate.[15]

Although by the mid-nineteenth century rural and urban, laboring and middle-class families had access to medical tracts and advertisements on methods to control fertility, most single women's access to birth control devices was probably sharply curtailed.[16] While respectable Americans appear to have valued nonprocreative sexuality in moderation rather than celibacy, marriage was still seen as the appropriate context for sexual activity. Despite the dampening effect of the 1873 Comstock "obscenity" law on the spread of information regarding fertility control and the marketing of advice literature and contraceptive devices, a black market in contraceptive devices flourished and "accommodated a broad spectrum of budgets" throughout the Gilded Age, but these products were not always reliable.[17] Even if working-class husbands and wives could afford condoms, female syringes, vaginal sponges, or diaphragms and could purchase them at druggists or through the mail, the cost of a diaphragm (several dollars) equaled a week's wages for a female domestic servant. Certainly, women handing over their wages to their mothers would have found it difficult to buy diaphragms, as would women who lived outside a family economy. Condoms were less expensive but their use required male participation and forethought. The practice of douching with vinegar or baking soda was also affordable but less well-suited to the perhaps unpredictable circumstances in which many single women had intercourse. Given the taboo against extramarital sexual intercourse in respectable middle- and working-class families, few sexually active young women would likely have used these practices; we know even less about single men's willingness to share responsibility for birth control.

Sexual respectability was an important indicator of social status for middle-class Philadelphians. Within working-class neighborhoods it played an equally significant part in elaborating distinctions between rough and respectable women. One historian has noted that among middle-class couples "physical demonstrativeness remained an accepted part of both casual courting and serious courtship" well into the mid-nineteenth century.[18] Such couples drew on an older tradition that deemed intercourse acceptable between betrothed couples. Other historians have argued that by the Civil War intercourse was no longer considered a normal part of courtship.[19] Although the boundaries of permissible behavior were more sharply drawn by the late nineteenth century, for at least some groups in the working class, sexual relations between an engaged couple were likely still considered appropriate if the couple married if the woman became pregnant. The possibility that even respectable working-class couples might engage in premarital sex is suggested by reformer Grace Dodge's admonition to members of a New York City working girls' club, "To keep a man's love you must keep his respect. . . . Until you are married you must not behave as if you were."[20]

The distinction between tacit acceptance of premarital sexuality within some working-class neighborhoods and its occasional consequence—illegitimacy—was significant. An unwed pregnancy that did not result in marriage was clearly a disgrace.[21] This was particularly so in working-class families with aspirations for social and economic mobility. The birth of an illegitimate child could label an entire family as "rough." While a young woman could try to hide her conduct from the watchful eyes of her family and neighbors to guard her reputation, an unwed pregnancy was a visible indicator of her misbehavior.

For African Americans of Philadelphia, sexual purity and its transgression may have carried a number of charged meanings particular to American blacks in the post-Civil War decades. Historians have chronicled the significance of marriage for African Americans immediately following Emancipation and Reconstruction. During centuries of American slavery, slaveholding states had not granted slave marriages legal recognition; for many emancipated slaves, therefore, legal marriage was an emphatic civic

statement as well as a personal and/or religious commitment.[22] Many black
men and women viewed sexual respectability as a strategy for fighting not
only representations of black men and women as oversexed and immoral
but also the predatory behavior of white men who viewed all black women
as fair game. In a strategy that paralleled the white male labor movement's
representation of white working-class "fallen" women as the victims of aristocratic rakes and overbearing employers, late nineteenth-century anti-
lynching activists bravely turned the notion of white purity and black
licentiousness on its head.[23]

In African American urban communities, respectable residents also
sought to distinguish themselves from those with "looser" morals who had
long-term sexual relationships but did not marry. In his sociological study
of African American life in turn-of-the-century Philadelphia, W. E. B. Du
Bois noted the prevalence of cohabitation in certain areas of the city and
claimed:

in distinctly slum districts, like that at Seventh and Lombard, from 10 to 25 per cent
of the unions are of this nature. Some of them are simply common-law marriages and
are practically never broken. Others are compacts, which last for two to ten years;
others for some months; in most of these cases the women are not prostitutes, but
rather ignorant and loose. In such cases there is, of course, little home life, rather a
sort of neighborhood life, centering in the alleys and on the sidewalks, where the children are educated. Of the great mass of Negroes this class forms a very small percentage and is absolutely without social standing.[24]

Despite their deep commitment to sexual respectability and desire to distinguish themselves from certain segments of the community, many African
American reformers explained "sexual immorality" and unwed motherhood as a consequence of social conditions. Some reformers like Du Bois
argued that cohabitation and common-law marriage resulted from the "lax
moral habits of the slave regime"; whether his comment refers solely to
slave behavior or to the behavior of masters as well remains ambiguous. Du
Bois also pointed to late nineteenth-century migration patterns, uneven sex
ratios, and under- and unemployment in Philadelphia. While also concerned with sexual harassment of black domestic servants and the risks of
urban life to the sexual purity of female migrants, female social purity and
anti-lynching activists pointed to the sexual exploitation of black women by
white men that continued after slavery's demise.[25]

Considerations of race, then, were central to African American attitudes toward unwed motherhood and illegitimacy in the 1880s and 1890s. Meanwhile, maternity homes run by white evangelical reformers typically provided fewer services for black women, using the claim that illegitimacy was widely accepted among African Americans to justify discriminatory practices.[26]

The records of the Philadelphia Haven for Unwed Mothers and Infants document just how serious most respectable families of all social groups considered reputation to be, and how deeply felt were the consequences of a daughter's pregnancy. Like SPCC records, evidence from the Haven also shows that the drama of respectability played out in two arenas: that of the disgraced family and the neighborhood. Young women appeared at the Haven with their infants after outraged parents had closed the doors of their homes. However, while the gossip of those who effectively policed the neighborhood led some parents to sever ties with their daughters, other respectable but sympathetic neighbors, family members, and friends sought placement in the Haven for unmarried mothers who would benefit from the chance to "hide their disgrace" while taking steps toward reform.

If virginity was central to both genteel and working-class codes of respectable womanhood, then unwed mothers breached the norms of both the dominant culture and their own communities. For some women and their families, the public, political meanings of female virtue and unwed motherhood may have become inextricable from their individual, private meanings. Perhaps just as single African American women from respectable families may have felt that their pregnancies undermined efforts to refute charges of African American sexual immorality, respectable white women from neighborhoods that boasted a significant labor movement presence may have felt more shame because their pregnancies were a public betrayal of working-class virtue.

An analysis of daily life at the Haven for Unwed Mothers and Infants in the 1880s and 1890s indicates that the effort to reform women was only partially successful. Although the institution's Lady Managers achieved their goal of providing temporary shelter and medical care for needy women and their infants, they were less able to remake their poorer sisters according to their own views of working-class respectability. Further, if the Home's prosperous founders and "fallen" working-class women rarely achieved cross-class sisterhood, neither did the Home's "inmates" create a cohesive working-class sisterhood. Records of life at the Haven for Unwed Mothers and Infants illuminate both the conflict between middle- and working-class standards of "true womanhood" and between competing standards within the working class.[27]

Another Tale of Urban Crisis and Family Disintegration

In 1882 a group of prominent evangelical Protestant women, sponsored by an exclusive Philadelphia church, established the Haven for Unwed Mothers and Infants on North Franklin Street in a German Jewish neighborhood.[28] Located two blocks north of the Pennsylvania and Reading Railroad depot, the three-story brick building with a picket fence was geographically accessible to young women who already lived in Philadelphia as well as to pregnant women who traveled to the city seeking anonymity. At full capacity the Haven housed some twenty women and thirty infants. The spacious structure included two parlors, a day room, kitchen, nursery, office, and infirmary.

In contrast to Philadelphia's reformers who labored to redeem hardened prostitutes, and still others who founded working-girls' clubs to prevent the downfall of respectable working women, the Haven served women who had already been "seduced" but who were still capable of return to decent society. The goal, as stated in the institution's annual reports, was the restoration of "seduced and abandoned" girls "to the holy principle of motherhood, which bewildering passion had almost plucked out of . . . [their] heart[s] in the madness of betrayal and desertion."[29]

While other historians have chronicled the development of homes for unwed mothers in the late nineteenth century, the concern with single mothers and their children should be read along with, rather than in isolation from, other post-Reconstruction reform stories of urban and family crisis. Like labor movement activists and SPCC reformers, the Haven's founders also told a story of the endangered family of the laboring poor. This story both resembled and differed from the charity reform and labor movement stories. The Haven's narrative of innocent single women's seduction and abandonment was a gendered story of male sexual aggression and female victimization that highlighted gender rather than class conflict. Where labor movement and woman's rights advocates called for higher wages so working women would not be driven to prostitution, the Haven's evangelical reformers called for an end to the double standard that absolved men who fathered children outside of marriage but left unwed mothers disgraced and without honest means of support.

Like charity workers and child welfare reformers, the Haven's leaders wanted to reconstitute laboring families around male providers, female homemakers, and innocent children. But the Haven's reformers defined the missing father as an irresponsible seducer and willful betrayer rather than as a vagrant, and sexually experienced women as vulnerable sisters at a turning point rather than as hardened prostitutes. The neglected child of their tale was not the victim of child labor, exploitation, or cruelty but the infant in danger of being abandoned or farmed out. Where the SPCC highlighted the significance of childhood environment in determining morality and argued that it was necessary to save poor children to save the Republic, the Haven's reformers focused on the child as key to maternal religious as well as social redemption.

Like the SPCC and other upper-middle-class reform groups, the Haven's founders believed that it was the responsibility of the wealthy to right the family wrongs of the poor. Yet while the SPCC lobbied for state intervention, the Haven's reformers committed instead to an older model of sisterly personal interaction between women of different social classes that had inspired the reform efforts of evangelical Protestant women since the antebellum era.

The Haven was originally established for foundlings as well as deserted and unwed mothers and their infants, and was an integral aspect of Philadelphia's campaign against infanticide. The SPCC also addressed the issue of infanticide, focusing on murdered and abandoned children as the victims of abuse rather than on the problems of the women forced to desert them. But within Philadelphia's reform circles, the Haven's reformers provided a unique perspective.[30] Although they worked with established reform efforts to rid the city of child desertion and infanticide, the Haven's founders approached these problems from the perspective of unwed mothers. At the heart of their philosophy was a simple but powerful insight: infanticide was as much a women's as a children's issue. Recognizing that the problems of poverty, illegitimacy, and abandonment were intertwined, the Home's founders sought to provide training and job placement as well as a temporary home for fallen mothers and their babies.

The Haven was influenced by two strands of the nineteenth-century woman's movement: that of female activists organized through the church, and that of the women's medical movement, which aimed to restore women and children to moral well-being as well as physical health.[31] Although the Haven was officially connected to a Protestant denomination and men handled its finances, it was in all other respects a women's institution, founded with the help of physicians from the Woman's Medical College, and staffed by a matron, nurses, and women physicians.[32] The Haven's Lady Managers also forged ties with the network of women's institutions that formed the infrastructure of late nineteenth-century Philadelphia's private charities, and used these connections to choose staff as well as inmates.

The Haven's Lady Managers and staff worked closely with the Maternity Hospital, Preston Retreat, the Temporary Home, the Midnight Mission, the Children's Aid Society, the Society to Protect Children from Cruelty, the Women's Directory, the Hebrew Society, and the United Hebrew Charities. This network, which supplied the Haven with inmates and provided placement services for women once they were released, attests to the strength of charitable and women's institutions, each forming "a link in the chain connecting the defences against sin and suffering so thickly set through the city of Philadelphia."[33]

The Haven's Lady Managers included some of the city's most prominent women. They lived in the city's elite neighborhoods or suburbs, in the fashionable Rittenhouse Square area, near the campus of the University of Pennsylvania, and in Germantown and West Chester. Of twenty-four women listed in the institution's *Sixth Annual Report* as board members, twenty-one were or had been married—to presidents of banks, corporations, and the railroad as well as professionals. While single women were often active in other charity and reform activities, rescue work with unwed mothers was probably considered more appropriate for married women.[34]

For the Lady Managers, work with unwed mothers—whose experience was similar to and yet reassuringly distant from their own—provided a safe forum in which to express their concerns about the need to regulate male sexuality and female fertility.[35] The demand for "voluntary motherhood"— the argument that married women should be able to choose when to become pregnant, and that couples should practice abstinence when pregnancy was not desirable—was a critical component of the nineteenth-century woman's movement and united a wide cross-section of female reformers; it was also a central tenet of middle-class Victorian marriage.

The Home's founders self-consciously located their charitable work in the context of the troubled economic conditions of the 1880s and 1890s. Although troubled by the distance between prosperous women and their poorer sisters, the Haven's reformers did not intend to eradicate class distinctions. Instead, they advocated personal contacts between women of different classes to alleviate the economic hardships of deserted and unmarried mothers. These activities were characteristic of socially conservative women whose radical appeal to other women across the boundaries of race, class, religion, and ethnicity nevertheless aimed to preserve the existing class order.[36]

Secure in their belief that their cultural values were morally superior to those of "fallen" working-class women, the Haven's reformers did not attempt to address needy unwed mothers from a position of equality, nor did they intend to let unwed mothers define their own needs. Reformers perceived these needs as embodying two related problems: the illicit sexuality of working-class daughters, and the inadequate maternal capabilities of young working-class mothers.[37] The Haven's program to restore inmates to true womanhood thus had two critical components: the inculcation of proper standards of infant care and domesticity.

Like woman's rights advocates, the Haven reformers believed that single women without male providers might be forced to resort to prostitution. In contrast to woman's rights activists, however—who argued that the low wages of domestic service drove women into "vice"—Haven reformers believed firmly in the suitability of domestic service, especially for young women in need of moral supervision. Familiar with domestic service as a model of cross-class interaction, convinced that domesticity was woman's true vocation, and aware that domestic service provided jobs for the majority of wage-earning women, the Haven's reformers sought to prepare fallen women for positions in households where they could retain custody of their children while working to support them. This situation would meet both the spiritual and practical needs of unwed mothers. The Haven's program therefore emphasized sewing, laundry, childcare, and other domestic tasks.

For late nineteenth-century reformers, strengthening the mother-child bond could restore even the most unnatural of mothers and keep her firmly fastened on the path of virtue.[38] The aim of keeping mother and child together was simultaneously a cherished goal of reform and a pragmatic means by which to attain it. If the loss of chastity could rob a woman of her womanliness, reformers believed that motherhood had the power to revive a woman's essential nature by awakening her maternal instincts, thus transforming biological mothers into caring social mothers as well. And the very presence of the child would serve as a constant reminder of her earlier sinfulness and a warning against future indiscretion. Indeed, the birth of a second illegitimate child was seen as an indication of a woman's inability to reform. Like the maternity wards in Philadelphia hospitals, the Haven for Unwed Mothers and Infants refused to admit a woman if she had borne a second child out of marriage.[39]

A staple of both reform ideology and practice, redemptive maternity is perhaps the most extreme example of the image of the child as innocent savior who guides his or her parents, that historian Karin Calvert has traced in nineteenth-century American culture. Yet reformers' concern for infants was not merely instrumental. They sought to discourage women from seeking abortions and to prevent the "grievous sin of infanticide" and hoped to save the lives of illegitimate infants otherwise likely to be abandoned.[40]

The desire to keep mother and child together at all costs flew in the face of earlier efforts that disrupted families in the name of social order and child protection. But childsaving underwent a significant transformation in the 1890s. As "charities and corrections" began to yield to the new discipline of social work, "home preservation" and casework replaced the earlier emphasis on the disruption of families. Even the SPCC began to emphasize the effort to preserve family relations in all but the most serious cases, making arrangements in 1894 to allow women sentenced to the House of Correction to bring their infants with them.[41]

Keeping Mother and Child Together at All Costs: A Contested Policy

Because of their commitment to redemption through motherhood, reformers insisted that mothers accompany their babies into the Haven. While fathers with ailing or absent wives were sometimes permitted to board infants so they could work for wages, wives in the same predicament with ill or absent husbands were not allowed this privilege. The only other infants admitted without their mothers were foundlings whose mothers were unknown; the Haven served as an informal adoption agency for these infants (although Catholics were not permitted to adopt foundlings until after the death of the organization's male religious leader in 1897).

The Haven's reformers believed that allowing a mother to relinquish her child would enable her to escape the consequences of her actions. But the policy of admitting unwed mothers and their children together had a more practical component as well: the admission of nursing mothers lowered the caretaker-child ratio and addressed the need for wetnurses for motherless foundlings, since inmates were expected to nurse another baby as well as their own. And as other historians of evangelical maternity homes have noted, reformers also believed that lengthy stays in the Home could facilitate religious conversion.[42]

Of all the Home's policies, the decision not to admit babies without their mothers sparked the most protest from the city's working-class women. Rejecting reformers' belief in the redemptive power of motherhood, many mothers drew instead on the customs of child boarding and informal adoption in some ethnic laboring communities.[43] The admissions policies became an arena for continual conflict, as women who wished to either board their infants or give them up for adoption attempted to redefine the Home's services.

Demands for childcare, temporary boarding, and permanent adoption formed a constant refrain. The Haven's records are filled with accounts of deserted and never-married women seeking facilities to board their children so they could "take in or go out sewing," earn money as weavers or wetnurses, or otherwise "work out." It was common for the matron to record, "There were 2 woman [sic] to get babies in without their mothers as they had to go out to work." In August 1884 the matron noted in her diary, "Friday two woman [sic] called and wanted to leave a baby and [I] told them there was [sic] no children here without its [sic] Mother." In another instance, the matron refused to admit the child of a deserted wife who had been unable to find work as a servant while retaining custody of her child. She noted, "I said we would take the child with the mother not with out."[44] And in the mid-1880s the matron noted, "Four ladies where [sic] here trying to get children into board it is a continual run at the door about getting children in to board."[45]

Because admissions decisions concerning infants could literally revolve around issues of life and death, despairing women resorted to ingenious performances to gain admission for their babies if necessary. Married women claimed to be single, single women claimed to be married, a neighbor pretended that her friend's child had been "farmed out" and then left on her hands.[46] Other women found it difficult to believe that the Home did not possess unlimited resources. In March 1884 the matron recorded how she was virtually shamed into accepting an infant into the Home: "Two young woman [sic] their names were Mrs. C. and Mrs. F. brought a babe about six months old looking very sick I first refused to take it they said its

mother was buried last Monday and the father is a complete drunkard and
a *poor* woman kept it and would not keep it any longer."[47]

Paradoxically, the Home's policy may have convinced mothers to abandon their infants so they might be admitted as foundlings. In July 1884 the
matron recorded how a baby bypassed the staff's previous refusal to admit
it: "There were two woman [sic] and one had a baby and was determined to
leave it here and we would not take it but it come in the evening about 7 o
clock a policeman from the falls of the Schuylkill [brought it]. it was left at
the Rev Alx Sloan 114 Queen Lane about 2.45 o clock PM had it rapt [sic] in
a bundle saying they would call for it but did not return. about four o clock
they examined it found to contain this baby it was brought."[48]

Reformers' refusal—in the face of persistent demands—to provide boarding and childcare facilities for the children of working mothers and adoption services for any but abandoned infants demonstrated their disapproval
of mothers who "deserted" their children by boarding or relinquishing
them for adoption or left their babies in the care of others for work outside
the home. Given the high mortality rates of bottle-fed babies, the need for
wetnurses to nourish infants rendered the Haven's policies practical, but
reformers' commitment to redemptive motherhood was ultimately more
salient in shaping their stance. Reformers focused on the uniqueness and
exclusivity of the relation between mother and child, but many single poor
mothers sought to enlarge the number of women who would accept responsibility for their children. While their determination to enable outcast
women who wanted to remain with their infants to do so was laudable,
reformers failed to understand that many other women seeking to board or
place children for adoption were not irresponsibly rejecting the institution
of motherhood. Some women who boarded their children sought to incor-
porate other caregivers into their children's lives; others who relinquished
infants for adoption were realistically appraising their ability to mother
under specific circumstances at a particular moment in their lives. Nonetheless reformers conflated desertion with almost any form of separation of
mothers and infants—whether children were boarded, placed with adoptive families, or left in the streets. For instance, when twenty-two-year-old
Bridget Q. bore the daughter of the "colored coachman in the family" where
Bridget lived at service, House Records noted that the child "was placed
with a light colored family in W. Philadelphia who are willing to adopt it if
the mother shall desert it."[49] In their unwillingness to heed the community's
view of its own needs—elaborated daily as women applied for aid—the

women who ran the Haven ultimately limited their ability to address the problems of working-class mothers and their children.

Seeking Respectability Among the Fallen

The Haven's inmates were chiefly white women who ranged in age from their late teens through their mid-thirties; most women were in their twenties when they sought admission. Although the Haven had been founded by devout evangelical Protestants, Catholics and Jews as well as Protestants from a variety of denominations were admitted. Even so, language barriers, mandatory Protestant religious services, and fears that Jewish children might be baptized or buried by Protestants probably kept some immigrant and Jewish women underrepresented. Recognizing the need to retain spaces for Jewish women, Philadelphia's Jewish charitable organizations donated money to the Haven. They also kept a close watch on Jewish infants, paying their board so that they could retain control over their eventual placement or, if necessary, their burial.[50]

Despite the Haven's official commitment to aiding African American as well as white women, racial tensions between inmates, discriminatory policies regarding black foundlings (whose admission hinged on the presence of African American inmates or white inmates' willingness to nurse a black infant), and black women's discomfort at entering a predominantly white institution kept the number of African American women and foundlings to a minimum.

Unlike charitable "rescue" homes in other cities that had private maternity wards, or small lying-in residences run for profit in their homes by Philadelphia midwives, the Haven for Unwed Mothers and Infants provided no obstetric services or immediate postpartum care. Thus women were often admitted directly from other institutions such as the Philadelphia Maternity Hospital, University Hospital, Philadelphia Lying-In Charity, Philadelphia Jewish Maternity, Pennsylvania Woman's Hospital, and the Homeopathic Hospital. Since many women were cast out of their families when they became pregnant, confinement in a hospital may attest to the desperate poverty of an unwed mother rather than the economic status of her family.

Scattered entries in the Haven's records attest to the jobs women had held and the ways they hoped to support themselves after their release. One deserted wife noted that both she and her husband were unemployed weavers. Other women had been domestic servants and seamstresses; at least one had worked as a candy-maker and another had "come from a beer saloon"; still another worked at a hosiery mill. The men the women were involved with worked as boilermakers, on the railroad, in foundries, and in shops. Others were unemployed skilled workers. Still others performed casual labor, taking whatever seasonal work was available. House Records noted of the man who had fathered Elizabeth P.'s baby that "last summer he drove a huckster wagon. said this winter he opened oysters in store in G. [Germantown]."[51]

For inmates, a stint in the institution provided time to assess their situations: to see if family members would allow outcast daughters or sisters to return, to figure out a scheme for combining wage work and motherhood, and, if they were lucky, to mend reputations. The Haven's diary entries contain many references to women whose outraged or humiliated families refused to allow them to remain at home with their infants. In July 1884 the matron recorded, "A Mr. W. call [sic] to see if we would take a babe only a few hours old as his old Mother would not consent to have the child at home she feel [sic] as if it was a dreadful disgrace."[52] Nonetheless, parents who refused to shelter their wayward daughters often sought admission there on their daughter's behalf. In September 1884 the matron noted, "One lady came to inquire about getting a baby here and another woman come [sic] to see about getting her daughter in with baby in a week or two she feels troubled greatly about it by the Lady Manneger [sic] told her she could bring her daughter when she is able to come."[53]

Other relatives claimed that they would be willing to permit their unwed daughter or sister to remain at home if the child was boarded or left permanently at the Haven. In January 1884 the matron noted in her diary that a woman had "called to see if we would take a baby in here the Mother wanted to hide her disgrace as she was young of a respectable family and he was young also."[54]

Institutionalization of women who became mothers in socially unacceptable ways was a strategy shared by reformers and some working-class family members alike. For some laboring families, maternity homes seem to have served the same purpose as other institutions for wayward girls who had not borne children.[55] While the Haven's very presence reinforced the stigmatization of unwed motherhood, laboring people's use of the institution to reform girls who had gone wrong—in tandem with reformers' commitment to redemptive maternity—also worked to clarify the distinction between "good" erring girls who could still be saved and sexually active women who were irredeemable prostitutes.

Since the number of applicants was almost always greater than the available places, applicants had to be weeded out. Private charities often skimmed off the "cream," sending other women to public charities such as the Almshouse. The Haven for Unwed Mothers and Infants was no exception. Every Wednesday from ten until noon, members of the board, the attending physician, and the matron interviewed candidates to choose those most "deserving." However, the applicant pool was not always composed of women the Lady Managers desired to aid: those whose personal histories could be encompassed in the phrase "seduced and abandoned."

House records reveal that a significant number of women applied for admission primarily because they were destitute and homeless. Many of the women were in immediate need of shelter and food rather than redemption.

There have been 3 or 4 woman [sic] in trying to get in with their babes have no home and no money.

two poor girls from the Alms-house come to be admitted in the home with their infants. no where to go. I admitted them until Wednesday.[56]

The recent tenure of homeless and penniless mothers in status-destroying institutions such as the Almshouse and the city's maternity wards clearly marked them as different from the "fallen" daughters of respectable working-class families. Board minutes indicate a desire to receive as few of these women as possible. Minutes for June 1891 note that

The question of admitting patients from the University Hospital was discussed. . . . The sense of the Board was felt to be that as under the circumstances of the Maternity Ward there having been instituted mainly as a Clinic and the cases admitted coming from the class of women from whom we are most anxious to keep the [Haven] free it is generally undesirable to receive them save when special reasons recommend them under our rules.[57]

Because they so obviously needed a roof over their heads, such women might find it difficult to convince the matron and Lady Managers of their sincere desire to reform. In August 1883 the matron noted in her diary, "Three girls call to get a home in the house but not suitable girls I think many of thease [sic] want one just for accommodation for awhile."[58] Women from maternity wards were frequently admitted, however, despite the preference for a different group of mothers. Board minutes for June 1891 noted, "A lady from the Womans [sic] Hospital brought 2 young woman [sic] with babies and where [sic] admitted by Mrs. B." [59]

Because a central aspect of their mission was to underscore the differences between prostitutes and otherwise respectable unwed mothers, the Lady Managers also screened prospective entrants to make sure that they were not dressed in the "gay" manner of "night-walkers." One of the earliest entries in the Haven's diaries reads, "A woman was here and wanted to leave her baby she was dressed up in a gay manner if she had a chance to leave it here that would have been the last."[60]

The admission of prostitutes threatened to lessen the Home's chance of success in reforming women, since such women might attempt to gain new recruits to their trade. This possibility was particularly threatening since one original impetus for the Home was the belief that unwed mothers were likely to support themselves by prostitution. Prostitutes were also notorious for their participation in a rough subculture that stressed drinking, carousing, self-indulgence, and raucous merriment as well as sexual activity.

The presence of prostitutes in the Home was certain to be resented by inmates hoping to preserve or mend their reputations. The admission of prostitutes might further jeopardize the ability of the institution to place its "graduates" in respectable families as domestic servants. Finally, the entrance of prostitutes threatened to shift the Home's priorities from reform and education to discipline.

Despite the Haven's refusal to admit them, there are hints that prostitutes were aware of the institution's existence and mentioned it when they traded information among themselves about the resources of the city's public and private charities. For instance, Fannie K. sought admission in April 1885, accompanied by "a gay girl [a prostitute] who met her on the train from Reading."[61]

The Home's admissions committee treated one group—widowed or deserted wives "in reduced circumstances through no fault of their own"—somewhat more sympathetically than others. Although these women were clearly seeking refuge rather than redemption, they were allowed to enter the Home if they appeared sufficiently worthy. For instance, in January 1885 Annie R., a twenty-eight-year-old Protestant, entered the Haven with her month-old infant when her husband was sent to prison for stealing. In December 1884 Addie N. and her son, both "hungry and poorly clad—the child having only a gown on"—were washed, clothed, and allowed to spend the night before being sent on their way because no places were available. In January 1885, Mary B., a Protestant, was admitted with her two-month-old baby after she found out that her husband, a boilermaker in Baldwin's Locomotive Works, had another wife and three other children. That same year, Lizzie H. was admitted with her newborn after they were deserted by Lizzie's husband, who also worked at Baldwin's Works.[62]

The women admitted to the Home as deserted wives strikingly illustrated the precariousness of economic dependence on men. One month a woman might be married to a man earning decent wages; the next month she and her children might be out on the street. Like the SPCC, the Haven was also confronted with the problem of abused wives. Although they had not originally intended to address this predicament, abused women and their children were sometimes admitted under the category of "deserted wives." For instance, Mary N. was admitted with her newborn daughter Kate after Mary's husband threatened to turn Mary and their two children out on the street.[63]

As they interviewed the candidates the Lady Managers established their right to judge the circumstances of each woman's pregnancy. Each interview was intended to establish the applicant's veracity, capacity for redemption, medical record, and ability to perform domestic chores as well as her need for aid. Some women were encouraged to press charges against the men who had "seduced" them in an effort to gain economic support for their children, underscoring the equation of fatherhood and breadwinning that was shared across classes. The matron also checked the details of the women's stories with previous employers, family members, and friends—investigations that occasionally led her on adventures into "low dives" not frequented by respectable women. Such an inquisition occasionally led some applicants to decline an offer of admission. A woman brought by the matron of the Maternity Hospital left her interview indignantly because the resident woman physician "inquired into all the case."[64]

The selective nature of the admissions process was marked by a paradox. Women who sought admission were clearly fallen women by both middle- and working-class standards. Yet to be chosen, women had to prove their essential respectability and potential for reform. Women frequently brought references from more established members of society who vouched for their character and earnest desire to reform. Ministers or priests, doctors, and family friends often served as intermediaries who sought admission on behalf of unwed mothers and their infants. In its reliance on character references and patronage, the Haven continued a long tradition in nineteenth-century benevolence.[65]

Women who employed domestic servants often used their status to reserve a place for unwed women who had given birth while in service. Indeed, just as industrial employers donated funds to charity hospitals to reserve "free beds" for victims of industrial accidents, the philanthropic concerns of many prosperous women probably grew out of their personal experience with unfortunate servant girls. Other women who interceded for unwed mothers did so out of a sentimentalized perception of their "fall." In February 1885 a Quaker, Annabella W., came to the Haven "to see how we took infants as they want to befriend a poor girl that got mislead [sic]."[66]

Women without character references had to represent themselves when trying to convince the Lady Managers to accept them. While the interviews do not seem to have been formally recorded, house records reveal that some women without references embroidered melodramatic tales that established their own innocence and victimization—either by men or by fate—in order to present themselves as suitable candidates for admission. For instance, Anna O. sought admission to the Haven a little over a month after her daughter's birth in the Maternity Hospital in November 1886. The matron noted, "Anna is 22 years old. has no friends in Phila. worked in Brewers Stationery Shop . . . and boarded with Mrs. T. 3524 Filbert St. She states that while in a restaurant with a friend and a man giving the name of Weaver. she was drugged and assaulted while unconscious."[67] While Anna may have been raped, her tale of being drugged and assaulted while unconscious was also a standard plot in sensational novels. Anna's use of the narrative of seduction and betrayal permitted her simultaneously to address and silence questions about her pregnancy; it erased the issue of her own sexuality while underscoring women's sexual, social, and economic vulnerability.[68]

While the details of women's stories often belied their tales of simple victimization, the matron and Lady Managers tended to overlook these discrepancies if the women appeared sincere. For instance, in May 1888, a Catholic woman born in Ireland "told a story about death of husband a brakes man [sic] on North Penn R.R. which is supposed to be false but as she is anxious to learn how to take care of her child she is admitted."[69]

The pervasive cultural narrative of seduction and betrayal provided a common language that enabled reformers and unwed mothers to speak about issues otherwise not openly addressed. Yet the perception that all unwed mothers were victims of male coercion or violence distorted some women's sexual experience and failed adequately to evoke the circumstances that surrounded extramarital sexuality and unwed motherhood for many working-class women.[70] Although even some "inmates" relied on the convention of seduction and betrayal to explain their pregnancies, the concept of seduction did not adequately convey the experiences of young women whose rowdy and rebellious behavior had resulted in pregnancy or whose anticipations of marriage had resulted in disaster. Moreover, "seduction" may have conveyed a different meaning for Lady Managers and inmates. Little direct evidence from the Haven illuminates how women of different social backgrounds understood seduction, but because some of the inmates were probably avid readers of working-girl novels in which the heroine's sexual purity was a central theme, we can look to popular fictional works in the 1880s and 1890s for clues.

Periodicals such as the *Fireside Companion* and the *Family Story Paper* published working-girl dime novels written by Laura Jean Libbey, Emma Garrison Jones, Charlotte M. Stanley, and others in serial form. Some sensational romance novels also sold as inexpensive paperbacks to both middle- and working-class readers.[71] Central to the plot of dime novel romances was the question: can a working girl be a lady? Dime novel romances confronted heroines with a series of perilous challenges in which they warded off attacks to their sexual purity by men of a higher social standing, and asserted emphatically that laboring single women "adrift" in the city could indeed be virtuous.[72] In the popular Laura Jean Libbey novels, for example, the heroines are resourceful "escape artists" who resist seduction and rape and never fail to defend themselves against villains, whether factory foremen or factory owners' sons. In fact, Michael Denning argues that the heroine's successful defense against an oppressor of a higher class may ultimately be more significant than the association of virginity and virtue, for working-girl novels served chiefly as gendered allegories of working-class resistance.[73]

While unwed mothers could appreciate tales that acknowledged the sexual dangers of the city for single and self-supporting women, working-girl fiction nonetheless established virginity as a marker of respectability and politicized the defense of working women's virtue as a matter of class pride—a stance that could not have encouraged readers who had "fallen." Yet dime novels that featured heroines confronting cross-class assaults on their physical integrity and reputations rather than inner temptation did not address consensual sexual relations between working-class couples.[74] Given the stigma they faced and the variety of circumstances in which they became illegitimate mothers, unwed mothers might have related to stories about women falsely accused of immorality. Perhaps women who became pregnant considered themselves simply less fortunate than the heroines who managed to escape disaster; perhaps they believed that like the resourceful heroines they read about, they could take action to improve their lives or marry in the future.

In contrast to both the sensational working-girl genre and most reform novels written by whites, some African American authors expressed a more flexible notion of respectability that allowed "fallen" women to redeem themselves. In *Contending Forces* (1900) by novelist Pauline Hopkins, Sappho, a single African American woman who bears a child in secret after she is raped by a white man, asks her friend Dora, "Then you are not one of those who think that a woman should be condemned to eternal banishment for the sake of one misstep?" And Dora replies, "I believe that we would hang our heads in shame at having the temerity to judge a fallen sister, could we but know the circumstances attending many such cases."[75] Unlike the fallen women in most novels written by middle-class white women, Sappho is not punished by death but marries and reclaims her child only after she realizes that her motherhood is not "contingent upon wifehood."[76]

Daily Life at the Haven: A "Dandy Place of Detention"?

The Haven's founders had anticipated ministering to a select group of girls reared in poverty, left friendless by virtue of their status as unmarried mothers, but eager to reform. If their insistence on viewing women as victims focused the blame on men, consequently it left reformers and staff ill-prepared for the rowdy behavior and misconduct of some of the inmates. The disparity between reform theory and practice—between the grateful young women the founders had imagined they would aid and the actual women who entered the Home—structured daily life at the Haven. While annual reports noted the gratitude of some women who returned to visit with their babies, other records reveal that institutional life was marked by unrest, insubordination, and a desire to leave the Home.[77]

Although a woman's stay at the Haven was voluntary, once within its walls she was forced to obey its rules if she wished to remain. Inmates were warned to refrain from profanity, drinking, fighting, leaving the Home without permission, and having any contact with men, including male relatives, without a staff chaperone. Visitors were permitted only once a month. Inmates were also required to participate in daily religious services, feed and care for their infants, and perform household tasks, including the detested washing in the Haven laundry—all those soiled diapers! Women who were physically capable of nursing two infants were expected to nurse a foundling as well. In late nineteenth-century cities, wet-nursing paid relatively well but was a temporary job of ambiguous status occupied by women with few or no other options.[78] The coercive requirement that women nurse another infant besides their own offended at least some inmates and potentially jeopardized their health, since some foundlings had congenital syphilis.

The Haven's reform strategy bore fruit for many women in practice as well as theory. Board minutes noted that the women entered "rude ignorant and untidy but in most cases soon change for the better in a way that seems permanent." Many former inmates returned to visit; board minutes for 1895 report that "Miss R. [the superintendent] . . . spoke of many visits from the older girls—all seeming happy and contented." One woman, doing well in the country when last heard from, was said to have referred to the Home as a Godsend that had "saved her from worse than death"—that is, prostitution.[79]

Nonetheless, at least a significant minority of the inmates refused to adhere to the standards of the staff and managers and had no intention of reforming their habits, on either a temporary or permanent basis.[80] House records, board minutes, and matron's diary all document that daily life was at times punctuated by profanity, "saucy" and impertinent remarks, an unwillingness to perform the required domestic tasks or to work without wages, and even by occasional brawls. Repeated pleas from the superintendent to the Lady Managers requesting more authority to discharge unruly women are sprinkled throughout the board minutes. At the heart of many of the conflicts between inmates and staff were competing definitions of womanhood and domesticity, as defiant women banded together and drew on the roughest aspects of working-class culture that valued very different standards of female behavior. Even as some women entered the Home to preserve their reputations by "hiding their disgrace," other inmates rejected at least some of the notions of respectability that were critical to the reformers' mission. In its place they struggled to achieve and maintain a sense of self-worth in a situation where they were doubly stigmatized: first as

unwed mothers and second as the recipients of charity in a moralistic institutional setting.

Rowdy behavior disrupted the institution's regimen, but it was symboli-
cally significant as well. By giving the lie to the inmates' desire to become
"holy mothers" such behavior threatened the very nature of the Haven's
mission. If staff and inmates did not share the conviction that unwed mothers and deserted wives could be reformed, the Haven would become less of
a Home where "the gentle influences of Christian women" would "fetch
fallen women back to a mother's duty" and more of a custodial institution
for incorrigible, deviant women.[81]

The passionate accounts of altercations between the staff and inmates
attest to the sincerity and commitment with which the reformers and staff
approached their mission, and to the intensity with which many working-
class inmates rejected both the Home's regulations and its founders' ideal of
an all-inclusive sisterhood. The fact that many inmates had entered the
Home only in need of shelter rather than out of expressed spiritual needs
also contributed to the problems the staff encountered. Discharges for
insubordination—most commonly a stubborn unwillingness to adhere to
the rules of the institution—were a frequent occurrence in the 1880s and
1890s.

Depending upon the nature of her offence, a woman deemed unruly
would usually have several chances to improve her behavior before being
told to pack her bundle and leave. In the winter of 1884 the matron noted,
"Lizzie P. went out without permission. I spoke to her about doing so and
she spoke back quit [sic] unbecoming for her to do so. but she made an apol-
ogy for doing so."[82] The tension between the two women built to a crescen-
do as Lizzie continued to chafe at the restrictions on her behavior. Shortly
after the first entry, the superintendent reported,

Lizzie P. and child left this morning with all her baggage every article that belongs to
her I told her she had better never come back to the institution. her reply was that she
did not intend ever to come back to the home again. We felt sorry to part with little
Lizzie. But her mother is a dreadful woman has a very ugly disposition. I said Lizzie
you went out with-out our leave and she spoke back very ugly indeed and tried to
make mischief among the girls.[83]

In the spring of 1884, the superintendent recorded her own attempts and
those of the minister and several Lady Managers to reason with the rebellious Mary McG., a mother of twins. The first entry reads, "Mr. McC. called

and gave some good advice to Mary McG. on account of her bad behavior. Mrs. M. called on the same errand to have her removed from the house." Five days later she confided: "Mary McG. keeps quiet but it is very hard for her to do so ready to burst out at any time." The next day a Lady Manager again attempted to reason with Mary, said to have "the demon in her," but to no avail. Instead, "she acted very sauceily [sic] and rude they are trying to remove her from the home."[84]

When the Reverend McGraff led services, all the "girls" were on record as enjoying them profusely, "with the exception of Mary McG. and she says she paid no attention to what he said." Her inability to appreciate the Reverend's fine preaching seems to have been the last straw, for the last entry records the superintendent's relief at Mary's departure: "Mary McG. and her two children left the home today which was a great relief to us all. . . . It feels like another house since that Mary McG. has left." In a later diary entry, the superintendent expressed her belief about Mary's unfitness for motherhood: "Mary McG. that had her twins here they are both dead which is a blessing."[85]

Numerous quarrels erupted in the laundry, which provided an immediate target for frustration as well as convenient weapons in the form of heavy irons. Quarrels between inmates could be both verbally and physically violent. Cursing and brawling were common forms of behavior for women in the city's rougher neighborhoods, and many women continued to swear and fight while in the Home. In August 1885 the matron noted "two of the girls have acted badly and used obsene [sic] language which gave me some trouble." Two days later, the "ladies" came to the Home and "talked to the girls on account of indecent language and bad behaviour."[86]

Although individuals scolded for "indecent" language and bad behavior were often given a second chance, misconduct by two or three inmates often resulted in immediate dismissal, particularly when such behavior involved drinking, or if a cluster of inmates appeared likely to spark discontentment and rebelliousness in others. The visits of an "old girl"—or former inmate— often provoked mischief. Entries in the superintendent's diary for August 1884 tell how "The ladies had some trouble with an old girl coming back to the home her name was Elizabeth G. is quite a bad girl the cause of turning two of them out Margaret L. O'C. with her infant. This bad girl treated them to drink for that reason both lost their place. . . . Kate F. left in the afternoon on account of drinking she was discharged."[87]

Like the original screening of applicants, the expulsion of troublemakers underscores the staff's efforts to prevent the development of a rebellious atmosphere in the Home. The decree against the discussion of one's past affairs at table, typically enforced at institutions for fallen women, was also useful in this regard. Yet the Haven's emphasis on discretion, isolation, and distance from the world outside the institution—all intended to promote female purity while in the Home—alienated residents and could encourage rebellion. However hostile to the institution, group pranks show that the Haven allowed some women to form friendships with other women in similar circumstances. This unofficial facet of institutional life was perhaps the most valuable, since it reduced the extreme social isolation of unwed mothers.[88]

Although rebellious inmates gained temporary power when they banded together, their diverse ethnic, racial, religious, cultural backgrounds, and reasons for entering the institution could also promote discord. For daughters of respectable families, the presence of rougher inmates who had spent time in the Almshouse or who drank, cursed, and brawled probably contributed to their sense of shame. "Fallen" women could demonstrate just as much sensitivity to the nuances of respectability as other women.

The Lady Managers encouraged this concern for reputation and insisted that inmates keep a low profile, particularly in public. Inmates were discouraged from speaking of the circumstances surrounding their pregnancies, especially at table, and were allowed to visit the park only in small groups. But circumspection was not intended as denial: Lady Managers were concerned when they discovered that a rumor that they discharged all inmates with "the protection of a black dress and married woman's title" had circulated among the institution's contributors.[89]

The inmates' concern for respectability also played out in regard to race. The admission of African American women and infants sparked dissent among white inmates, indicating that working-class women did not share the founders' belief that sisterhood encompassed all women. The avowal that the Haven accepted women and infants without regard to race was repeatedly put to the test, as the white inmates refused to nurse black foundlings. While the official policy never wavered, its implementation depended on the decisions of staff and the cooperation of white inmates, as well as the willingness of African American women to enter a predominantly white institution. In September 1883 the matron recorded how "A colored woman called and wanted to leave a black child and said it was deserted and left on her hands. The Doctor was here at the time and said no not take it at all could not ask a white girl to nurse it."[90]

The following spring a Lady Manager was called to the Home to "see about Elizabeth G. she refused to nurse a colored baby." And shortly after an African American foundling was admitted, another inmate left "because she refused to nurse a foundling." The presence of Rachel J., one of the few "colored" women admitted to the Haven in the 1880s and 1890s, provoked many "disgraceful fights" for the duration of her stay. Finally she was deemed "no longer a safe occupant of the home" and was sent to the House of the Good Shepherd, although her baby was permitted to remain.[91]

When daily life was disrupted, the Lady Managers chose to change staff and inmates rather than rethink their program, which remained virtually unchanged throughout the 1880s and 1890s. Stung that some inmates perceived the Haven as a prison for wayward girls, in February 1894 the Lady Managers determined to do their best to convince their charges that "This is not a 'dandy place of detention.'" By 1898 the Lady Managers conceded that "much discontent and a desire to leave" the Haven "after a few weeks, was very much the custom among the inmates."[92]

Temporary respite from their troubles and exposure to the institution's strict regimen sometimes rekindled women's desire to survive as best they could on her own. Three weeks after the superintendent had rejoiced at Mary McG.'s departure, Eliza N. "eloped" after she was given permission to go out on an errand from which she never returned. Hannah H. and her infant left shortly after her arrival because "she was two [sic] fanciful to live her [sic] was disgusted to change a napkin off of an infant." When Sarah K. was reprimanded for discussing "her private affairs at table," she left with her child of her own accord to make a home with her sister. Sarah R. was discharged when she "refused to take the children out in a large coach" that would have publicly identified her as an inmate of the institution. Katie Q. and child left when Katie refused to accept a position in the country. Another woman managed to skip her stint of reformation completely, when she realized that instead of waiting for the Haven's staff to send her to the Children's Aid Society for placement as a servant when they deemed fit, she could initiate the placement process on her own.[93]

When they could arrange ways to combine motherhood and wage work, inmates often chose to do so. In 1884, Kate M.—said to be "to [sic] lazy to work"—"left to go to board," claiming "she could work at her trade among candies and leave her child in the day nursery." In February 1885, Anne H. and her infant "left to live with a friend of hers and go out days work" so she could save enough money to return to Scotland. Three years later, Emma S. took her child with her when she left, stating for the record that "she did not want to work without wages."[94]

Reformers encouraged departing residents to seek work as domestic servants in households that would permit their children to accompany them. Such placements, arranged with the assistance of the Children's Aid Society, enabled single mothers to support themselves while remaining with their children, returned female-headed families to the ostensible protection of a male household head, and, in theory, prepared working-class women to be good wives and mothers. When they could, however, many single mothers rejected domestic service in favor of work that was better paid and less constraining. Furthermore, although African American women often found work in domestic service or not at all, they did not share the reformers' belief that white households provided a safe and sheltered environment. Wary of the risks of domestic service stemming from whites' widespread belief that black women were innately promiscuous, African American women openly discussed sexual harassment by white men and shared strategies for avoiding it.[95]

Other inmates cemented alliances with men as a way out of the Haven, rejecting respectable notions of sexuality and legal marriage along with their opportunity to reform. In February 1884, the matron noted a Lady Manager's attempt to convince Eva Du P. to remain in the Home instead of returning to the man who had "seduced her": "Mrs. C. called this mornning [sic] and had a talk with Eva Du P.—she left today; go she would she has gone to New Brunswick supposing the father of her child will keep her in cash."[96]

And in December 1886 she noted in the diary, "Mary Rose E. left to live with a man who she say [sic] is her husband. and willing to care for her child. Her Aunt says she is not married. and the Committee have tried very hard to persuade her to remain but without avail. child Henry E. went with his mother."[97]

Other women left when they managed to make a successful transition to marriage and respectability. The Haven celebrated weddings, viewed as successes by the staff and quite possibly by some of the inmates as well.[98] In at least some laboring communities, marriage could render a previously sexually active girl or an unwed mother respectable. Board minutes for February 1898 noted, "One woman, Barbara M., was married to Frederick G. He, although not the father of her child, was anxious to marry her, and is able to keep her and her child in comfortable circumstances." [99]

Other women returned home as daughters and sisters rather than as wives when their families relented. In November 1884, Annie F.'s mother and sister came to the Haven to take Annie and her "babe" home with them.

In June 1892 the matron reported that "two very young girls not 16 or 17 were forgiven and received by their families." Catherine Mc K.'s family had rejected her when she first informed them of the birth of her son; her brother had sent her a letter telling her never to return to Wilkes-Barre, for "the news would kill the Mother." But in November 1885 the matron reflected that the "parties became reconciled" after the intervention of a Catholic priest."[100]

In the end, if reformers' belief in redemptive motherhood and the power of sisterhood fell far short of the mark, and if they refused to let single mothers define their own needs, still their efforts are noteworthy. For in the same city in which evangelist Russell Conwell assured audiences that "To sympathize with a man whom God has punished for his sins . . . is to do wrong," the devout reformers of the Haven for Unwed Mothers and Infants asked rhetorically, "And so in hunger and cold and pain . . . these young unhappy mothers, with their babies in their arms, come to our doors. Shall anyone among us say, 'I am not thy keeper'?"[101]

Yet homes for unwed mothers reinforced the category of illegitimacy and the consequences of illicit maternity even as they provided much-needed aid. By newly emphasizing distinctions between married and unmarried mothers that already existed, reformers at private institutions like the Haven helped create policies around the special category of the single mother. Moreover, because they clarified the distinctions between illicit and legitimate sexual expression and maternity, homes for unwed mothers affected all women.

The majority of Philadelphia's late nineteenth-century single mothers never entered a maternity home or other rescue institution. These women had to invent their own creative strategies to handle the often incompatible demands of wage earning and caring for young children. The Haven's founders worked to provide unwed mothers with an alternative to placing their children out to board. For many single mothers, however, "baby farming"—the practice of boarding infants and toddlers so their mothers could work for wages outside the home—provided a welcome alternative to institutional life. Like single motherhood itself, this practice directed attention to the supposed problematic mothering of working-class women, or what reformers and many middle-class Americans saw as the dangerous maternity of the poor.

Chapter 5
Murderous Mothers and Mercenary Baby Farmers?

IN JULY 1879, Caroline L.'s neighbors in a working-class district of Philadelphia had good reason to view her boarding establishment for infants with suspicion. Case records of the SPCC revealed that "There is every reason to believe that d'fndt is engaged in 'baby-farming'; she has now 2 or 3 babies on hand—within the last two months, 3 or 4 babies have been seen taken out of the house dead; the little coffins were placed in a private carriage, and rapidly driven away. There has been no sign of a doctor or undertaker attending the house—no crepe ever appeared on the door or shutters."[1] "Greatly annoyed by the crying of the infants," the neighbors told the SPCC investigator that eight burials had taken place in as many weeks. None of the deaths had been acknowledged by mourning rituals common in working-class neighborhoods, such as hanging crepe or staging elaborate funeral processions. Instead the defendant—who ironically claimed to board infants from the Society to Protect Children from Cruelty—had buried the corpses while accompanied by a Mrs. S. of Bainbridge Street. Moreover, the defendant had been heard to remark "that it was a good neighborhood for *that* business and that she was going to take some more." What did Philadelphians mean when they referred to "*that* business"?[2]

In the last decades of the nineteenth century, baby farming—as the boarding of infants was popularly known—was a controversial and risky business for all involved. The term captures the misgiving with which Philadelphians viewed the trade, for "baby farming" was used interchangeably to refer to the boarding of infants in exchange for a fee, and to their murder in pursuit of profit.[3] Convinced that childcare for the children of working mothers in poor neighborhoods was linked to the wholesale murder of infants, working- and middle-class men and women alike feared that many baby farmers provided childcare services only as a camouflage for the flagrant destruction of unwanted infants that was also believed to take place on their premises. Indeed Dr. John Parry, a physician at the Children's

Department of the Philadelphia Hospital in the 1870s, almost equated baby farming with deliberate infanticide. Pointing out that the children of unwed mothers were the primary victims of both infanticide and baby farming, Parry commented, "The poor victims of misplaced confidence have no sooner given birth to their children than they are abandoned by their heartless seducers and turned into the world outcasts from society. . . . One of two courses is open to them—to rid themselves at once and summarily of their burden—by criminal means, or to delegate the care of their children to others, and go forth and earn a livelihood for both. The result is almost equally fatal to the child in either case."[4]

Infanticide and abandonment, its sister crime, had long been traditional recourses for unwed and deserted mothers and couples too destitute to care for an additional child. But tales of a trade organized around the systematic destruction of unwanted babies, with well-known practitioners and stipulated fees, shocked Philadelphians in a way that individual cases of infanticide had not. In the Gilded Age, baby farming was denounced in the press and annual reports as a lucrative profession in which a woman could literally make a killing. Lurid accounts by journalists, doctors, and reformers drew on class, ethnic, and racial stereotypes of the poor, the Irish, and African Americans and featured working-class mothers who were intent on destroying the infants they had thoughtlessly borne and unscrupulous baby farmers who murdered the children of unwitting mothers. Both the practice of baby farming and the concerns it raised coupled the already charged issues of childcare, working mothers, and infant mortality with those of race and ethnicity in two ways: poor immigrant and African American mothers were already suspect by virtue of their location outside the boundaries of respectable womanhood, and they were also the chief clientele served by baby farms.

The need for women to work, coupled with the low wages of women's work; the precariousness of the family economy, particularly for widowed, deserted, and single women with children too young to earn wages; the stigma of illegitimacy; and the shortage of appropriate childcare—all pointed to the increased likelihood of child abandonment or abuse. The SPCC recognized the dire consequences of working-class mothers' reliance on the services of baby farms when it told readers of its 1883 *Annual Report*, "The inadequate provisions existing in this City for the care of infants belonging either to the very poor or the degraded classes, is the occasion of much suffering and cruelty towards the children and of fearful temptation to the crimes of desertion and infanticide on the part of those who are by nature or complication of circumstances charged with their care."[5]

Infamous female practitioners were believed to "surreptitiously put...away young infants, whose birth and existence entail a disgrace under the specious pretext of affording accommodation for nursing children." As the SPCC 1887 *Annual Report* explained, "the parties so engaged receive them often when only a few hours old, and by a systematic neglect, usually contrive to put them away within a few months."[6]

Seeking to explain the staggering rates of infant mortality among African Americans in Washington, D.C., the District's Health Commissioner also pointed to "the reprehensible custom of committing little impoverished waifs to hired nurses and foul feeding bottles rather than allow them the food that nature has provided."[7] Throughout the nineteenth century, the marked difference in infant mortality rates by race was accentuated in American cities, a consequence of crowding, poor sanitation, and inadequate nutrition, as well as the shorter interval that infants were breastfed—all of which were in turn related to poverty.[8] In Washington, D.C., for example, the mortality rate among African American children in 1888–92 was almost three times greater than among whites.[9] Because more African American than white mothers worked outside the home and infant mortality rates were highest for African American children, race was central to the controversial practice of baby farming, even when not explicitly addressed by reformers.

Although cases of cruelty in baby farms were not isolated incidents, baby farms belong as much to the history of late nineteenth-century childcare arrangements as to the history of child abuse. Indeed the two aspects of baby farming are inseparable historically. Suspicions of notorious baby farmers influenced perceptions of legitimate boarding establishments. Furthermore, the routine licensing of childcare establishments grew out of the surveillance of illicit baby farms.

In spite of their unsavory reputation, baby farms were a prominent feature of working-class life in Philadelphia, as in other late nineteenth-century cities. In probably the majority of cases, baby farming was a legitimate occupation that merely formalized the informal childcare arrangements of single mothers and other laboring women. Boarding infants enabled some women to earn a living while remaining at home, while making it possible for others to go out to work to do the same. Despite rumors concerning the lucrative nature of the trade, baby farms were run by poor women; the working mothers who availed themselves of their services were often even more hard pressed.

The controversy over baby farms and the attempt to regulate their use can only be understood when placed in the wider context of the "discovery" of child abuse in the 1870s and of reformers' subsequent concern for infant welfare. In the Gilded Age, members of Philadelphia's reform community campaigned to abolish infanticide, child neglect, and abandonment, to license homes where babies were boarded for profit, and to provide accommodations for the city's foundlings, or abandoned babies. There was also a good deal of community regulation, as the residents of poor neighborhoods monitored the childcare establishments in their communities that catered to working mothers.

How are we to understand the controversy over baby farming and the widespread confusion over what it actually entailed? Why did many Victorians so readily believe in the perfidy of the mothers and childcare providers of the laboring poor? The anxiety over baby farming was as much a cultural phenomenon as it was a reflection of an uncontrolled institutional situation. Although focused specifically on poor, immigrant, and African American women, it both embodied and contributed to concerns about women of all classes and their relationship to sexuality, reproduction, and childrearing. The outcry about baby farming rested on representations of fallen women, mercenary caretakers, and nonmaternal, dangerous, and possibly murderous destitute mothers—representations that served as a cautionary tale warning women not to leave the confines of proper Victorian womanhood and motherhood. Transgressions included wage work outside the home, sexual relations or pregnancy outside of marriage, attempts to separate sexual activity from reproduction and childrearing, and rejection of maternal self-sacrifice in the face of the conflicting needs of mothers and children.

Infanticide and Child Abandonment

After studying the coroner's reports for Philadelphia for several years in the 1860s and 1870s, Dr. John Parry of the Children's Department of the Philadelphia Hospital was convinced that, although infanticide usually went undetected and unpunished, it was not a rare crime in the city. As he told the members of the Philadelphia Social Science Association in 1871, "It must be remembered . . . that very many of the bodies of murdered infants never come under the notice of the Coroner, but thrown down cesspools, into culverts, or into the rivers upon the east and the west, they rest until the sea and the earth shall give up their dead."[10] Philadelphia's medical and moral reformers estimated that hundreds of the city's infants were victims of abandonment, infanticide, and deliberate starvation each year.[11] Thrust down sewers, deposited in alleys or empty lots, these children swelled the already high infant mortality rates in nineteenth-century Philadelphia, where out of every 1000 infants born in 1870, roughly 175 would die within their first year of life.[12] In an age in which Americans sentimentalized motherhood and childhood innocence, newspapers reported frequent accounts of infants drowned in inlets, abandoned on doorsteps or in empty lots, or left in the arms of unwitting strangers. Between 1861 and 1901 the annual average of infants found dead outdoors was greater than fifty-five, or more than one a week, a figure that does not take into account those abandoned infants discovered alive.[13]

Because Philadelphia's coroners frequently rendered a verdict of "death by unknown causes" in inquests of infants found dead in yards, inlets, lots, and culverts, on the docks, and under bridges—in essence using the category of "unknown causes" for unlabeled infanticides—it is impossible to know just how many infants perished in this way. Some suspicious deaths of infants under one week of age were labeled death by strangulation, suffocation, "exposure and neglect," or "found drowned" while in other equally suspicious cases the cause of death was deemed unknown. A verdict of death by "unknown cause" for an infant who died at home could also simply signify the lack of medical observation and treatment, since a coroner's inquest followed all unattended deaths.[14]

The number of suspicious deaths labeled "unknown causes" indicates the difficulties inherent in prosecution of the crime and in ascertaining the extent of infanticide in the late nineteenth century. Despite the criminality of infanticide, most of its perpetrators were never discovered. In other cases of infanticide the responsible parties were arrested and charged with committing infanticide or with the lesser crime of child desertion.[15] If convicted of child abandonment, they could be imprisoned for twelve months and fined $100.

Although the annual register of deaths in the mayor's reports does not consistently differentiate causes of infant mortality by ethnicity or race, the overrepresentation of Irish and African American women among the poor and their consequent lack of access to medical attention—as well as possible disinclination to seek a physician's care for infants clearly dying of incur-

DEATHS OF INFANTS UNDER ONE WEEK OLD ON WHICH INQUESTS WERE HELD BY THE CORONER.

November 1st, 1863, to December 31st, 1863.

(*Out of 119 inquests held during the same period.*)

Verdicts.	White. Male	White. Female	Total.	Colored. Male	Colored. Female	Total.	Grand Total.	Remarks.
Unknown Causes	2		2				2	One found in a water closet.
Still-Born.......	4	1	5	1		1	6	
Want of Medical Attention......	1	2	3				3	
Exposure and Neglect..........					1	1	1	
Totals	7	3	10	1	1	2	12	10 per centum of all the inquests.

January 1st, 1864, to December 31st, 1864.

(873 *inquests.*)

Verdicts.	White. Male	White. Female	Total.	Colored. Male	Colored. Female	Total.	Grand Total.	Remarks.
Unknown Causes	12	4	16	2		2	18	One probably still-born.
Still-Born.......	24	13	37	10	4	14	51	
Exposure and Neglect..........	1		1				1	
Infanticide......	1	1	2				2	The male was thrown out of the window by its mother. The female was killed with laudanum.
Totals	38	18	56	12	4	16	72	8¼ per centum of all the inquests.

Charts from Dr. John S. Parry, "Infant Mortality and the Necessity of a Foundling Hospital in Philadelphia," paper read to the Philadelphia Social Science Association, May 5, 1871. Courtesy of Urban Archives, Temple University, Philadelphia. Philadelphia coroners frequently rendered a verdict of "death by unknown causes" in inquests of infants found dead in rivers, lots, and other places.

January 1st, 1865, *to* December 31st, 1865.

(931 *inquests*.)

Verdicts.	White.		Total.	Colored.		Total.	Grand Total.	Remarks.
	Male	Female		Male	Female			
Unknown Causes	19	9	28	11	3	14	42	Includes colored twins, male and female.
Still-Born.......		1	1	1		1	2	One caused by injury to the mother.
Exposure and Neglect........	6	3	9	1		1	10	
Asphyxia. }.....	1	1	2				2	
Suffocation. }.....	2		2				2	
Debility.........		2	2	1	1	2	4	
Accidentally drowned......	1		1				1	
Hemorrhage....		1	1				1	
Natural Causes...				1		1	1	
Totals..........	29	17	46	15	4	19	65	7 per centum of all the inquests.

January 1st to October 31st, 1866.

(829 *inquests*.)

Verdicts.	White.		Total.	Colored.		Total.	Grand Total.	Remarks.
	Male	Female		Male	Female			
Unknown Causes	11	10	21	1	4	5	26	
Exposure and Neglect.........				1		1	1	
Asphyxia. }.....	9	9	18		2	2	20	
Suffocation. }.....	1		1				1	
Debility.........				1		1	1	
Found Drowned.	4	1	5				5	
Natural Causes...	1		1	2		2	3	
Want of Medical Attention......		1	1				1	
Spasms..........	2		2	1		1	3	
Violence.........	1	1	2				2	One supposed to have been strangled by the umbilical cord.
Totals...........	29	22	51	6	6	12	63	7 3-5 per cent. of all the inquests.

From *November* 1, 1869, *to December* 31, 1870—15 *months.*

(1153 *inquests.*)

Verdict.	White.		Total.	Colored.		Total.	Grand Total.	Remarks.
	Male	Female		Male	Female			
Unknown Causes	25	10	35	6	2	8	43	Found in yard, 2; cellar, 1; culvert, 1; lot, 3; street, 2; dock 1; alley, 1; bridge, 1; 1 died in almshouse.
Still-Born	6	2	8	10	2	12	20	One found in a field.
Inanition	5	5	10	1	4	5	15	
Asphyxia........	6	3	9	3	3	6	15	One found in cesspool, one found in lot.
Suffocation......	2		2				2	One a premature birth, suffocated in a cess-pool.
Debility	2	3	5	3		3	8	One case—death accelerated by being thrown into Cohocksink Creek.
Found Drowned.	2	1	3				3	
Premature Birth.	1	*	1		1	1	2	
Strangulation ...	2		2				2	One strangled by unknown person, found in a water-closet.
Gunshot wound..		1	1				1	Killed by its feeble-minded mother.
Exposure and neglect..........	5	3	8		1	1	9	
Want of Medical Attention......		1	1				1	
Spasms	1		1		3	3	4	
Pneumonia......				1		1	1	
Cholera Morbus..	1		1				1	
Totals...........	58	29	87	24	16	40	127	11 per centum of all the inquests

January 1 to March 31, 1871.—191 Inquests.

Verdict.	White. Male	White. Female	Total.	Colored. Male	Colored. Female	Total.	Grand Total.	Remarks.
Unknown Causes	11	4	15				15	One found in inlet, one in culvert, one in run, one in pond.
Still-Born......	3	1	4	3		3	7	Two found in boxes, both colored males.
Asphyxia.......	1	1	2	2		2	4	
Strangulation....	1	2	3				3	One strangled by umbilical cord, found in water-closet. One by doctor, or the mother. One found in an ash-pile with a string around its neck.
Exposure and neglect.........		1	1				1	
Want of medical attention......		2	2				2	
Difficult Labor..	1		1				1	
Totals.........	17	11	28	5		5	33	$17\frac{1}{3}$ per centum of all the inquests.

TOTAL SUMMARY OF INQUESTS BY THE CORONER
From November 1, 1863, to October 31, 1866, and from November 1, 1869, to March 31, 1871.

PERIOD.	No. of Months.	No. of Inquests on Infants.	Average No. of inquests each month on Infants.	Total No. of inquests for the same period.	Average No. of inquests each month on infants and adults.	Percentage of inquests on infants compared with the total No.	No. of infants unknown.
Nov. 1 to Dec. 31, 1863........	2	12	6	119	$59\frac{1}{2}$	10	5
Jan. 1 to Dec. 31, 1864.........	12	72	6	873	$72\frac{3}{4}$	$8\frac{1}{4}$	30
Jan. 1 to Dec. 31, 1865..........	12	65	$5\frac{5}{12}$	931	$77\frac{7}{12}$	7	18
Jan. 1 to Oct. 31, 1866..........	10	63	$6\frac{3}{10}$	829	$82\frac{9}{10}$	$7\frac{3}{5}$	22
Nov. 1, 1869, to Dec. 31, 1870..	14	127	$9\frac{1}{14}$	1153	$82\frac{5}{14}$	11	63
Jan. 1 to March 31, 1871.......	3	33	11	191	$63\frac{2}{3}$	$17\frac{1}{3}$	21
Totals.....................	52	372	$7\frac{2}{13}$	4096	$52\frac{10}{13}$	$9\frac{1}{11}$	159

About 40 have the ages specified—varying from 2 hours to 7 days.

able conditions—make it likely that their infants were overrepresented among those whose deaths were labeled "unknown causes" throughout the Gilded Age.[16] It is possible that in at least some cases doctors otherwise labeled the deaths of native-born, middle-class white infants that resulted from "unknown causes" to protect their families. Nonetheless, in the years immediately following the Civil War, African American infants were clearly overrepresented in deaths attributed to unknown causes; in 1869 the 49 deaths reported represented "roughly ten times what proportionate numbers would suggest."[17]

Infanticide and abandonment can be viewed as reproductive strategies to avoid motherhood used chiefly by women lacking social and/or economic resources who believed they had no viable alternative.[18] Both practices were used by single mothers trying to preserve their reputations as well as by couples who could not afford another mouth to feed. Even more than other reproductive strategies, they were practiced in secret, not only because discovery could lead to criminal prosecution and popular opprobrium, but because when the motive was to preserve a single mother's reputation and her family's honor, secrecy was itself the crime's intent.

Significantly, although abandonment could sometimes be traced to the actions of either a man or a couple, cultural convention emphasized women's role to the exclusion of their partners. As bearing and rearing children were female responsibilities, so infanticide and abandonment were female abdications of responsibility. Men were represented chiefly by their absence, since it was the refusal of men to acknowledge their responsibilities as fathers and husbands that allegedly led most women to abandon or kill their children. Although male violence was highlighted in the temperance narrative in which drink led to economic ruin, domestic abuse, and death, cautionary tales about infanticide featured murderous mothers instead of fathers.

The belief in infanticide as an act of desperate women was bolstered by vivid newspaper accounts that publicized details of a crime that, although committed in secret, was nonetheless a highly visible phenomenon for the city's residents. One Sunday morning in January 1877, William Bentley left his home before daybreak to begin delivering newspapers. Bentley paused in his yard as he noticed that his dog was barking wildly and that the door to the outhouse was fastened, indicating someone inside. Breaking the door open, he found a woman sheltered within. As the *Public Ledger* recounted, "She begged to remain there until daylight, and said she had no home, meant no harm, was sick, and had no place to go. She gave her name and stated where she had last resided, and appeared to be in distress."[19] Satisfied with her responses, Bentley gave the woman permission to stay until morning. He then left to deliver the papers. Several hours later, the female residents of the house found a trail of blood leading from the out-house and a newborn female child lying dead in the outhouse sink. The coroner's report stated that the child had been born healthy; the cause of death was declared "infanticide by throwing down a cess-pool."

In a similar case a month later, Mary Kee was arrested and called to account for the death of her newborn son. The infant had been discovered in a well at 918 Hamilton Street, where Mary resided. At the station house, Mary confessed that she "was the mother of the child and had disposed of it in the manner indicated, and that the child was born in the outhouse."[20] The cause for the child's murder appeared evident when her sister testified that Mary was single.

Although popular belief held that only single women abandoned or killed their infants, some couples did so as well. A month before Mary Kee's confinement in the outhouse, the *Ledger* reported that "John and Clara John-son, colored, . . . were heard at the Central Station on Saturday, charged with child desertion." Lucy Painter, who lived in the same house as the cou-ple, testified that Clara Johnson had become a mother on the previous Wednesday. The next day, Lucy listened and watched while John Johnson "took the babe away, saying he was going to find a more comfortable home for it." Lucy Painter claimed that that was the last she had heard of the child. Further testimony on the part of other witnesses revealed that on Thursday morning "a colored baby was found in Horst Street, bundled up in some rags." Although the child had not been identified as the one which John Johnson had removed from his home that very day, "the magistrate thought the circumstances sufficient to justify a holding of the accused, and he fixed the bail at $1000."[21]

Detective work on the part of police, SPCC agents, and staff from the Haven for Unwed Mothers and Infants revealed that many of Philadelphi-a's foundlings had been born in the wards of the Woman's Hospital, Wom-en's Homeopathic Hospital, Lying-In Charity, and Maternity Hospital. Babies born in hospitals and then abandoned after their mothers' release were easily identified by the clothing they wore, stamped with the markings of the hospital in which their mothers had been confined. When called upon, staff of these institutions could identify the children of women who had "worked the charities" during their confinements. Such a case was that of Margaret A. and her child. Two days after she exited the Maternity Hospital in a carriage, police found Margaret's baby abandoned in a lot on Camac Street.[22] Another foundling whose clothing was marked with the insignia of Woman's Hospital was easily identified after its discovery in a churchyard, shortly after its mother had been refused boarding privileges for the child at the Haven earlier that day.[23]

The fact that so many foundlings were born in the maternity wards of Philadelphia hospitals testifies both to the extreme poverty of women who abandoned their children and the likelihood that many of these infants had indeed been born to unwed mothers. Because hospitalization bore a stigma in the late nineteenth century, only very poor and unmarried women made use of maternity wards. In the late 1860s, of roughly 246 infants born each year in the Philadelphia Hospital—the medical facilities of the Almshouse— about 188 or 76.5 percent were assumed to be illegitimate.[24] The destitution and poor prenatal care of Philadelphia's child deserters is also indicated by the ill-health of those foundlings who survived abandonment. Foundlings were often "rachitic, syphlitic, half dead from drugging or neglect, or from ante-natal or post-natal abuse."[25] Infants brought to the Haven for Unwed Mothers and Infants suffered from congenital syphilis and marasmus—a deadly form of malnutrition—and were susceptible to cholera infantum (diarrhea and enteritis). While some infant health problems were a direct result of neglect and abandonment and then congregate care, where infants risked a lack of attention and exposure to contagious disease, others seem attributable to the poor health of their mothers during pregnancy.

Illegitimacy and destitution often went hand in hand. If marriage could act as the catalyst that set in motion a system of supports that aided an expectant mother and encouraged her to obtain adequate care, the stigma of illegitimacy could disrupt whatever support already existed. If it resulted in an eventual marriage, a premarital pregnancy might invoke only a tempo- rary loss of face.[26] But as a premarital pregnancy evolved into single moth- erhood, family members' feelings of shame and anger could intensify markedly. Hard-pressed families could ill afford another mouth to feed and the loss of income that a daughter might bring home. A child born outside of marriage was thus not merely a social liability but an economic one as well.

Although abandonment was most often the resort of extremely poor women, the stigma of illegitimacy appears solely responsible in some cases. The Haven superintendent mused in her diary one evening,"There was a baby left on the doorstep at half past seven o clock PM clothed nicely and quite a bundle of good clothes on it. Could find no clue to it." Clearly, some infants were abandoned by women or families who could afford the financial expense of an illegitimate child but not the social stigma.[27]

Because the Haven provided a shelter for the city's abandoned babies, the institution's records note details of numerous cases of abandonment. These surprisingly rich sources make it possible to reconstruct the circumstances and possibly the meanings surrounding the practice in the 1880s and 1890s. To read the Haven records is to realize how pervasive the foundling problem was. Citizens brought foundlings they had discovered to their local police station houses; policemen and night watchmen found abandoned infants as they walked their beats. An entry for September 1884 is typical of many in the Haven's records. "A foundling was brought here twelve o clock PM by a policeman . . . it was in an Alleyway on 10th between Brown and Parrish a little girl."[28] Brought in a basket, this African American infant died four days after she was admitted to the Haven. Children brought to the institution in this manner were frequently named after the policemen who carried them to the Haven, or after the streets in Northern Liberties, Kensington, Spring Garden, Southwark, Moyamensing, and other sections of the city in which they had been found. Indeed, the names given to foundlings provide a crude lesson in the social geography of poor neighborhoods and a register of the policemen who walked those beats.

The act of abandonment embodied in acute form the same cruel conflict of interests between mother and child that caring for the child entailed. Without a child a woman could barely support herself if she was not part of a family economy; a woman solely responsible for both mothering and breadwinning faced an even more monumental challenge. This dilemma was especially keen in those cases where a loss of respectability and the access it might provide to charity and employment were involved.[29]

Although abandonment could lead to an infant's death because of exposure to cold and lack of nourishment, child desertion was not necessarily as final as infanticide, nor was it always certain that whoever abandoned the child did so in order to kill it. It is likely that many parents who abandoned infants intended to save rather than destroy their children. Some overwhelmed women, torn between their commitment to older children and the desire to respond to the needs of a newborn, risked the life of one child for the sake of the rest. An entry recorded in the Home's diary noted tersely, "A Lady came to inquire about Catherine K. she deserted the child on account of starvation has 2 or 3 others."[30] Other evidence suggests that some parents saw abandonment as a temporary measure during a period of economic hardship and hoped to reclaim their babies when their financial situation improved. Nonetheless, the need for secrecy worked against the child's chances for survival.

The terrible ambivalence provoked by such a predicament is apparent in the cases of two female infants, abandoned, respectively, in a lot and in a lumber pile, both with names pinned to them.[31] Perhaps those who abandoned the infants in these out-of-the-way places hoped, nonetheless, to reclaim the girls when they were able. But parents who sincerely believed that they would one day reclaim their abandoned babies were clinging to an illusion. By the time they were ready, the children might no longer be living. In May 1884, a week-old boy was left on the steps of the Home with a note saying that the child would be reclaimed in the future. By August 1 the child was dead.[32]

The Haven staff routinely ignored the implicit request to call foundlings by the names that identified them on the notes pinned to their clothing. Instead, they duly recorded the names in the record book and then assigned the children new ones. If a baby was fortunate enough to be adopted, he or she would likely be renamed once again. When one baby was left at the door of the Home in a basket with forty dollars wrapped in paper—a considerable sum in the 1880s and 1890s that approximated the fee midwives charged to place infants for adoption—and a request that the child be named Alice L., she was promptly dubbed Martha B.[33]

Unfortunately for the children, the circumstances that made it more likely that infants would be discovered promptly and given shelter tended to increase the deserter's chances of detection. By abandoning a child where its presence was likely to pass undetected, a woman protected herself at her child's expense. By deserting a baby in a way that increased its chances for survival, a woman increased her own risk of detection in a criminal act. By bundling a child in clothing that could be identified, pinning a name to it, leaving it in a busy, well-lit street where it would be sure to attract attention, or even remaining nearby until the child was discovered, a woman provided clues for the special police detectives to follow. For instance, one foundling taken from the alley of 1530 North Twelfth Street in May 1885 and brought by a policeman to the Haven for Unwed Mothers and Infants was reportedly "left there 1/4 after five o clock AM a girl. by the name of Annie Caster saw a stout woman go up the alley with a bundle in her arms."[34]

Women who wished to ensure the survival of their infants employed a strategy of desertion that greatly increased their own visibility, but left them with the knowledge that their child was in safe hands. The method involved a certain element of deception similar to that employed in nineteenth-century con games: a man or woman would enlist the aid of a stranger in either minding the baby or holding a "bundle" while he or she then went on an errand, never to return. Gradually, the person whose aid had been enlisted would grasp the situation, and drop the child at the nearest station house.[35] From there, the child would probably be taken to the Haven for Unwed Mothers and Infants. Several entries in the institution's records illustrate this pattern:

March 15 1885- A foundling was brought in by a policeman. . . . It was left in the arms of an old woman as the girl said she was going to get a bundle but never returned so it was taken to the station house and afterwards brought here.

June 18 1885- A foundling was brought by police officer . . . and Mrs. Jane Steel brought it in her arm [s]. She lives . . . this side of the station house. Three boys brought it to the station house a man came up to the boy ask to hold a bundle while he went away and gave him a few pennies.[36]

Similarly, the entry for a male infant who was named after the police officer who brought him to the Haven in February 1884 reads, "A veiled lady deposited this child in the arms of an old woman at a street corner, promising to return for it."[37]

Other fortunate abandoned infants quickly drew the attention of passers-by. Mitchell A. was found in an ash barrel by a couple of boys playing on Marshall Street; another infant was discovered when several boys kicked a bundle blocking their path across a vacant lot and were startled to hear it cry.[38] This child was brought to the local police station, then taken to the Haven by a poor washerwoman with eight children and a grandchild living with her who had kept the child for a few days before determining that her house was too crowded to keep the foundling. The infant was adopted that same day by a bricklayer and his wife who lived on Mascher Street, near the scene of her earlier abandonment.[39]

Sometimes infants were abandoned in saloons and brothels. Elizabeth D. was brought to the Haven by a policeman after she was "left in vestibule of lager beer salon [sic] by two boys in an old chip basket." One seven-month-old baby girl was found "deserted in a house of ill-fame" by the Society to Protect Children from Cruelty and was sent to the Haven, only to die the following month. Another infant, three-day-old Clarence L., was deserted in similar circumstances. Records reveal he was "deserted by Mother, in a low-house in 511 Gillis Alley, and brought to the Home at midnight of June 3-83 by policeman"; he died sixteen days later.[40]

Some parents scouted out likely neighboring families or strangers who seemed willing and able to take charge of a child, and then left the infant in a basket or wrapped in a shawl on the steps of a dwelling. Other women left their babies in the care of those who had offered both mother and child temporary food and shelter, perhaps rationalizing that such people were better able to provide for an infant's needs. James P. was brought to the Haven after his "mother asked for a nights [sic] lodging and in the morning left before the family were up."[41]

Landlords and those who employed domestic servants were occasionally confronted with the offspring of tenants and servants left behind when their mothers departed. In October 1887, a baby subsequently dubbed Mabel B. was brought to the Haven by the "little daughter of Mrs. B." The baby's mother had been employed as a housekeeper by Mrs. B. Two months after the birth of her child, she disappeared, leaving her baby behind. And in January 1884, another "destitute babe" deserted in a house on Federal Street was admitted into the Haven after "Mrs. B. brought it as it was left by one of her tenants a room in her house. . . . It was very dirty when she brought it all over."[42]

Many foundlings were left in churchyards or on the pavement in front of police stations and other public buildings in an implicit declaration that the poor children of the city were rightfully public charges. Emma F. was admitted to the Haven after her discovery in a public schoolyard at Fifth and Federal Streets; she was dropped off at the Home "by a woman who had taken it home but whose husband refused to keep it." One foundling sent from the Northern Home, an orphanage, to the Haven had been tossed out of a carriage as it was driven past the entrance of the House of Refuge.[43] If its caretakers had hoped to deliver the child to a place of safety while protecting their own identities, they had sadly miscalculated. Within several days after its flight from the carriage, the child died of its injuries.

Abandonment of children in public places provided a pointed critique of the lack of social services outside of institutions for poor women and their infants. But abandoning an infant in a churchyard or on the steps of a station house not only demonstrated which agencies and organizations poor families held accountable for infant welfare; it also displayed their hope that these institutions would care for their children.

Paradoxically, the policy of institutions like the Haven for Unwed Mothers and Infants, which admitted foundlings but refused to admit other babies unless their mothers were willing to enter the Home, forced some mothers to abandon their infants in order to ensure their care. Numerous babies were left in baskets or wrapped in shawls and placed on the steps of the Haven. In early November 1885, "a basket was left on the doorstep about half past five o clock in the evening. it contained a newborn infant not washed or any clothes on it a little girl." One Sunday the superintendent recalled how "Dr. F. called and had services with the household. during the service the doorbell rang violently and there was a bundle laying on the steps which proved to be an infant 6 weeks (colored). The Doctor was much surprised to see it when he got through."[44]

Reformers did not intend their policies to encourage women to abandon children, however. In 1871 and again in the late 1890s, Philadelphia child welfare reformers considered and rejected proposals to establish a foundling asylum to care for the city's deserted infants, believing it would encourage "viciousness" and immorality.[45] When private philanthropists began to provide services to enable unmarried mothers to care for their infants in the 1880s and 1890s, they did so in adamant opposition to foundling hospitals that permitted mothers to desert their infants and insisted that women enter institutions along with their children. Others, particularly doctors, opposed establishing a foundling hospital on the basis that aggregate care of infants was conducive to disease and death.[46]

In the early nineteenth century, Philadelphia's public welfare officials had paid wetnurses to care for foundlings in their own homes and provided a weekly cash stipend to unmarried mothers to allow them to care for their babies at home. Although the Blockley Almshouse began to place abandoned babies with foster families in 1883, by the late nineteenth century the practice of paying unwed mothers to nurse their infants at home had been eliminated as the city cut back on "outdoor relief." In these same years the Society to Organize Charity condemned illegitimacy as immorality and refused material aid to the undeserving poor. While mothers could attempt to surrender their infants to the Guardians of the Poor, who would deliver the baby to the Almshouse, it was widely and correctly believed that infants were likely to die there. Moreover, not all babies were accepted by the

Guardians of the Poor, and those mothers who relinquished their infants could be liable later for the support of their children if they married.[47]

Certainly some if not most women who abandoned infants would have preferred to raise their children, given appropriate financial and social support, or relinquish them for adoption. Clearly, the lack of diverse options for single mothers—ranging from material aid to enable women to keep their children at home, to safe and affordable childcare, to temporary child placement or adoption—often resulted, directly or indirectly, in death.

Child Care and Child Neglect: Baby Farming in Philadelphia's Late Nineteenth-Century Working-Class Neighborhoods

Despite the refusal to condone single motherhood in laboring poor communities, the traditions of mutual aid and informal adoption and childcare supported many unwed or deserted mothers determined to fulfill their responsibility to their children. Perhaps the most urgent need of women raising children on their own—after food, shelter, and employment—was childcare. The urgent need for child care was also shared by extremely poor wage-working wives whose husbands had deserted them, were unemployed, or had left the city to "tramp" in search of work. Here the concerns of single, destitute, and deserted mothers and baby farmers intersected.

While more than 20 percent of married women in Philadelphia's African American families worked full-time for wages, only the most destitute of the city's white families sent mothers outside the home to earn wages. Instead most families relied on the earnings of male breadwinners, coupled with the critical contributions of children as secondary wage-earners.[48] When married women of the laboring class contributed cash to the family economy, they usually did so by taking in laundry, running speakeasies in their front rooms, or managing cheap lodging houses and brothels. Other women worked as midwives, turning their homes into lying-in establishments or places in which to birth and board the babies of poor and especially single mothers.

Throughout the nineteenth century, Philadelphia's single young women were far more likely to work for wages outside the home than were their mothers, often contributing to the family economy while they lived out at service or remained as members in their parents' households for an extended period of time to assist in supporting their families. Irish, German, and African American daughters, in particular, had high rates of labor force participation.[49] While racial prejudice confined black women chiefly to work in service occupations, Irish and German women worked not only as domestic servants but as seamstresses, as weavers and millworkers in the city's textile industry, and in other industries and trades open to women in Philadelphia's diversified economy.

Philadelphia's unwed mothers formed a striking contrast to this portrait of dutiful daughters remaining within their parents' household to contribute to the family economy. Such women faced restricted economic opportunities and the possible loss of family support just when they needed to support not only themselves and their families but a baby as well. Because illegitimacy posed an acute crisis of reputation for unwed mothers and their families, many parents refused to allow unwed mothers to remain at home with their infants. For instance, a young German woman, Matilda G., was admitted to the Haven for Unwed Mothers and Infants in September 1884 with her two-week-old infant because "her mother was dreadful worried about her and don't allow her to come home on account of the disgrace."[50] Other parents were willing to shelter a wayward daughter only if she could arrange other accommodations for her child.

In an effort to prevent public disgrace, many women tried to place their infants in private institutions, but most were unwilling to care for the children of "fallen" women. By the 1890s day nurseries provided childcare for the children of the city's working mothers for five cents a day, but philanthropists refused admission to "any child whose legitimacy could not be proven."[51] Most orphanages accepted neither infants nor the children of unwed mothers and rescue homes required mothers to be institutionalized along with their babies.[52] Although the Haven's policies prohibited admission of illegitimate babies whose mothers were unwilling to accompany them, the Home was barraged by a steady stream of applicants—accompanied sometimes by their mothers or represented by their doctors—seeking to relinquish their babies. Such women sought to "hide the disgrace" or in the matron's words, "to get it away to hide the shame."[53]

Unwed mothers who were unsuccessful in placing their children or wished to avoid the stigma of institutionalization—or who preferred to attempt motherhood and wage-work on their own—comprised the chief clientele of the city's baby farms, along with their infants. These women boarded their infants and young children to retain jobs as live-in domestic servants, work in other occupations, including prostitution, accept positions as wetnurses in the homes of employers who insisted they board their own babies, or remain within the households of parents who would accept a fallen daughter but not her newborn baby. For single mothers already living outside family economies, the need to board an infant to permit the mother to work was more pressing than the need to preserve her reputation. Yet the ability to find work often hinged on a woman's respectability, so unwed mothers might be forced to board their infants to keep their motherhood a secret.[54]

Wetnursing—an occupation born of poverty, misfortune, and circumstance—was open to unwed mothers despite their fall from respectability, but wetnurses who lived in private homes were often required to board their infants.[55] The limited economic options available to poor mothers without the support of a male breadwinner might force a woman to nourish another woman's baby at the expense of her own, exemplifying the impact that the combination of poverty and illegitimacy could have on an infant's chances for survival.[56] During the depression of the mid-1880s, the superintendent at the Haven for Unwed Mothers and Infants recorded in her diary how "Two ladies call to get a wetnurse and this poor girl had been in only a half day so these ladies were very anxious to get her; to save their baby as it was very sick & the Doctor said that was all that would save it they wanted her to put her baby out to board and nurse theirs first she was not willing but they come back in the evening and persuaded her to go and promised to get a place for her child to board so she left with them this evening."[57]

In the late nineteenth century, wetnurses suckled infants in public and private charitable institutions, in private families, and in their own homes.[58] While deserted wives, homeless women, and unwed mothers nursed foundlings in institutions and in private homes, poor married women whose babies had died sometimes took infants to nurse in their own homes, serving a working-class clientele that included the infants of wetnurses employed by private families. Extremely destitute married women with living infants also used the comparatively high wages paid to live-in wetnurses to support their families and pay boarding fees for their own infants. While wet-nursing another woman's baby enabled single and destitute married mothers to compensate for the lack of a male breadwinner's wage, the consequences for the wetnurses's own infant were frequently devastating, especially if the infant was bottle-fed.

SPCC records document the use of baby farms by native-born white and African American women and by Irish, German, English, and Jewish immigrants, but the extent of their use of baby farms depended on the interaction of a number of factors affected by the household and occupational structures of each group. These included illegitimacy rates; the need for married women with young children to earn wages; the availability of other household members who could provide childcare or relatives willing to take a child into their own home; the presence of other wage-working family members and the nature and regularity of their employment; and the accessibility of institutional sources of aid. In each racial and ethnic group, the poorest of the city's wage-working mothers relied heavily on baby farms as places in which to board their young children, paying between $1.50 and $3.00 per child each week depending on the age of the child.

How well did baby farming serve the needs of such women and their children? How did women reconcile their need for safe and affordable childcare with the reputation of baby farms as houses of murder? Since baby farming was widely understood to be a means of abandoning an unwanted infant and legitimate care was readily confused with illicit practices, women who ran baby farms and women who boarded their children both needed to clarify the ambiguous nature of baby farming. How did mothers seeking childcare distinguish between murderous baby farmers and women who provided decent childcare? How did women who ran legitimate boarding establishments protect themselves from customers interested in disposing of unwanted babies?

To answer these questions, we must situate baby farming within the context of working-class women's networks of scrutiny, gossip, and mutual aid. While respectable working-class women condemned illegitimacy and used verbal criticism and neighborhood gossip to affirm the boundaries of acceptable sexual behavior, networks of the city's "rougher" women provided some measure of support for women in need of childcare with enough money to pay for it.

Baby farming resembled other neighborhood-based exchanges of cash, goods, and services but involved more than a simple commercial transaction. Baby farms embodied an extensive system of mutual aid among working-class women. In many cases, the baby farmer and her customer were clearly friends, relatives, or neighbors. Such women pooled social and economic resources critical to their survival, as the following example from SPCC case records illustrates.

When the SPCC received a complaint from the coroner that a child had died at Emma F.'s baby farm in West Philadelphia in the winter of 1896, the Society sent an agent to investigate. The agent's report documents a complex interplay among a group of African American women who pooled money and services accordingly, as the variables of health and employment changed over time. Emma F. usually cared for four children, who at the time of the investigation ranged in age from seven months to eight years and belonged to three different mothers. Her charges were three-year-old

Edith S., two-year-old Gertrude Q., Gertrude's seven-month-old brother Clarence, and Rachel, age eight. Emma claimed that Edith had lived with her about two and one half years, and that Edith's mother, Martha S., lived at service and paid $1.50 per week to board her child. Gertrude and Clarence Q. were boarded with Emma while their mother, Eliza Q., worked out as a cook, earning $4 per week. Emma had adopted Caroline T.; George W., the child whose death had prompted the investigation, was the son of another adopted daughter of Emma's, who worked at service in a home near the University of Pennsylvania. The SPCC agent noted, "Defendant [Emma F.] is suffering with a milk-leg. and is [word missing, possibly "hard-pressed"] at times, to follow her business; and Eliza Q. then comes there, and stays with her and does her work. such as Dfndt cannot do. and they put their earnings together & they live in common; but when Mrs. Q. is employed, cooking, she pays Dfndt $2 per week for the children. . . . The woman Q. sleeps at Dfndt's house when not at service."[59]

Commenting that "Dfndt is very poor. and does whatever she can to make a living," the agent also noted that Emma relied on two other home-based sources of income. Emma and the children occupied "a good-sized room with one single and a large double bed-stead" that was "comfortably furnished"; she rented out two rooms on the second floor of her six-room house. In her front room, Emma kept a number of trunks "belonging to colored girls who are out at service," who paid Emma money to store their worldly possessions.[60]

Clearly baby farming was not always as impersonal and cold-blooded as depicted in sensational accounts. In African American communities in particular, the practice appears to have been part of a larger pattern of female wage-earning and collective childrearing.[61] While many wary baby farmers under investigation by the SPCC claimed they "did not know the name of mother or child. or where to find the mother," baby farmers were unlikely to accept charge of an infant without being certain of who would pay the fee.[62] Records also reveal that some working women who were able to visit their children did so, indicating that baby farmers and their customers were likely to know each other's whereabouts. When Rachel M.'s boarding establishment, which catered to African American women and children, was under investigation, she told an SPCC agent that Martha J., who boarded her two-year-old daughter Eda, "works every day and comes there at night and takes care of the child."[63]

Kin ties frequently underlay both group and individual child-boarding arrangements. For instance, Norah D., a single mother who lived at service, paid her sister $1.50 per week to board her eight-year-old daughter Bridget.[64] In the 1880s a female servant in Philadelphia might earn about two dollars in cash a week as well as her room and board. This economic arrangement between sisters illustrates two significant points about baby farming and the provision of child care for older children. First, in some ways baby farming was no different from other economic arrangements between working-class relatives, in which family members pooled income and services to increase the resources of the entire family. Some women who had routinely contributed their wages to a family economy before the birth of their children continued to do so in an altered form once they became working mothers. When a woman's child care provider was her sister or adopted mother, baby farming became merely a different variation of an earlier family economy, albeit one that now centered around the needs of working women and their children. This knowledge that often baby farmers were well-known and trusted family members or neighbors rather than practitioners of a deadly trade explains the willingness of working women to board their children.[65]

At the same time, baby farming was also a home-based occupation. Although some baby farmers were boarding the children of a neighbor or a sister on a temporary basis and accepting money to cover their expenses, other women remained in the business for years, seeking new infants to replace those who died or were removed by their mothers. While couples very occasionally managed boarding establishments, almost all the cases brought to the attention of the SPCC mentioned a female proprietor. Like other women working in predominantly female occupations, baby farmers appear to have been initiated into the trade by other women, usually relatives. Case records note mother-daughter teams as well as establishments run by sisters.[66]

If baby farming had advantages as a home-based source of income, boarding other women's infants for profit also entailed occupational hazards. These ranged from nonpayment of fees, to the difficulties involved in caring for bottle-fed infants in an era when bottle-feeding entailed significant health risks, to the abandonment of infants by their mothers.

Medical observers in the late nineteenth century clearly recognized an obvious correlation between infant survival and breastfeeding, and infant mortality and bottle-feeding. Denied immunities passed from lactating women to breastfed infants and endangered by contaminated water and milk, bottle-fed infants were more susceptible to gastrointestinal diseases and malnutrition. Although expensive commercial infant food was marketed in the second half of the nineteenth century, bottle-fed infants were typically given a mixture of cow's milk diluted with water and sweetened with sugar.[67] While some doctors advised boiling the water and milk, contaminated water supplies, unpasteurized milk, and unsterile conditions made bottle-feeding a hazardous undertaking. For many low-birthweight infants born to poorly nourished women, bottle-feeding set up a dangerous cycle of bacterial infection and chronic diarrhea that led quickly to dehydration, malnutrition, and death. Infants boarded together in the same facility were also vulnerable to fatal contagious infections as well as neglect.

Late nineteenth-century doctors lamented the reluctance of the poor to rely on their services and claimed that many infants died from want of proper medical advice. As Dr. Parry commented, "Among the poorer classes it is not uncommon to postpone sending for the doctor until near the close of the life of the child, and every physician has often been told, when called to one of these patients, that it was not expected that he would cure the infant, 'but you must come, you know, as we must have a line to bury the little darlint' ."[68] Indeed many poor families and baby farmers may have found the doctor's ability to issue a death certificate that would lessen the likelihood of a coroner's inquest more valuable than medical advice.

Although baby farmers were accused of deliberately starving infants and neglecting to seek medical attention for the children in their care, physicians were powerless to cure diarrheal diseases such as cholera infantum until the 1920s and 1930s, when they began to develop effective fluid and electrolyte therapies.[69] Access to clean water and pasteurized milk and improved sanitation in poor neighborhoods, along with better control of infectious diseases, would have more impact in reducing infant mortality in Philadelphia in the first third of the twentieth century than would medical compliance and the regulation of childcare facilities.

In the last decades of the nineteenth century, though, the high mortality of bottle-fed infants ensured that death was a frequent visitor to Philadelphia's baby farms, posing significant risks to both child care providers and their charges. Based on his clinical experience treating single mothers at the Philadelphia Hospital, Dr. John Parry estimated that approximately 90 percent of the infants who were boarded—typically at four to six weeks of age—so their mothers could work as wetnurses would die before their first birthday.[70] The age at which a child was boarded out was significant, for older children who were less dependent on artificial feeding had better chances for survival than very young infants. While ethnic background or custom may have influenced at what age mothers and baby farmers began feeding infants solid foods—making them less dependent on bottle-feeding and so at less risk of disease—reformer Helen Campbell noted that working-class families typically began giving solids at six months or so.[71]

Rather than growing rich off murders committed for profit, many baby farmers were themselves vulnerable to abuse by their customers. Abandonment of infants at baby farms was a common mode of desertion throughout the 1880s and 1890s in Philadelphia, as mothers burdened with an infant they could not care for disappeared without paying weekly fees. In this way, baby farmers often served as unwitting and unwilling agents in the process of abandonment. Dr. Charlotte Abbey—physician at a home for unwed mothers in the early 1890s and Superintendent at the Women's Directory after 1893—noted, "In work among deserted children a frequent source of infant suffering has been recognized. Those who have taken an infant to board and failed to receive payment have great difficulty in being relieved of the care of the child, and the little one suffers."[72]

Many women who brought infants to the Haven for Unwed Mothers and Infants claimed that they had arranged to board the child for a fee, but that payments had stopped after several weeks, with no news of either the mother or her intentions. Nonpayment of fees allowed a mother to abandon a child gradually, and from a distance. An indirect form of desertion, it removed the responsibility for determining the infant's fate from the shoulders of one woman, and placed it on those of another. Because baby farming was widely perceived as intimately related to the disposal of unwanted children, some mothers who deserted their infants at legitimate boarding establishments may have misunderstood the nature of their agreement.

Possibly, some of the women who left babies at the Haven were not baby farmers seeking to rid themselves of their charges, as they claimed, but the mothers of the infants instead. However, collaborative investigations by police and Haven staff uncovered few of these cases. Evidence supports the contention of baby farmers that—whether deliberately or inadvertently—mothers did desert infants at childcare establishments; when they did so, their caregivers often sought other placements.[73] In January 1885 a Spring Garden baby farmer seeking to admit an infant told the matron at the Haven how "She had taken a baby to board and the woman had deserted the child and she was not able to keep it so she wanted to get it in here."[74] Less than four months earlier, the matron noted " A girl . . . called to get a deserted child in saying it was left on her hands as she had taken it to board and suppose [sic] the mother was dead."[75] A policeman brought another infant to the Haven after it was deserted at the Day Nursery on Diamond Street.[76]

Some women had never intended to desert their infants but were simply unable to make the weekly payments. Afraid to inform the baby farmer of her plight for fear that she would refuse to board the child on credit, such a mother might be forced to rely on her baby farmer's goodwill and hope that maternal instincts would triumph over business acumen. In December of 1881, a two-year-old boy was left at the mayor's office. Taken by a policeman to the Haven, the circumstances of his abandonment were clarified when his relieved mother came to claim him a week and a half later, paying his board before bringing him home.[77] The child's mother, Mrs. K., had boarded him with a woman who lived in the vicinity of Fourth and Spruce Streets. When Mrs. K. fell behind in her payments, the baby farmer had deposited the child at the mayor's office, a center of the city's public life.

The possibility of becoming a dumping ground for unwanted babies was a serious occupational hazard of baby farming. Since most women who ran baby farms were quite poor themselves, they could ill afford to raise the infants left on their hands when mothers defaulted on payments. As businesswomen as well as surrogate mothers, many baby farmers were firm in their conviction that their responsibilities for the infants ended with the final payment. Such women were adamant in their refusal to take no for an answer when they sought to dispose of their "stock" at the Haven. In late December 1883," a colored woman came to leave a child that was left on her hands wanted to leave it wether [sic] or no." Another time, Mrs. C., a Lady Manager, threatened to send a detective after an "elderly German woman a pedler [sic] she called herself brought an infant saying it was left on her hands and insisted to leave it here saying [otherwise] she would leave it on the street."[78]

Some baby farmers did desert infants on the streets, although some took pains to ensure that the babies would be found. The SPCC Annual Report for 1883 recounted "a woman was seen in the vicinity of 5th and Christian Sts. with a bundle in her arms which she appeared to be anxious to conceal by the wrappings of her shawl. She was noticed to be acting in a suspicious manner, to frequently look around and behind her as if she were being watched; finally she was observed to lay her bundle carefully down on a stone step of a dwelling-house and walk stealthily away. In that bundle was wrapped an infant a few months old, deserted in the middle of winter in the open streets."[79] When investigators traced the woman "who had perpetrated this outrage" to her house, they found a number of malnourished infants "all suffering from . . . the confined unhealthy atmosphere of the improvised nursery." In an adjoining room, they discovered an infant corpse lying on a table "awaiting the undertaker's care." SPCC agents learned that the baby farmer had been boarding babies for some time; "if reports were to be believed, it was a common thing for her to dispose of her stock" by deserting infants in alleyways.[80]

Clearly this baby farmer was trying to secretly abandon infants left in her care. Although she abandoned the baby on the steps of a dwelling, suggesting she wanted the infant to be discovered alive, her choice of location nonetheless placed the baby in danger of death from exposure. The number of infants found in her care is also revealing, for women who boarded numerous infants at a time were less able to care for them than women who tended only one infant along with several toddlers or older children, as in the cases of apparently legitimate child care arrangements described above.

In yet another instance reported in the *Public Ledger*, an African American midwife named Susannah P. was charged in the summer of 1896 with abandoning the corpse of a three-day-old black infant in a vacant lot. Several hours before her arrest, a stranger had followed Susannah home, after watching her deposit a bundle in a lot at 19th and McKean Streets. Suspecting foul play, the young man had notified Patrolman McFarland, who searched the lot and discovered a package containing a dead infant. In prison awaiting the coroner's report, Susannah refused to divulge any information concerning either the mother of the child or her own reasons for abandoning the infant's corpse. An official from the coroner's office informed the police that "there was peculiar evidence indicating that death resulted from violence." [81]

In the wake of Susannah's arrest, another complaint followed to strengthen the evidence that Susannah was indeed a notorious baby farmer. On July 2, her next-door neighbor called at the office of the SPCC to charge that a neglected infant who "cried a great deal" was being kept in Susannah's house. Upon investigation, SPCC agents discovered a three-month-old girl. Susannah's husband claimed that his wife had taken the child to board some time ago and that he did not know who she belonged to. With his wife in prison he had no way to care for the child and was quite "willing that Agents should take it." His married daughter brought the infant to the local station house and from there the tiny boarder was taken to the Philadelphia Hospital.[82]

It is difficult to determine in such instances which of a number of possible scenarios was most likely to have been played out. A baby farmer whose boarder baby had died from diarrhea and dehydration might bury the evidence out of fear of facing arrest for infanticide. On the other hand, she might be responding to nonpayment, whether deliberate or unintentional, or she might be fulfilling an implicit agreement with the mother to destroy the child after payments ceased. Although neighboring women readily pressed charges at the SPCC office against mothers they suspected had struck such deadly bargains, explicit agreements of this sort remain hard to document.[83] A desperate mother could place her child with a notorious baby farmer fully aware of the risks involved, without articulating her desire to be rid of the child. Still other women who unwittingly placed their children with negligent baby farmers were clearly trying to do the best they could under difficult circumstances.

The case of Lillie G., a one-month-old infant brought to the Haven by the turnkey of the 16th District Station House, demonstrates what could happen when a baby inadvertently fell prey to a baby farmer more criminal than incompetent. Shortly after her birth in November 1885, Lillie was placed to board because her mother was too ill to nurse her. In early December, Lillie's caretaker was discovered lying intoxicated on the street with the baby; Lillie was found "feeding out of a bottle containing soap and water."[84]

In the fall of 1877, a wetnurse switched baby farmers after she became the target of an SPCC investigation for allegedly boarding her child with a negligent baby farmer. Case records noted, "Mrs. G. F. B. . . . states a case of alleged cruel desertion of a baby boy by its mother, a woman named Mrs. K. . . . and states that this woman left her child and goes out to wetnurse another infant while her own is starving—Upon investigation we find this poor woman in very destitute circumstances does this for a living and pays a board of $2 a week for her own child—and if it was not properly taken care of—it was not her fault."[85] "Quite indignant that she should be charged with neglect," Mrs. K. promised to provide another caretaker for her child, but the chance that her baby would survive as a boarder was slim at best.

The Regulation of Baby Farming

In the Gilded Age, the practice of baby farming was significantly shaped by the sensational accounts of baby farming in the press and the efforts of reformers to regulate the trade. While boarding establishments for children existed in the early nineteenth century, in a very real way "baby farming" as urban late Victorian Americans understood the term, was constructed as reformers attempted to regulate the trade. As concern over the "evils of baby-farming" became more pervasive, boarding establishments for children were regarded with suspicion, so that even the wail of a baby could suggest the ghoulish possibility of criminal violence. It was then incumbent on women who boarded children to prove that they did not engage in criminal acts. In these decades baby farmers began to rely on the medical services of physicians, in order to demonstrate their concern for the children entrusted in their care in a way that middle-class reformers could understand and so protect themselves against charges of infanticide.[86] Regulation of baby farms, in turn, served to transform the traditional exchange of social and financial resources among neighboring women into a formal system of child care.

If part of the cultural construction of the crime of baby farming focused on working-class indifference or resistance to medical supervision of infants' health, illness, and death, for reformers the logical solution was supervision of baby farms to ensure that needy infants received medical attention.[87] After May 1885, the advent of licensing in Philadelphia subjected informal networks among women to legal regulations concerning the amount of space and number of caretakers required to board a given number of children. This legislation was intended to promote infant health and safety and set the terms by which a baby farmer could be considered criminally negligent. Reformers also intended regulation to weed out practitioners who killed through incompetence as well as the more notorious baby farmers who deliberately murdered unwanted infants.

The Society to Protect Children from Cruelty was instrumental in lobbying for this legislation and SPCC agents worked closely with the police to enforce the law. Before the law passed, agents had found it "almost impossible to put a stop to the practice of baby-farming, which was known to exist to a considerable extent, but there were such inherent difficulties in successfully tracing the ill-treatment, that the injury done by the unscrupulous was left unpunished."[88] While the 1885 legislation did not necessarily make it easier to track down criminal baby farms, it required individuals who boarded infants under two years of age to possess a license. The license could be revoked at any time by the Court of Quarter Sessions. Most significantly, the legislation authorized members of the State Board of Charities and officers of the SPCC to inspect the premises of baby farms.

While the regulations did not stipulate that baby farmers had to engage doctors if their charges became ill, evidence that a baby farmer had sought medical attention could constitute a strong defense against charges of neglect or infanticide. An investigation of a baby farm in the vicinity of Sixth and Parrish Streets in Northern Liberties, an Irish and German Jewish section of Philadelphia, illustrates the value of maintaining relationships with medical practitioners. In July 1893, Isaac K., a German Jewish man, informed the SPCC that his neighbor, Janet S., was a baby farmer.[89] As evidence he noted that one Saturday night "two coffins were taken in the house in a bag, and taken out again in 10 or 15 minutes." Although two children had died, agents found nothing suspicious to report. The children had been attended by a doctor, and the other children appeared well cared for. Although Janet S. had no license, she was willing to apply for one. Janet stated that she had taken children to board for the last two years, and that she received them routinely from local doctors and a midwife. There is no evidence that Janet S.'s baby farm was exploiting unwed mothers and their infants.

Unlike similar proposals elsewhere, the 1885 legislation permitting designated officials to inspect private residences where women were engaged in baby farming generated little public consternation in Philadelphia. In England the topic attracted considerable public debate in the late 1860s. Lydia Becker of the National Society for Woman's Suffrage, a vocal opponent of bills to regulate baby farms, argued that such bills would prevent single mothers from leaving children with friends and neighbors. Couching her opposition in references to the cherished principles of laissez-faire, she decried the police interference and espionage that would result from efforts to regulate a home-based occupation. But Becker's most significant criticism pointed to the increased legal control of women by men that would result from the regulation of this form of women's work. Becker angrily pointed out, "*Men only* are to grant the licenses—*men only* are competent to certify to the qualifications of the license—and *men only* are to visit the babies in their own nurses' charge. This minute and galling supervision by men of the domestic and nursery arrangements of women, would be felt as grievously vexatious by the women of this nation, especially by the poorer classes."[90]

In Philadelphia, responsible baby farmers responded with apparent equanimity to demands that they procure licenses, although they often failed to comply with the law until after a visit from an SPCC agent. After coroner Samuel Ashbridge held an inquest in 1896 on the body of a two-month-old infant boarding with Rachel and John J., an African American couple, he informed SPCC agents, "There was no evidence . . . that the woman Defdt was not a proper person to keep children or that her house was not cleanly.

. . . She was keeping children without a license and he deemed it his duty to notify the Society."[91]

Rachel claimed that she tried to procure a license from several magistrates without success, but was willing to try again. Similar investigations of other establishments in the 1880s and 1890s uncovered no evidence of wrongdoing except the failure to procure a license. During these years, applicants shuttled from the police station to the SPCC office and back again, as women who applied directly at their local station houses were referred back to the SPCC for an inspection and approval of their facilities before a license would be issued.

Some baby farmers may have welcomed the opportunity to distinguish their premises from more illicit establishments. Clearly, the issue of safety concerned the prostitutes, wet nurses, domestic servants, and other mothers who actually boarded their children at least as much as it concerned the city's more prosperous late Victorian reformers.[92]

Notorious baby farmers faced strong condemnation in the poor neighborhoods where their trade was based. Neighbors who were close-mouthed and uncooperative when SPCC investigators inquired about the sexual and drinking habits of their neighbors considered the abuse of baby farming a far different matter. The eagerness of neighbors to inform the authorities when they believed infants were being abused—and their readiness to bring complaints to the SPCC, an upper-middle-class agency alternately feared and hated by a significant minority of the city's working class—testifies to their disapproval of the seamier side of baby farming.[93]

The licensing of baby farms was closely related to reformers' efforts to regulate private lying-in facilities, which were associated with the abuses of baby farming. In the 1890s, investigations linked private maternity homes or unlicensed lying-in facilities to a deplorable "traffic in children." In the Gilded Age the market for adopted babies was limited, compelling some unwed mothers to pay other women to take permanent charge of their babies.[94] It was easier for unscrupulous midwives to abandon or farm out the infants instead, however, while claiming that they would provide good homes.

Most nineteenth-century women gave birth within their own homes, attended by midwives or doctors. Women who could not afford the fees of medical practitioners, and unwed women whose families had cast them out, could seek institutional help in the maternity ward of charity hospitals or in the medical wards of the city's almshouse. Poor pregnant women who were able to remain outside of institutions or were unwelcome because of prior illegitimate births utilized unlicensed lying-in facilities. Because homes in which women had just given birth had to care for newborns as well as their mothers, and because women often needed long-term childcare arrangements to return to work, women who ran lying-in homes sometimes provided facilities for boarding infants, as well as adoption services.[95] However practical this arrangement, reformers regarded these joint lying-in/baby farming establishments patronized chiefly by unwed mothers with great alarm.

In the 1890s investigations by reformers from the SPCC and the Women's Directory linked private lying-in facilities to a deplorable "traffic in children." Of twenty-eight adoptions from lying-in homes investigated in 1898 by the Women's Directory, for example, thirteen addresses had proved fictitious and two infants had been "given into the hands of questionable characters."[96] Dr. Charlotte Abbey of the Women's Directory discovered that "Fifty dollars is the usual amount paid by an unfortunate mother to the proprietor of a private lying-in hospital for the disposal of her child."[97] Calling the sale of infants a "terrible evil," Dr. Abbey pointed out that although the Board of Health ensured that the sanitary condition of lying-in homes was satisfactory, no comparable effort was ever made to oversee the well-being of the adopted children.

As they recognized the links between lying-in homes, the sale of infants, and the boarding of infants at disreputable baby farms, reformers expanded their efforts to encompass the regulation of lying-in facilities too. The SPCC *Seventeenth Annual Report* recounted:

Additional enactments at the last session of the legislature authorizes [sic] the Society's Agent, appointed under sanction of court, to visit unchartered Lying-In Hospitals and exercise a surveillance over them. By such scrutiny, and the enforcement of the penalty of the law, it is believed much criminality and infanticide will be prevented. Doubtless crimes are perpetuated in some of these so-called hospitals which exist under the guise of offering a home for women in the hour of their extremity. . . . In the last year several houses of this character have been stripped of their flimsy veil and their true character exposed. The proprietors were brought to justice and are now suffering the penalty of their misdeeds by confinement in the State prison.[98]

Undercover work revealed that babies were bought and sold at private maternity hospitals as some midwives and baby farmers sought to profit from the determination of unwed mothers to put their children up for adoption. Promising confidentiality, the proprietors of lying-in hospitals received a "surrender fee" to cover the alleged expenses of confinement and adoption. But instead of placing infants with appropriate families, midwives boarded them with baby farmers or paid other women small sums to adopt the infants after they themselves received larger sums, usually about a fifty dollar "surrender fee" from the baby's mother. Although some mothers undoubtedly believed their children would be adopted, advertisements in English and foreign language newspapers offering babies for adoption probably served as coded messages indicating a midwife's willingness to place—and perhaps dispose of—an infant.[99]

Like investigations by the Haven and Women's Directory, SPCC records also linked midwives and the proprietors of lying-in homes to the sale of infants. While investigating charges of misconduct leveled at a mother, SPCC agents incidentally discovered "that the defendant was not the mother of this infant, only by adoption. . . . She purchased the baby from Mrs. Dr. B.____for ten dollars, one-half of which went to the real mother to meet the expense she incurred at the doctor's house, and the remaining half, to the practitioner who brought it into the world."[100]

Another case investigated by the SPCC in 1901 clearly establishes the seamier side of baby farming and its ties to the traffic in children at illicit lying-in homes. When the SPCC received reports that an infant had died in a baby farm "in a miserable shanty on Fitzwater St." in South Philadelphia and that several other children were slowly starving to death, they alerted the coroner and dispatched an agent to the house under suspicion. The agent issued the following report regarding the baby farmer and her practice: "She is a drunken, worthless person. The man is entirely under her control, and she obtained three children from midwife houses. One of the children is almost dead, and she has no means of caring for them. She received a bonus for taking them."[101] At first, the defendant claimed to be the mother of one of the children, but after sharp questioning she admitted that she had obtained each of the children from three separate midwives, one of whom had advertised in the *Stern* under the name of Dr. Janne. She stated that she had no license to board babies but had "adopted the children to comfort and cheer her in her old age."[102] She confessed nonetheless that she was usually paid ten dollars for each child she adopted. In exchange she signed an agreement "stipulating that for the sum of $10, she would take the child, keep it, and not return it."

At the coroner's inquest, Dr. Janne was called to the stand. She testified that her name was Yanne, and that the *Stern* had made an error when printing her name that she had not corrected. Indignant, the coroner "reprimanded her severily" [sic] for using the name of a prominent Philadelphia physician. "Dr. Janne" admitted that she had received fifty dollars for her services, and thirty-five dollars for taking the child before selling it for ten dollars. One of the other midwives, Mrs. Kerpardt, declared that she had received twenty dollars for her services to the mother and another forty dollars for adopting it, before she paid the baby farmer five dollars to take the child off of her hands. As the SPCC *Annual Report* explained: "The hearing developed the fact that a regular traffic in infants was carried on and that the midwives, many of them unscrupulous and mercenary made charges of $50 for caring for unfortunate women, and $25 for the adoption of the infants, of which they paid to the baby farmer ten dollars. Of course, the sooner the infant dies the better these people like it, and the children are left to starve to death."[103]

This particular incident was resolved when the judge asked the Board of Health to revoke the licenses of Mrs. Yanne and Mrs. Kerpardt. The baby farmer was held until she could pay a fine of seventy-five dollars and costs, and the children were brought to the Philadelphia Hospital.

Of course, some midwives worked very hard to place unwanted babies. In November 1893 the SPCC received an "anonymous communication" requesting agents to investigate the case of a fifteen-year-old girl allegedly soon to become the mother of her father's child. An agent called on several neighbors who claimed to know "nothing further than the rumor that was going around the neighborhood." Proceeding to the home of the defendant, the agent found his daughter, who had been " delivered of a child" earlier that month. She maintained that last winter in February, "on a Sunday afternoon whilst Defdt [her father] and the children were absent 3 young men entered the house. & took her to the water closet and there had criminal intercourse with her." The tale she told differed from the "story the neighbors heard," for they placed the blame not on three strangers but rather on a young man employed by her father; the neighbors claimed her attacker had fled to Italy.

Further investigation revealed that a German midwife, Mrs. H., had attended the girl in labor and delivery and had taken the newborn to the Haven but the institution had refused to "receive it." Undeterred, the midwife had continued on to the Tenth District Station House. There she was told to bring the infant to the Guardian of the Poor, "which she did & they refused to take it." Finally, St. Vincent's Home had agreed to admit the baby.[104]

Although case records noted the activities of women doctors in the traffic

in children, it is highly doubtful that members of the "regular" medical profession were so involved. While the presence of the Woman's Medical College of Pennsylvania assured Philadelphians of a steady supply of female
physicians, these practitioners of "regular" medicine supported the work of
institutions such as the Women's Directory and the Haven for Unwed
Mothers and Infants that provided an alternative to the city's baby farms. Of
forty-five doctors who issued a public statement in support of the Women's
Directory in 1893, six were women. Similarly, homes for unwed mothers
and their infants relied on the services of women physicians, who provided
medical care for the inmates.[105] In late nineteenth-century American cities,
the phrase "woman doctor" typically referred to midwives who performed
a variety of reproductive services, including abortions; some also ran lying-
in homes. SPCC case records probably refer to these women.[106]

Cautionary Tales: Unnatural Mothers, Mercenary Baby Farmers,
and Children at Risk

If concrete examples of infanticide and abandonment and of child abuse
within baby farms abounded, baby farming was also notorious for other,
less tangible reasons. There were cultural as well as practical foundations
for Victorian disapproval of the practice. Whether they were regarded as
dens of iniquity or merely as facilities for the children of working mothers,
the establishment of baby farms violated cherished Victorian ideals about
the proper relation of women to children, and about women's relation to the
workplace. The separation of mothers and their children was disturbing to
many Victorians, who believed proper motherhood essential to the
upbringing of virtuous citizens. At a time when the birth rate of middle-
class women was declining substantially, so that middle-class families were
raising fewer children more intensively, the idea of caring for infants wholesale was particularly appalling to many middle-class Americans, especially
if money tainted the transaction. Baby farms appeared to be based on the
premise that woman's sacred duty of raising children could be turned over
to the lowest bidder.[107]

The poor reputation of baby farms as dens of wickedness can be attributed in part to the disreputable reputations of the women and children who
resorted to their use. The fact that so many of the infants were illegitimate
mocked the sanctity of Victorian motherhood. Baby farms served a population consisting chiefly of the children of prostitutes, wetnurses, unwed

mothers, and those destitute and deserted wives who, although mothers of small children, were compelled nonetheless to earn a living through wage-work performed outside the home. In different ways, each group of women appeared to repudiate the social construction of good mothering and was therefore suspect.

These women became the stock characters in the late nineteenth-century morality play that shaped social policy for women and children. Greedy baby farmers subjected childrearing to the cash nexus and tended young children for profit rather than out of love; hardened prostitutes severed sexuality from reproduction and linked money and sex. Wetnurses' reliance on baby farms underscored the mercenary rather than maternal nature of working-class women, who relinquished their own maternal duties—and possibly traded the lives of their own infants—in exchange for hard cash.[108] As economic rather than moral agents, all wage-earning women challenged Victorian constructions of normative womanhood; as women who earned money for what should have been labors of love performed within their own households for their own husbands and children, prostitutes, baby farmers, and wetnurses in particular exposed the instability of dominant assumptions about female nature.[109] Prostitutes, baby farmers, and wet-nurses, then, each provided cautionary tales about what happened to calculating women who took money for sex or for rearing children or nursing babies and in so doing, became what anthropologist Anna Tsing has termed "enemies of nurturance" who placed children's lives at risk.[110] Unwed mothers had no rightful claim to maternity. Furthermore, by exemplifying the potentially conflicting needs of mother and child that self-sacrificing "good motherhood" obscured, their dilemma heightened their transgression. By abandoning the infants they so recklessly conceived, they ensured that the public would pay for their indiscretion. Destitute mothers and deserted wives came the closest, perhaps, to those deserving of pity rather than scorn, for they were forced into the labor market by the inadequacy of a male provider.

Each of these constructs—the baby farmer, the prostitute, the wetnurse, the unwed mother, the wage-working mother—combined to create the trope of the dangerous, possibly murderous poor mother that emerged at a critical moment in the late nineteenth century. This suspicion of destitute single mothers resonated in laboring communities as well as among the upper and middle classes. Baby farmers were watched carefully in working-class neighborhoods, and unwed mothers were clearly scorned by men and women of the respectable poor. Nonetheless, the identity, meaning, and significance of the dangerous mother was contested as upper-middle-class social observers and child protection workers and labor reformers attributed the problems of working-class childrearing to different causes. In working-class communities, the dangerous mother was specifically defined in relation to her lapses from respectability; for the middle and upper classes, the category was expansive enough to include large numbers of working-class women.

In this way the controversy over the dangerous poor mother, her suspicious childrearing practices, and their link to baby farming was also part of a larger concern about the role of the family and child nurture in an ostensibly republican society beset by increasing class tensions. In the Gilded Age, upper- and middle-class reformers located the source of urban social problems in the family relations of the poor. For upper- and middle-class men and women, and particularly for medical reformers, doubts about the maternal instincts and abilities of working class women to mother underlay criticism of baby farms; single and working-class women were portrayed as either unfortunate victims or as unnatural mothers and deadly killers intent on destroying their own young. The exposés of baby farms fit neatly into the dominant cultural tendency to portray the family life of the poor as destructive. Baby farming fell into a larger category of suspect working-class childrearing practices, highlighted in this period by the SPCC's focus on child exploitation, cruelty, and neglect.

In contrast to mainstream social welfare and medical reformers, male labor leaders writing in the labor press and testifying before Congress refused to blame the incompetence or deliberate negligence of working-class mothers for the high rates of infant and child mortality in poor neighborhoods. Instead they insisted that it was the poor conditions of working-class life that were hazardous to women and children and that created child neglect and exploitation. Labor activists did not take up the cause of safe child care for working mothers, however, not only because of the relatively small proportion of white as compared to African American mothers in the labor force, but because of their overriding commitment to the gendered division of labor and the family wage.[111] Instead, they linked the controversial issue of child neglect to the demand for the eight-hour day and claimed that by overworking men and women, employers were indirectly creating the inmates of orphanages and juvenile houses of correction.[112] In this context, child neglect dramatically highlighted the impact of economic inequality on working-class family life, while the fact that some mothers had to leave the home to earn wages emphasized the economic instability of the city's poorest families and pointed to the need for the family wage—a family wage paid to male providers that would not have helped single mothers and their children.

The alarm about child abuse at baby farms resonated because it touched directly and indirectly on a cluster of related issues that troubled late Victorian men and women of all classes: motherhood outside of marriage; the relationship of women to paid labor; the vulnerability of working-class children and their exploitation through child labor; ongoing negotiations between and within classes over the meaning of childhood and the familial obligations of parents and children, and the relationship of the poor to the authority of the state and the state's relationship to the provision of social services.

The cultural anxiety over baby farming also served to identify, criminalize, and punish transgressions of good mothering, while reinforcing the definition of good mothering in working-class neighborhoods. Just as the activities of the SPCC problematized the family relations of the laboring poor, the baby farming alarm highlighted suspicions about working-class single mothers and childcare providers. Abandonment, infanticide, and baby farming were all seen as "unnatural" working-class alternatives to more appropriate forms of motherhood. But concern over the improper mothering in the city's poor neighborhoods was a class-specific elaboration of a more general cultural preoccupation with the definition and enforcement of good mothering in regard to women of all classes.

In the years following the Civil War, "regular" medical professionals gained an influential voice in public discussions of sexuality, motherhood, and child welfare. Advocating state intervention in a variety of previously "private" issues, "regular" doctors were leading figures in campaigns to regulate prostitution and criminalize abortion. Philadelphia's medical community joined the nationwide effort to medicalize social and moral issues and subject them to legislative control. For instance, the leading text in the crusade to criminalize abortion, *Foeticide,* was authored by Dr. Hugh Hodge, a prominent Philadelphia physician and medical reformer.[113] Whether they drew on traditional concepts of medicine as a moral science or on newer beliefs in the scientific nature of medicine, doctors concerned with infant mortality found it imperative to change female attitudes and behavior toward children.

In a lecture on infant mortality and illegitimacy to the Philadelphia Social Science Association in 1871, Dr. John Parry called for a "kindly hand to aid" unwed mothers to help preserve the lives of their children. Many of his colleagues, however, blamed married as well as single mothers for the high mortality rates of their babies. Richard Ashurst, in the audience during Parry's lecture, commented, "I fancy that among foundlings there are very few who are the children of the seduced and the seducer. There is a vast number of foundlings who are the children of the degraded and criminal classes, born to the life in which they, perhaps, naturally take their places." And a Dr. Ludlow claimed that the problem affected all classes, although in each class the situation was somewhat different. Commenting that "the great deficiency, not only in the lower, but in the higher classes, is the want of sufficient responsibility on the part of the parents in regard to the rearing of children," he went on to indict the mothers of the more prosperous, laboring, and destitute classes. Wealthy women were unable to care properly for their children, "jaded" as they were from "long walks, midnight revels, and fatiguing exercise;" or else in their "anxiety to get rid of the care of the child" they put the child in the charge of a "hireling." Parents in the laboring class were overworked and intemperate; "mothers rush from their work, to take care of their children, when they are unfit to nourish them." He concluded that mortality was greatest in the "lower classes" "where we have the illegitimate; they are anxious to get rid of them, they are thrown upon the public, and taken to our public institutions to be reared."[114]

Significantly, at the same time that the mothering—indeed the very womanhood—of poor women became problematized and scrutinized, medical reformers began to create a discourse that focused on the selfish and unnatural proclivities of more prosperous women. In medical reform literature written by men, criticism of unnatural women who were unwilling to mother was class-specific. By the mid-nineteenth century, infanticide was perceived as a crime of poor and degraded single women, while abortion was believed to be a crime of respectable married women of the middle and upper classes.[115] In the same years that doctors addressed infanticide and infant mortality among the poor, they campaigned to criminalize abortion before as well as after "quickening." This attempt by physicians to effect changes in the legislation pertaining to criminal abortion was successful in most states by the last third of the nineteenth century. Casting "medical men" as the "guardians of the rights of infants," physician Hugh Hodge made repeated parallels between infanticide and abortion. Both were "hideous, unnatural" crimes which violated "every natural sentiment."[116]

Although the dangerous poor mother was defined in sharp contrast to the good mother of the middle and upper classes, in considerations of abortion, doctors found the same perturbing qualities of single, poor and disreputable women present in prosperous respectable married women. Anti-abortion rhetoric of the period was filled with images of unnatural aborting women who were otherwise respectable, women whose crimes were made even more unthinkable because of their unquestioned social status and apparent devotion to the children they had previously carried to term. The charges against dangerous poor mothers and unnatural aborting women of the middle and upper classes were surprisingly similar. These women were selfish rather than maternal. They failed to respect either fetal or infant life or medical authority, they placed their own concerns above those of their offspring and potential offspring, they sought to separate sex from reproduction in order to experience pleasure without responsibility, and they repudiated maternal (and no doubt wifely) self-sacrifice. At the same time, in discussions of the deleterious impact of higher education on the reproductive capacities of young women, male doctors discovered a repudiation of motherhood in middle-class daughters as well.[117]

Thus there was an analogue to the sensationalized concern over baby farming and the dangerous maternity of the poor for women of the middle class as well. It was expressed in concerns over the persistence of abortion despite its criminalization, the declining birthrate, the growing political and social activity of women, and the willingness of an increasing number of young women to allegedly risk ruining their reproductive health and their marital prospects in the pursuit of higher education. The repudiation of motherhood by women of all classes that was identified by male doctors in the late nineteenth century, addressed in discussions of infant mortality and abortion, and alluded to in discussions of the impact of higher education on women's reproductive capacities, was figurative as well as literal: the alarm was as much about unnatural women who disdained self-sacrifice and rejected a lifetime spent nurturing husbands and children as it was about risks to fetuses and children.

While pejorative attitudes toward single mothers and class, racial, and ethnic prejudice framed perceptions of child desertion, infanticide, and baby farming, they also contributed to Philadelphia's high rates of infant mortality and helped determine which infants would be dead before their first birthday. Although poverty and the stigma of illegitimacy played a critical role in determining which babies would be abandoned or boarded, the two conditions were usually intertwined. Poverty was both a contributing factor to unwed motherhood and a consequence of it. Birth control and abortion were frequently unavailable or unreliable. High rates of male unemployment and unsteady work at low wages could disrupt the best-laid plans, as men went "tramping" in search of work and left behind pregnant wives and sweethearts. Unwed mothers and deserted wives found it extremely difficult to support both themselves and children outside of a family economy. Left to their own resources, they combined wage-work and motherhood as best they could. The sometimes unfortunate outcome of their efforts is compelling testimony to the limitations within which they shaped their lives.

Women in this position faced a number of difficult options. They searched for positions as domestic servants in homes that would accept their infants, and they resided with other family members, exchanging wages for childcare. Barring that, they might board a child with friends or relatives or at a neighborhood baby farm. Recognizing the hardships confronting unwed and deserted mothers, institutions such as the Haven for Unwed Mothers and Infants and the Women's Directory provided shelter, limited vocational training, job placement, and legal and medical care. Many working-class women eagerly sought out these resources. Yet others shunned them to avoid the stigma of charity and institutionalization. Some women were considered unsuitable candidates for aid, were unaware of the services, or had long-term needs that these institutions could not fulfill.

Some women resorted to abandonment or infanticide or surrendered their infants for adoption, paying an exorbitant fee for the confidential delivery and placement of the child. Along with the deliberate starvation and neglect of infants, this traffic in children provided the material context—however misinterpreted—for sensational tales of a working class that destroyed its own young and threatened to destroy the fabric of American society as well. Well-publicized cases of infanticide and abandonment contributed to the baby farming controversy by attributing these practices to the worst kind of criminal motivation. In fact, abandonment was most often a response to the problems of poverty, the stigma of illegitimacy, and inadequate provisions for child care. Legitimate baby farming was an alternative to abandonment; yet this neighborhood system of group child care still posed certain risks and dangers for parents, children, and baby farmers.

Child abuse within baby farms mobilized not only Philadelphia's middle-class residents, but working-class men and women as well. As the city's professional and reform community used their skills and influence to regulate baby farming and provide services for destitute mothers and their children, working-class Philadelphians monitored baby farms within their own neighborhoods. They scrutinized boarding establishments, noting the quality of medical care provided and the display of appropriate signs of mourning when an infant died. They took notice when too many mothers went in and too few children came out. They watched for evidence of suspicious burials and listened for incessant crying that might indicate abuse or neglect. Most of all, they informed authorities such as the SPCC when they suspected malpractice.

The resort of unwed mothers to infanticide, abandonment, and abusive baby farming in order to "hide the disgrace" of an illegitimate child testifies to the power of respectable working-class matrons to define neighborhood sexual morality and enforce strict Victorian standards of female sexual behavior in some of Philadelphia's working-class neighborhoods. Working-class reliance on neighborhood childcare establishments also demonstrates the significance of rougher women's local networks in providing much-needed services and financial and emotional support for unwed mothers and widowed and deserted wives. Legitimate baby farming reveals the strength of working-class women's networks of mutual aid, yet the resort of unmarried mothers to illicit baby farms and infanticide and abandonment also reveals the heavy burden and consequences of neighboring women's criticisms of sexual misconduct, as well as the deadly policies of public and private institutions that discriminated against unwed mothers and their children.

Instead of exposing a working-class population intent on destroying its own children, an examination of abandonment, infanticide, and baby farming in late nineteenth-century Philadelphia attests to stark patterns of inequality between men and women, blacks and whites, natives and newcomers, and rich and poor. For every child who ostensibly died by drowning, suffocation, or deliberate neglect at the hands of a notorious baby farmer, many more were killed in effect by the harshness of life for the city's destitute, deserted, and single mothers and their children. The late Victorian penchant for sentimentalism and scandal encouraged popular perceptions of "unscrupulous" and "mercenary" midwives and "unfortunate" and "unnatural" mothers and their "innocent babes." It was easier for Philadelphians to conceptualize the abuses of baby farming as a problem of criminals and their victims, to be solved by legislation, licensing, and law enforcement. Yet as some reformers themselves understood, this approach had limitations. Legal regulation was important. But regulation alone could not eradicate the underlying problems of poverty, the inadequate childcare provisions for working-class mothers and their infants, and the stigma of illegitimacy that drove unwed mothers to baby farms and illicit lying-in homes.[118]

Through the policing of working-class mothering, a particular ideal of motherhood was made normative at the expense of poor, single women. By locating the threat to children in individual unnatural women, criminalizing individual women whose children died, and circulating spurious tales about the entire class of women whose children faced the greatest risk, the focus on murderous mothers individualized a social crime and obscured the social epidemiology of infant mortality. Meanwhile the elaboration of the dangerous, possibly deadly mother of the poor contributed to the vilification of women in an era when women were suspect but motherhood was sacrosanct.[119]

Conclusion

IN THE 1890S Caroline Pemberton declared James, the central character of her novel *Your Little Brother James*, to be a member of the American family and challenged her readers to take responsibility for his welfare. Over one hundred years later, it would be difficult to convince many readers of either their "familial" relationship to the poor or their responsibility for the well-being of those in poverty. Rather than accepting public accountability for the welfare of all citizens, the Personal Responsibility and Work Opportunity Reconciliation Act of 1996 (PRA) that heralded welfare's demise implies that poor people are responsible for their own troubles and for any efforts to overcome them. In the United States, the late twentieth and early twenty-first centuries have witnessed what one scholar has called a "nostalgia for stigmatization," accompanied by a renewed emphasis on the distinction between the deserving and undeserving poor and an insistence that the eradication of poverty and its attendant problems can only be accomplished not by addressing the structural inequality of the U.S. economy but by the modification of the personal behavior of the poor.[1] The demonizing of poor women—coded as single black mothers in the public discourse despite the preponderance of white women and children receiving public aid—and the criticism of their maternal abilities, has been coupled with an assault on the material assistance that contributed to their well-being and that of their children. In the words of legal scholar Dorothy Roberts, "the chief behavior to be reformed by the new policies is poor women's mothering."[2] To this end legislative reforms have included family caps to curtail childbirth among women already receiving aid, regulations that coerce women into disclosing the paternity of their children's fathers in order to receive assistance, and work requirements that force mothers to leave home for employment at low-paying jobs that do not cover the cost of childcare for their own children. The public debate over welfare reform and its consequences and the determination to push poor mothers of even very young children into the work force has revealed the vastly different value attributed to the mothering and domestic labor performed by women of different classes and races, highlighting the presumed inadequacy of poor women's mothering and their dependence on the state, rather than their children's dependence upon their care. Similarly, the belief that poor single mothers are harmful to their children became public currency again in the mid-1990s, as evidenced by then Republican Speaker of the House Newt Gingrich's memorable argument that government funds directed at children born to mothers on welfare would be better allocated if diverted to programs that would place them in either orphanages or adoptive families.[3]

My engagement with the late nineteenth-century debate over the laboring family in part grew out of my attempt to understand American culture and social policy at the end of the twentieth century and my fascination with the powerful way popular cultural meanings shape people's experience of themselves, their society, and social policies concerning families, reproduction, and sexuality. The contemporary familiarity of nineteenth-century representations of tramps, unfit mothers, and neglected children—today's racialized perception of an urban underclass of unemployed men, absent fathers and deadbeat dads, single mothers, welfare queens, and crack babies—is striking. Indeed the debate over welfare reform in the 1990s exemplifies the power of cultural representations and their meanings to frame public perceptions of complex social issues. Ultimately, it was the representations of the poor and the corresponding assertion that the origin of social problems are located within individuals that made it possible for otherwise decent Americans to believe patently false information about who the recipients of Aid to Families with Dependent Children were and what kind of lives they led, and that justified the punitive policies aimed at their reform. In the late nineteenth century, charged terms like "tramp," "fallen woman," and "waif" and the stories these terms told similarly limited Americans' abilities to formulate compassionate and constructive solutions to the problems the nation faced.

As the crusaders against the poor in the mid-1990s grew more strident, despite frequent media coverage of the issues it became more difficult to hear the voices of those most affected by welfare reform and most knowledgeable about the multiplicity of reasons women and children become recipients of public relief.[4] *Tramps, Unfit Mothers, and Neglected Children* clearly demonstrates the importance of considering diverse outlooks on social welfare issues and listening to poor men, women, and children as they define their own needs. Any discussion of intervention in all its different forms must begin by addressing the frequently conflicting perspectives of all of those most closely affected by it.

Similarly, renewed attention to concerns about state intervention into family life that have vexed child welfare workers for over a century is even more pressing, given the possibility that with welfare's end more children may end up in foster care.[5] In New York City in the fall of 1995, the violent death of Elisa Izquierdo at the hands of her mother brought new publicity to the problems of an overburdened child welfare system. In the months following Elisa's death, as caseworkers and the courts removed more children from households under investigation in order to err on the side of safety, the pendulum of public opinion swung. Concern about the inadequacy of efforts to remove children from dangerous households and demands for more state intervention into families and households gave way to charges that children were being removed from families without proper investigation. Questions about the quality of legal representation for poor parents seeking to regain custody of their children mounted. Intervention necessarily raises complicated and ongoing questions about the frequently conflicting needs, rights, and obligations of children, parents, and the state. The critical issues are not whether or not or how much or how little the state should intervene, but rather who decides what forms "intervention" should take and what particular policies should be enacted.[6] Any intervention must be informed by the diverse needs, experiences, and voices of those most affected by its processes and outcomes.

Historians' heightened awareness of the social and historical contexts that shape daily life mandates that we consider carefully the circumstances in which some parents fail their children.[7] When destitute families sent their children out to peddle, or when E. O., the "unnatural mother" who could not afford childcare, left her eighteen-month-old infant unattended all day while she was at work, even when Clara Johnson and her husband abandoned their infant wrapped in a bundle on the street or when Mary Kee delivered her baby in an outhouse and then left him for dead—these actions must be understood in the context of the larger society, and they caution us to look closely at the wider context in which "crimes against children" are committed today. As reformers and many residents of Philadelphia's poor neighborhoods recognized in their different ways a century ago, commitment to children's well-being requires both individual and collective responsibility. It also requires commitment to the well-being of their parents—especially their mothers, given women's disproportionate responsibility for children. By labeling some citizens—or even entire groups of people—as deadbeat dads and unfit mothers, we fail to address the social problems of substandard and unsafe housing, failing schools, inadequate childcare, and persistent racial, gender, and economic inequality, and thereby deflect attention from the social crimes that harm not only children but ultimately the entire society.

An overview of the range of social problems debated during the "family crisis" of the late nineteenth century demonstrates that contemporary debates that ponder the risks of overly intrusive intervention versus the failure to intervene, or raise questions about cross-cultural perspectives on childrearing and child welfare, or ask what a family is or what makes a woman a mother, all have rich historical antecedents that can illuminate and enrich our current understandings of American family life and social welfare. Perhaps by listening to the tales told long ago by late nineteenth-century Philadelphians on city streets and in the offices of social welfare reformers we can begin to devise a more nuanced and creative approach to solving the problems of families today.

Abbreviations and Archival Sources

The following list includes the major files cited from the Urban Archives, Temple University, Philadelphia. Parentheses indicate source abbreviations in the Notes.

Pennsylvania Society to Protect Children from Cruelty

Annual Reports, 1877–1930 (SPCC *Nth Annual Report*, 188x (188y))
Case Records, 1877–1901 (SPCC CR, 188x)
Board Minutes (SPCC Board Minutes)

Haven for Unwed Mothers and Infants (pseudonym)

Annual Reports, 1882–1912 (broken series) (Haven, *Nth Annual Report*, 188x)
Diary, 1883–1887 (Haven Diary, 188x)
Correspondence, 1881–1882
Minute Book, 1889–1903 (Haven Board Minutes, 188x)
House Records and Register, 1881–1890 (Haven House Records, 188x)

Notes

Introduction

1. Caroline Hollingsworth Pemberton, *Your Little Brother James* (Philadelphia: George W. Jacobs and Co., 1898), 16, 18, 41, 44. Within several years of the novel's publication, Pemberton joined the Socialist Party of Philadelphia. Her later novel, *The Charity Girl*, published in serial installments in the *International Socialist Review* from March 1901 through February 1902, served as an indictment of the scientific charity and organized child welfare work to which she had devoted herself for thirteen years.

2. For background on Pemberton, see Caroline Pemberton, "How I Became a Socialist," *The Comrade* 1, 9 (June 1902): 202; Philip Foner, "Caroline Hollingsworth Pemberton: Philadelphia Socialist Champion of Black Equality," *Pennsylvania History* 43, 3 (1976): 239–46.

3. George E. McNeill, ed., *The Labor Movement: The Problem of Today* (Boston: M.W. Hazen, 1887), 455–56.

4. For a critique of the social control model, see Walter Trattner, ed., *Social Welfare or Social Control?* (Knoxville: University of Tennessee Press, 1983); Michael B. Katz, *Poverty and Policy in American History* (New York: Academic Press, 1983), 183–210; John Mayer, "Notes Toward a Working Definition of Social Control in Historical Analysis," in *Social Control and the State*, ed. Stanley Cohen and Andrew Scull (Oxford: Blackwell, 1983), 17–38; Barbara M. Brenzel, *Daughters of the State: A Social Portrait of the First Reform School for Girls in North America* (Cambridge, Mass.: MIT Press, 1983); Linda Gordon, "Family Violence, Feminism, and Social Control," *Feminist Studies* 12, 3 (Fall 1986): 453–78; Peggy Pascoe, *Relations of Rescue: The Search for Female Moral Authority in the American West, 1874–1939* (New York: Oxford University Press, 1990), xix–xxi; Elizabeth Pleck, *Domestic Tyranny: The Making of American Social Policy Against Family Violence from Colonial Times to the Present* (New York, Oxford University Press, 1987), 74; David Rothman, "The State as Parent: Social Policy in the Progressive Era," in *Doing Good: The Limits of Benevolence*, ed. Willard Gaylin et al. (New York: Pantheon Books, 1981), 69–96; Linda Gordon, *Heroes of Their Own Lives: The Politics and History of Family Violence* (New York: Viking, 1988), 6. As Brenzel, Pleck, and Gordon have argued, along with Christine Stansell, *City of Women: Sex and Class in New York, 1789–1860* (New York: Knopf, 1986), Mary E. Odem, *Delinquent Daughters: Protecting and Policing Adolescent Female Sexuality in the United States, 1885–1920* (Chapel Hill: University of North Carolina Press, 1995), and Eric C. Schneider, *In the Web of Class: Delinquents and Reformers in Boston, 1810s–1930s* (New York: New York University Press, 1992), working-class family members themselves frequently sought out reform intervention. Gordon's work on the Massachusetts SPCC offers an explicit challenge to the social control model while still self-consciously retaining much of its framework in order to formulate a feminist model of

social control. Although Gordon emphasizes that the relationship between reformers and their clientele was a dynamic interaction rather than a one-sided imposition of middle-class morality and notes that clients had their own ideas about good family life, her work does not situate working-class people in their own ideological context. See the exchange between Linda Gordon and Joan W. Scott in *Signs* 15, 4 (Summer 1990), 848–60, 851, 853; Maureen A. Mahoney and Barbara Yngvesson, "The Construction of Subjectivity and the Paradox of Resistance: Reintegrating Feminist Anthropology and Psychology," *Signs* 18, 1 (Autumn 1992): 44–71, 63, 69, 70; Gordon, "Family Violence, Feminism, and Social Control," in *Gender and American History Since 1890*, ed. Barbara Melosh (New York: Routledge, 1993), 282–308, 295, 288, 300, 302. Also see Barbara Melosh, "Introduction," in *Gender and American History*, ed. Melosh, 11, 282. For discussions of how categories construct agency by attributing it, see Joan W. Scott, review of Linda Gordon, *Heroes of Their Own Lives*, *Signs* 15, 4 (Summer 1990), 851; Parveen Adams and Jeff Minson, "The 'Subject' of Feminism," *m/f* 2 (1978): 43–61. For exchanges among feminist scholars about the value of the application of poststructuralist methodologies to historical scholarship, see Sonya O. Rose, with comments by Kathleen Canning, Anna Clark, Mariana Valverde, and Marcia R. Sawyer, "Women's History/Gender History: Is Feminist History Losing Its Critical Edge," *Journal of Women's History* 5, 1 (Spring 1993): 89–128; Judith R. Walkowitz, Jehlen, et al., "Patrolling the Borders," *Radical History Review* 43 (Winter 1989); Judith Newton, "History as Usual? Feminism and the 'New Historicism,'" in *The New Historicisim*, ed. H. Aram Veeser (New York: Routledge, 1989).

5. At the request of the social service agency that currently owns the records of the institution I refer to as the Haven for Unwed Mothers and Infants, I have given a fictive name to this organization and to those who applied to the institution for aid, while preserving historical accuracy in all other details and assigning names that preserve individuals' gender and ethnic identities. The Haven was an agency, now defunct, affiliated with a Protestant church in Philadelphia. The name of the agency has been disguised to protect the identities of its clients. The records themselves are the property of a private Philadelphia social work agency affiliated with the Protestant church and are housed at the Temple University Urban Archives.

6. I read every Pennsylvania SPCC case record for the years 1877, 1878, 1879, 1880, 1887, 1893, 1896, and 1901, which amounts to roughly ten thousand cases, and read cases selectively in the records in 1881–86, 1888–92, 1894–95, and 1897–1900. In addition I also read through SPCC Annual Reports from 1877 through 1930 and Board Minutes from 1876 through 1926. My strategy was to read closely rather than to quantify. For quantitative analyses of SPCC case records, see Gordon, *Heroes*, and Pleck, *Domestic Tyranny*. In late November 1876 Mrs. Henry Jackson Turner organized a meeting held at the Hicksite Friends Meeting House to found a Pennsylvania Society to Protect Children from Cruelty to aid Philadelphia's "suffering children," similar to the organization that had been established in New York City in 1874 by another Quaker reformer, Elbridge Gerry. Although the SPCC publicized tales of "anger, cruelty, and oppression" within Philadelphia's families and even exhibited "instruments of torture" confiscated from abusive parents and guardians, the rescue of children from physical abuse comprised only a small part of its child welfare work, its chief aim being to reform the family life of the laboring poor and aid those children of the

"unworthy poor" who would otherwise be neglected by charity societies because of their parents' alcohol abuse and lack of industry. Tracing the problems of child labor, begging, scavenging, prostitution, drunkenness, and child neglect to their perceived source in impoverished families, SPCC reformers turned to the state to embody in law their own vision of proper family relations at home and in the streets. SPCC reform efforts encompassed legislative activities, investigations into cases of reported abuse, and when warnings proved insufficient, the arrest and separation of family members. Although a privately chartered corporation, the SPCC first lobbied to pass legislation and then worked closely together with the Philadelphia police to enforce state laws. A special police officer served as a liaison to the SPCC, directing its attention to particular cases where intervention might be useful. SPCC agents requested and were issued warrants by the Philadelphia police and—once given permission from the city's magistrates and/or help from the police—they had the power to arrest lawbreakers. If they deemed it necessary, the SPCC arrested and prosecuted abusive parents in order to remove children at least temporarily from their custody. They then took an active role placing the children in the homes of relatives and neighbors, or if necessary, placed the children in one of the city's many institutions devoted to the care of orphaned or errant children. The founders of the Pennsylvania SPCC were ecumenical in intent and were careful to include a Catholic and a Jewish member on their board. Throughout the late nineteenth century SPCC members were primarily upper- and upper-middle-class Protestants—chiefly Quaker and Episcopalian—men and women with a sense of social obligation, who created an organization in which men and women with shared social and class interests could work together in reform activities, although men and women reformers had distinct, clearly defined gender-specific roles. The board of twenty-eight managers was evenly divided between women and men. Male officers of the organization included a secretary, a treasurer, a president, vice-presidents, legal counselors, and medical and surgical advisors. Although the women's work was integral to the daily work of the organization, the men's work was more visible to the public. Within the organization, men offered legal and medical advice and handled financial matters as well as the public presentation of material, such as writing the annual reports and speaking at anniversary fundraisers. Women were in charge of overseeing child placements and were responsible for much of the day to day fundraising as well as special fundraising events. In this way some men reformers donated their professional skills, while women relied on the skills they had honed through voluntarist work in other organizations or had developed as mothers and managers of households. In the first decades of the SPCC's existence, most board members lived as neighbors in two residential clusters in the heart of the city: on Walnut, Spruce, and Pine Streets and De Lancey Place in the wealthy Rittenhouse Square area, and in the Quaker neighborhood centered around Arch Street. In rejecting sectarian moral reform, the SPCC implicitly aligned itself with a new breed of postbellum reformers across the nation who were creating the new discipline and practice of social science. As part of a national reform network, SPCC members attended national conferences of charities and corrections and were in contact with childsaving agencies in other states and with other charitable and reform organizations and institutions in Philadelphia.

7. Stephanie Coontz, *The Way We Never Were: American Families and the Nostalgia*

Trap (New York: Basic Books, 1992), is an excellent exception that explores these issues in the nineteenth- and twentieth-century United States. The burgeoning literature on gender and the state in the late nineteenth and early twentieth centuries also explores the historical antecedents of contemporary welfare and family policy, although scholars have chiefly overlooked the connections between social policy and labor protest. They have addressed maternalism, women's contribution to the creation of the welfare state, the gendered nature of the welfare state, and the ways that social redistribution has different consequences depending on one's class, race, gender, and family status. For a sampling of this vast and growing field see Theda Skocpol, *Protecting Soldiers and Mothers: The Political Origins of Social Policy in the United States* (Cambridge: Cambridge University Press, 1992); Molly Ladd-Taylor, *Mother-Work: Women, Child Welfare, and the State, 1890–1930* (Urbana: University of Illinois Press, 1994); Linda Gordon, *Pitied But Not Entitled: Single Mothers and the History of Welfare, 1890–1935* (New York: Free Press, 1994); Seth Koven and Sonya Michel, eds., *Mothers of a New World: Maternalist Politics and the Origins of Welfare States* (New York: Routledge, 1993); Mimi Abramovitz, *Regulating the Lives of Women: Social Welfare Policy from Colonial Times to the Present* (Boston: South End Press, 1988); Linda Gordon, ed., *Women, the State, and Welfare* (Madison: University of Wisconsin Press, 1990); Gwendolyn Mink, ed., *Whose Welfare?* (Ithaca, N.Y.: Cornell University Press, 1999) and *The Wages of Motherhood: Inequality in the Welfare State 1917–1942* (Ithaca, N.Y.: Cornell University Press, 1995); Robyn Muncy, *Creating a Female Dominion in American Reform, 1890–1935* (New York: Oxford University Press, 1991); Joanne L. Goodwin, *Gender and the Politics of Welfare Reform: Mothers' Pensions in Chicago, 1911–1929* (Chicago: University of Chicago Press, 1997); Barbara Machtinger, "Shaping the Maternalist Welfare State: Mothers' Pensions and the U.S. Children's Bureau, 1912–1939," PhD dissertation, Boston College, 1995.

8. Recent works that have used case records include Regina G. Kunzel, *Fallen Women, Problem Girls: Unmarried Mothers and the Professionalization of Social Work, 1890–1945* (New Haven, Conn.: Yale University Press, 1993); Marion Morton, *And Sin No More: Social Policy and Unwed Mothers in Cleveland, 1855–1990* (Columbus: Ohio State University Press, 1993); Julie Berebitsky, *Like Our Very Own: Adoption and the Changing Culture of Motherhood, 1851–1950* (Lawrence: University Press of Kansas, 2000); Emily K. Abel, "Valuing Care: Turn-of-the-Century Conflicts Between Charity Workers and Women Clients," *Journal of Women's History* 10, 3 (Autumn 1998): 32–52; Odem, *Delinquent Daughters*; Gordon, *Heroes*; Pleck, *Domestic Tyranny*; Beverly Stadum, *Poor Women and Their Families: Hard-Working Charity Cases* (Albany: SUNY Press, 1992). Christine Stansell, *City of Women: Sex and Class in New York, 1789–1860* (New York: Knopf, 1986) also uses material from the Children's Aid Society of New York.

9. See Pleck, *Domestic Tyranny*, 70–89; Nancy Cott, *Public Vows: A History of Marriage and the Nation* (Cambridge, Mass.: Harvard University Press, 2000), 130; Eric Foner, *Reconstruction: America's Unfinished Revolution, 1863–1877* (New York: Harper and Row, 1988), on increased state intervention in the post-Civil War period.

10. For works on laboring families, reform, and the state see Gordon, *Heroes*, and *Pitied But Not Entitled*; Brenzel, *Daughters of the State*; Katz, *Poverty and Policy*; Odem, *Delinquent Daughters*; Stadum, *Poor Women*; Schneider, *In the Web of Class*; Anna R.

Igra, "Likely to Become a Public Charge: Deserted Women and the Family Law of the Poor in New York City, 1910–1936," *Journal of Women's History* (Winter 2000): 59–81. Ardis Cameron refers to the "gendered landscape of working-class life" in her excellent study of working-class neighborhoods and labor protest, *Radicals of the Worst Sort: Laboring Women in Lawrence, Massachusetts, 1860–1912* (Urbana: University of Illinois Press, 1993), 9. See Joan W. Scott, *Gender and the Politics of History* (New York: Columbia University Press, 1988); Alice Kessler-Harris, *A Woman's Wage: Historical Meanings and Social Consequences* (Lexington: University of Kentucky Press, 1990); Ava Baron, ed., *Work Engendered: Toward a New History of American Labor* (Ithaca, N.Y.: Cornell University Press, 1991); Mary H. Blewett, *Men, Women, and Work: Class, Gender, and Protest in the New England Shoe Industry, 1780–1910* (Urbana: University of Illinois Press, 1988 and *Constant Turmoil: The Politics of Industrial Life in Nineteenth-Century New England* (Amherst: University of Massachusetts Press, 2000); Eileen Boris, *Home to Work: Motherhood and the Politics of Industrial Homework in the United States* (New York: Cambridge University Press, 1994); Joanne Meyerowitz, "Sexual Geography and Gender Economy: The Furnished Room Districts of Chicago, 1890–1930," in *Gender and American History*, ed. Melosh, 43–71; Kathy Lee Peiss, *Cheap Amusements: Gender Relations and the Use of Leisure Time in New York City, 1820 to 1920* (Philadelphia: Temple University Press, 1986); Stansell, *City of Women*; Judith R. Walkowitz, *Prostitution and Victorian Society* (New York: Cambridge University Press, 1980) and *City of Dreadful Delight: Narratives of Sexual Danger in Late Victorian London* (Chicago: University of Chicago Press, 1992); Ellen Ross, *Love and Toil: Motherhood in Outcast London, 1870–1918* (New York: Oxford University Press, 1993). Molly Ladd-Taylor, *Mother-Work: Women, Child Welfare, and the State, 1890–1930* (Urbana: University of Illinois Press, 1994); Ellen Ross, "New Thoughts on 'the Oldest Vocation': Mothers and Motherhood in Recent Feminist Scholarship," *Signs* 20, 2 (Winter 1995): 395–413; Marianne Hirsch, "Feminism at the Maternal Divide," in *Representations of Motherhood*, ed. Donna Bassin, Margaret Honey, and Meryle Mahrer Kaplan (New Haven, Conn.: Yale University Press, 1994), 352–68, 363, call for an examination of motherhood in all its specific contexts and practices or to use Hirsch's term, "local, multi-vocal" analyses of motherhood. For a sampling of the voluminous literature on motherhood see Julia E. Hanigsberg and Sara Ruddick, eds., *Mother Troubles: Rethinking Contemporary Maternal Dilemmas* (New York: Beacon Press, 1999); Dorothy Roberts, *Killing the Black Body: Race, Reproduction, and the Meaning of Liberty* (New York: Pantheon Books, 1997); Evelyn Nakano Glenn, Grace Chang, and Linda Rennie Forcey, eds., *Mothering: Ideology, Experience, and Agency* (New York: Routledge, 1994); Ross, *Love and Toil*; Martha A. Fineman and Isabel Karpin, eds., *Mothers in Law: Feminist Theory and the Legal Regulation of Motherhood* (New York: Columbia University Press, 1995); Alexis Jetter, Annelise Orleck, and Diana Taylor, eds., *The Politics of Motherhood: Activist Voices from Left to Right* (Hanover, N.H.: University Press of New England, 1997); Cynthia Garcia Coll, Janet L. Surrey, and Kathy Weingarten, eds. *Mothering Against the Odds: Diverse Voices of Contemporary Mothers* (New York: Guilford Press, 1998); Maureen Reddy, Martha Roth, and Amy Sheldon, eds., *Mother Journeys: Feminists Write About Mothering* (Minneapolis: Spinsters Ink, 1994); B. O. Daly and M. T. Reddy, *Narrating Mothers: Theorizing Maternal Subjectivities* (Knoxville: University of Tennessee Press, 1991) ; Martha

Albertson Fineman, *The Neutered Mother, the Sexual Family, and Other Twentieth Century Tragedies* (New York: Routledge, 1995); E. Ann Kaplan, *Motherhood and Representation: The Mother in Popular Culture and Melodrama* (New York: Routledge, 1992); Molly Ladd-Taylor and Lauri Umansky, eds., *"Bad" Mothers: The Politics of Blame in Twentieth-Century America* (New York: New York University Press, 1997); Nancy Scheper-Hughes, *Death Without Weeping: The Violence of Everyday Life in Brazil* (Berkeley: University of California Press, 1992); Rickie Solinger, *Wake Up, Little Susie: Single Pregnancy and Race Before Roe v. Wade* (New York: Routledge, 1992); Rima D. Apple and Janet Golden, eds., *Mothers and Motherhood: Readings in American History* (Columbus: Ohio State University Press, 1997); Boris, *Home to Work.*

11. See Cameron, *Radicals of the Worst Sort*, 2–5; Ava Baron, "On Looking at Men: Masculinity and the Making of a Gendered Working-Class History," in *Feminists Revision History*, ed. Ann-Louise Shapiro (New Brunswick, N.J.: Rutgers University Press, 1994), 146–71, 148, on tendencies in earlier labor history to see male workers as representative of the working class and to focus on the workplace rather than on neighborhood and family.

12. See Jennifer Terry, "Theorizing Deviant Historiography," in *Feminists Revision History*, ed. Shapiro, 276–303, 278–82; Joan W. Scott, "The Evidence of Experience, " *Critical Inquiry* 17 (Summer 1991): 773–97; Richard W. Fox, "Intimacy on Trial: Cultural Meanings of the Beecher-Tilton Affair," in *The Power of Culture: Critical Essays in American History*, ed. Richard Wightman Fox and T. J. Jackson Lears (Chicago: University of Chicago Press, 1993), 103–32; Renato Rosaldo, "From the Door of His Tent: The Fieldworker and the Inquisitor," in *Writing Culture: The Poetics and Politics of Ethnography*, ed. James Clifford and George E. Marcus (Berkeley: University of California Press, 1986), 77–97; Natalie Zemon Davis, *Fiction in the Archives: Pardon Tales and Their Tellers in Sixteenth-Century France* (Stanford, Calif.: Stanford University Press, 1987), 20, 25 on shared authorship; Scott, review of Gordon, *Heroes*, on case records as representations.

13. Fran Olsen, "The Politics of Family Law," in *Family Matters: Readings on Family Lives and the Law*, ed. Martha Minow (New York: New Press, 1993), 336–43, 336; Hanigsberg and Ruddick, eds., *Mother Troubles*, xvi.

Chapter 1. Tramps, Fallen Women, and Neglected Children

1. James Sylvis, ed., *The Life, Speeches, Labors, and Essays of William H. Sylvis* (Philadelphia: Claxton, Remsen, and Haffelfinger, 1872; New York: A.M. Kelley, 1968), 208–9.

2. Charles Loring Brace, *The Dangerous Classes of New York and Twenty Years' Work Among Them* (New York: Wynkoop and Hallenbeck, 1872; Montclair, N.J.: P. Smith, 1967), ii.

3. Eric Foner, *Reconstruction: America's Unfinished Revolution, 1863–1877* (New York: Harper and Row, 1988), 468–69.

4. John Swinton, *A Momentous Question: The Respective Attitudes of Labor and Capital* (Philadelphia: A.R. Keller, 1895), 288.

5. For exceptions see Ava Baron, ed., *Work Engendered: Toward a New History of*

American Labor (Ithaca, N.Y.: Cornell University Press, 1991); Eileen Boris, *Home to Work: Motherhood and the Politics of Industrial Homework in the United States* (New York: Cambridge University Press, 1994); Alice Kessler-Harris, *A Woman's Wage: Historical Meanings and Social Consequences* (Lexington: University of Kentucky Press, 1990); and Michael B. Katz, *Poverty and Policy in American History* (New York: Academic Press, 1983) and *In the Shadow of the Poorhouse: A Social History of Welfare in America* (New York: Basic Books, 1986). See Boris, 6–8, for discussion of the need for labor and policy historians to reconceptualize work and family and Ava Baron, "Introduction to Symposium on Eileen Boris, Home to Work," with additional contributions by Evelynn Nakono Glenn, Sybil Lipshultz, Daniel R. Ernst, Judith G. Coffin, Eileen L. McDonagh, and Eileen Boris, *Labor History* 39 (1998): 407–34, 413.

6. David Montgomery, *Beyond Equality: Labor and the Radical Republicans, 1862–1872* (New York: Knopf, 1967), 28–30, 91; Sean Wilentz, "Against Exceptionalism," *International Labor and Working Class History* 26 (Fall 1984): 13; Eric Foner, "Workers and Slavery," in *Working for Democracy: American Workers from the Revolution to the Present*, ed. Paul Buhle and Alan Dawley (Urbana: University of Illinois Press, 1985), 27; Alexander Keyssar, *Out of Work: The First Century of Unemployment in Massachusetts* (New York: Cambridge University Press, 1986), 37.

7. George McNeill, *The Labor Movement: The Problem of Today* (Boston, 1887; New York: A.M. Kelley, 1971), 459. Also see the testimony of Isaac Sturgeon in the *Report of the Committee of the Senate upon the Relations between Labor and Capital, and Testimony Taken by the Committee*, United States Congress, Senate Committee on Education and Labor, 4 vols. (Washington, D.C.: GPO, 1885), 2: 395.

8. Thomas Bender, *Toward an Urban Vision: Ideas and Institutions in Nineteenth-Century America* (Baltimore: Johns Hopkins University Press, 1975), 109; John L. Thomas, *Alternative America: Henry George, Edward Bellamy, Henry Demarest Lloyd, and the Adversary Tradition* (Cambridge, Mass.: Belknap Press of Harvard University Press, 1984; Paul Avrich, *The Haymarket Tragedy* (Princeton, N.J.: Princeton University Press, 1984; Sidney Harring, *Policing a Class Society: The Experience of American Cities, 1865–1915* (New Brunswick, N.J.: Rutgers University Press, 1983); Katz, *In the Shadow of the Poorhouse*.

9. See Elizabeth Pleck, *Domestic Tyranny: The Making of American Social Policy Against Family Violence from Colonial Times to the Present* (New York: Oxford University Press, 1987), chapter 4, "Protecting the Innocents."

10. Joshua Freeman, Bruce Levine, et al., eds., *Who Built America: Working People and the Nation's Economy, Politics, Culture, and Society*, vol. 2, *From the Gilded Age to the Present* (New York: Pantheon Books, 1992), 22.

11. Walter Licht, *Getting Work, Philadelphia, 1840–1950* (Cambridge, Mass.: Harvard University Press,1992; Philadelphia: University of Pennsylvania Press, 2000), 16; Susan Levine, *Labor's True Woman: Carpet Weavers, Industrialization, and Labor Reform in the Gilded Age* (Philadelphia: Temple University Press, 1984), 17.

12. Katz, *Poverty and Policy*, 157; Keyssar, *Out of Work*, 132; Michael Denning, "Cheap Stories: Notes on Popular Fiction and Working-Class Culture in Nineteenth-Century America," *History Workshop* 22 (Fall 1986): 1–17, 9–10.

13. Michael Davis, "Forced to Tramp: The Perspective of the Labor Press, 1870–1900," in *Walking to Work: Tramps in America, 1790–1935*, ed. Eric Monkkonen

(Lincoln: University of Nebraska Press, 1984), 141–170, 161; Katz, *Poverty and Policy*, 157–58.

14. Katz, *Poverty and Policy*, 91–93.

15. Jeanne Boydston, *Home and Work: Housework, Wages, and the Ideology of Labor in the Early Republic* (New York: Oxford University Press, 1990), 29, 55.

16. Mary E. Richmond, "Married Vagabonds" (1895) and "Charity and Homemaking" (1897), in *The Long View: Papers and Addresses* (New York: Russell Sage Foundation, 1930), 71, 79.

17. Ellen Ross, " 'Not the Sort That Would Sit on the Doorstep': Respectability in Pre-World War I London Neighborhoods," *International Labor and Working Class History* 27 (Spring 1985): 39–59, 52–53; Ross, "Response to Harold Benenson's 'Victorian Sexual Ideology,'" *International Labor and Working Class History* 25 (Spring 1984): 32. See Beverly Stadum, *Poor Women and Their Families: Hard-Working Charity Cases* (Albany: State University of New York Press, 1992), for an excellent analysis of the work required of charity recipients.

18. Richmond, "Charity and Homemaking," 85.

19. Henry Martyn Boies, *Prisoners and Paupers: A Study of the Abnormal Increase of Criminals and the Public Burden of Pauperism in the United States* (1893; Freeport, N.Y.: Books for Libraries Press, 1972), 205, 209.

20. Frank Watson, *The Charity Organization Movement in the United States: A Study in American Philanthropy* (New York: Macmillan, 1922), 191. See the Annual Reports of the Philadelphia Society for Organizing Charitable Relief and Repressing Mendicancy, 1879–1895, Urban Archives, Temple University, Philadelphia.

21. See SPCC CR, 1896, #15856.

22. Philadelphia Society for Organizing Charity and Repressing Mendicancy, "Concerning Tramps and Beggars" (Philadelphia, 1901; Urban Archives, Temple University, Philadelphia, 18.

23. Keyssar, *Out of Work*, 256; Alice Hamilton, in *Alice Hamilton: A Life in Letters*, ed. Barbara Sicherman (Cambridge, Mass.: Harvard University Press, 1984), 80.

24. Amos Griswold Warner, *American Charities: A Study in Philanthropy and Economics* (New York: Thomas Crowell and Co., 1894), 68, 73; Mary P. Ryan, *Cradle of the Middle Class: The Family in Oneida County, New York, 1790–1865* (New York: Cambridge University Press, 1981), 157, 182.

25. William Rhinelander Stewart, ed., *The Philanthropic Work of Josephine Shaw Lowell* (New York: Macmillan, 1911), 357–59.

26. Howard Rock, *Artisans of the New Republic* (New York: New York University Press, 1979), 139, 309, 311 and Sean Wilentz, *Chants Democratic: New York City and the Rise of the American Working Class, 1788–1850* (New York: Oxford University Press, 1984). For a discussion of manliness and the dignity of labor, see David Montgomery, *Workers' Control in America: Studies in the History of Work, Technology, and Labor Struggles* (New York: Cambridge University Press, 1979), 13; *Trades* (Philadelphia), 1879.

27. Keyssar, *Out of Work*, 37.

28. Ava Baron, "On Looking at Men: Masculinity and the Making of a Gendered Working-Class History," in *Feminists Revision History*, ed. Ann-Louise Shapiro (New

Brunswick, N.J.: Rutgers University Press, 1994), 162; Ardis Cameron, *Radicals of the Worst Sort: Laboring Women in Lawrence, Massachusetts, 1860–1912* (Urbana: University of Illinois Press, 1993), 65.

29. See Kessler-Harris, *A Woman's Wage*, chap. 1, on the family wage.

30. Sylvis, *Life*, 361.

31. Sylvis, *Life*, 267; F. Waters, "A Plea for the Toilers," *Tocsin*, November 3, 1886.

32. F. Waters, "Appropriate Philanthropy," *Tocsin*, August 14, 1886.

33. For a discussion of tramping, see Paul Ringenbach, *Tramps and Reformers 1873–1916: The Discovery of Unemployment in New York* (Westport, Conn.: Greenwood Press, 1973); Keyssar, *Out of Work*; Monkkonen, ed., *Walking to Work*. Actual treatment of tramps varied in different locations. Even within the same city, the enforcement of vagrancy laws could coexist with the provision of public or charitable shelter for tramps or the temporarily homeless. See Keyssar, *Out of Work*, 137, for discussion of the complexity of tramp legislation; Monkkonen, ed., *Walking to Work*; and Monkkonen, *Police in Urban America, 1860–1920* (New York: Cambridge University Press, 1981), chap. 3, on the role of police station houses in providing shelter for vagrants.

34. Jacqueline Jones, *The Dispossessed: America's Underclasses from the Civil War to the Present* (New York: Basic Books, 1992), 24–27, on the black codes of the late 1860s and 1870s.

35. "The Tramp Law," *Trades*, August 23, 1879, 1.

36. *Trades*, April 3, 1879.

37. "On Tramps," *Trades*, April 3, 1879.

38. "Where Are the Unemployed?" *Trades*, March 6, 1880.

39. "The Tramp Law," *Trades*, August 23, 1879, 1.

40. *Public Ledger*, January 2, 1877; Julia Rauch, "Unfriendly Visitors: The Emergence of Scientific Philanthropy in Philadelphia" (Ph.D. dissertation, Bryn Mawr College, 1974), 104, 295.

41. Edward Aveling and Eleanor Marx Aveling, *The Working-Class Movement in America* (London: Sonnenschein, 1891; Amherst, N.Y.: Humanity Books, 2000), 84, 98, 100–115.

42. Kirchner, as cited in "Advocating Shorter Hours," *Tocsin*, February 28, 1885.

43. Keyssar, *Out of Work*, 177, 204, 192.

44. See Montgomery, *Beyond Equality*, 238; Roy Rosenzweig, *Eight Hours for What We Will: Workers and Leisure in an Industrial City, 1870–1920* (New York: Cambridge University Press, 1983); Philip Foner, ed., *We the Other People: Alternative Declarations of Independence by Labor Groups, Farmers, Woman's Rights Advocates, Socialists, and Blacks, 1829-1975* (Urbana: University of Illinois Press, 1976), 22.

45. Barbara Meil Hobson, *Uneasy Virtue: The Politics of Prostitution and the American Reform Tradition* (New York: Basic Books, 1987), 49, 51, 54; Carroll Smith-Rosenberg, "Beauty, the Beast, and the Militant Woman," *American Quarterly* 23 (1971): 562–84; Barbara Berg, *The Remembered Gate: Origins of American Feminism* (New York: Oxford University Press, 1978), 179; Ellen Du Bois and Linda Gordon, "Seeking Ecstasy on the Battlefield: Danger and Pleasure in Nineteenth-Century Feminist Sexual Thought,"in *Pleasure and Danger: Exploring Female Sexuality*, ed. Carole S. Vance

(Boston: Routledge and Kegan Paul, 1984), 33; Christine Stansell, *City of Women: Sex and Class in New York, 1789–1860* (New York: Knopf, 1986); Patricia Cline Cohen, *The Murder of Helen Jewett: The Life and Death of a Prostitute in Nineteenth-Century New York* (New York: Knopf, 1998); Timothy J. Gilfoyle, *City of Eros: New York City, Prostitution, and the Commercialization of Sex, 1790–1920* (New York: W.W. Norton), 1992.

46. Hobson, *Uneasy*, 64, 75; Smith-Rosenberg, "Beauty."

47. Joanne Meyerowitz, *Women Adrift: Independent Wage Earners in Chicago, 1880–1930* (Chicago: University of Chicago Press, 1988); John D'Emilio and Estelle B. Freedman, *Intimate Matters: A History of Sexuality in America* (New York: Harper and Row, 1988), 151.

48. Ryan, *Cradle*, 157, 182; Gail Bederman, "'Civilization,' the Decline of Middle-Class Manliness, and Ida B. Wells' Anti-Lynching Campaign (1892–94)," *Radical History Review* 52 (Winter 1992): 5–32.

49. Mary Poovey, *Uneven Developments: The Ideological Work of Gender in Mid-Victorian England* (Chicago: University of Chicago Press, 1988).

50. Stansell, *City of Women*; Hazel Carby, *Reconstructing Womanhood: The Emergence of the Afro-American Woman Novelist* (New York: Oxford University Press, 1987).

51. David Roediger, *Wages of Whiteness: Race and the Making of the American Working Class* (New York: Verso, 1991), 133; David Montgomery, *The Fall of the House of Labor: The Workplace, the State, and American Labor Activism, 1865-1925* (New York: Cambridge University Press, 1987), 25.

52. Hobson, *Uneasy*, 113; Cynthia Eagle Russett, *Sexual Science: The Victorian Construction of Womanhood* (Cambridge, Mass.: Harvard University Press, 1989), 131.

53. Mari Jo Buhle, "Needlewomen and the Vicissitudes of Modern Life: A Study of Middle-Class Construction in the Antebellum Northeast," in *Visible Women: New Essays on American Activism*, ed. Nancy A. Hewitt and Suzanne Lebsock (Urbana: University of Illinois Press, 1993), 145–65.

54. See Ellen Ross, "Good and Bad Mothers: Lady Philanthropists and London Housewives Before the First World War," in *Lady Bountiful Revisited: Women, Philanthropy, and Power*, ed. Kathleen D. McCarthy (New Brunswick, N.J.: Rutgers University Press, 1990), 174–98.

55. For an excellent summary of the voluminous literature on women and reform, see Paula Baker, "The Domestication of Politics: Women and American Political Society, 1780–1920," *American Historical Review* 89 (June 1984), and Mari Jo Buhle, *Women and American Socialism, 1870–1920* (Urbana: University of Illinois Press, 1981), 49–104. See Ellen Du Bois, *Feminism and Suffrage: The Emergence of an Independent Women's Movement in America, 1848–1869* (Ithaca, N.Y.: Cornell University Press, 1978, and Elisabeth Griffith, *In Her Own Right: The Life of Elizabeth Cady Stanton* (New York: Oxford University Press, 1984), on the mid-century woman's movement.

56. Caroline Dall, *Woman's Right to Labor, or, Low Wages and Hard Work* (Boston: Walker, Wise, and Co., 1860), 58; Cameron, *Radicals*, 25–27.

57. Dall, *Woman's Right to Labor*, 58, 4–6.

58. D'Emilio and Freedman, *Intimate Matters*, 149; see Linda Gordon and Ellen Du Bois, "Seeking Ecstasy on the Battlefield: Danger and Pleasure in Nineteenth-Century Social Thought," in *Pleasure and Danger: Exploring Female Sexuality*, ed. Carole S. Vance (Boston: Routledge and Kegan Paul, 1984), 35, for a discussion of prostitution

and the nineteenth-century woman's rights movement and the use of "legalized prostitution" to discuss marital rape.

59. Helen Campbell, *Prisoners of Poverty* (Boston: Little, Brown, 1887).

60. Campbell, *Prisoners of Poverty*, 19, 23, 20. See Buhle, "Needlewomen and the Vicissitudes of Modern Life"; Ellen Ross, *Love and Toil: Motherhood in Outcast London, 1870–1918* (New York: Oxford University Press, 1993), 76, for a discussion of the music hall comic ballads of late Victorian London, in which wives regularly go through the pockets of their drunken husbands.

61. Campbell, *Prisoners*, 26–27.

62. Campbell, *Prisoners*, 29.

63. A small but significant group of activists in the woman's movement also turned to socialism for a solution to the woman question, and developed an analysis of prostitution that took the factors of class and gender into account. See Buhle, *Women and American Socialism*.

64. Also see Baron, "On Looking at Men," 152.

65. See Baron,150–52 for a similar analysis.

66. Sylvis, *Life*, 220.

67. F. Waters, "Our Working Women," *Tocsin*, September 18, 1886.

68. Caroline Pemberton makes this point in the *Charity Girl*, published in serial installments in *International Socialist Review* from March 1901 through February 1902.

69. Waters, "Our Working Women."

70. Leon Fink, *Workingmen's Democracy: The Knights of Labor and American Politics* (Urbana: University of Illinois Press, 1983), 11, Sylvis, *Life*, 220, Levine, *Labor's True Woman*, 110, 132–33.

71. Levine, *Labor's True Woman*, 132–33.

72. Levine, *Labor's True Woman*, 108.

73. Levine, *Labor's True Woman*, 121.

74. Levine, *Labor's True Woman*, 135, 111.

75. This discussion is indebted to Susan Levine's formulation of "labor feminism" and her analysis of the role of women in the Knights of Labor. See Mary Blewett, *Men, Women, and Work: Class, Gender, and Protest in the New England Shoe Industry, 1780–1910* (Urbana: University of Illinois Press, 1988) for an analysis of women's labor activism in the nineteenth century.

76. See Levine, *Labor's True Woman*, 129–32, for an excellent analysis and the entire "Song of the Carpet Weavers."

77. Levine, *Labor's True Woman*, 129–32. Significantly, the theme of the virtuous working girl and her superiority to "gilded butterflies of fashion" was also elaborated in the working-girl romance novels of Laura Jean Libbey. For an analysis of Libbey's novels, see Meyerowitz, *Women Adrift*, 59–60; Michael Denning, *Mechanic Accents: Dime Novels and Working-Class Culture in America* (New York: Verso, 1987), 188–200.

78. See Montgomery, *Workers' Control*, 13.

79. This contention is amply documented in the SPCC case records as well as in the work of other historians of working-class families. See Meyerowitz, *Women Adrift*, xvii; Kessler-Harris, *Out to Work*, 77, and Cameron, *Radicals*, 37; Kathy Lee Peiss, *Cheap Amusements: Gender Relations and the Use of Leisure Time in New York City, 1820*

to 1920 (Philadelphia: Temple University Press, 1986); Judith E. Smith, *Family Connections: A History of Italian and Jewish Immigrant Lives in Providence, Rhode Island, 1900–1940* (Albany: SUNY Press, 1985).

80. "The American Wage-Worker's Declaration of Independence," July 4, 1886, in *We, the Other People,* ed. Foner, 134–35.

81. Stansell, *City of Women,* 193–216, and Steven Schlossman, " The 'Culture of Poverty' in Antebellum Thought," *Science and Society* (Summer 1974): 150–66; Ellen Ross, "Good and Bad Mothers," 192.

82. See Deborah Gorham, "'The Maiden Tribue of Modern Babylon' Re-examined: Child Prostitution and the Idea of Childhood in Late Victorian England," *Victorian Studies* (Spring 1978): 358–69. See Bernard Wishy, *The Child and the Republic: The Dawn of Modern American Child Nurture* (Philadelphia: University of Pennsylvania Press, 1968); Karin Calvert, *Children in the House: The Material Culture of Early Childhood, 1600–1900* (Boston: Northeastern University Press, 1992), 108–9; Joan D. Hedrick, *Harriet Beecher Stowe: A Life* (New York: Oxford University Press, 1994), 191, 222, 223.

83. See SPCC CR, 1878, 451; Ryan, *Cradle,* chap.2, esp. 99–100; Pleck, *Domestic Tyranny,* 76; Stephen Mintz, *A Prison of Expectations: The Family in Victorian Culture* (New York: New York University Press, 1985); Calvert, *Children in the House,* 122.

84. SPCC, *Twentieth Annual Report,* 1896 (1897), 11.

85. Brace, *Dangerous Classes,* i–ii, 30.

86. Joseph F. Kett, *Rites of Passage: Adolescence in America, 1790 to the Present* (New York: Basic Books, 1977); Michael B. Katz, *The People of Hamilton, Canada West: Family and Class in a Mid-Nineteenth-Century City* (Cambridge, Mass.: Harvard University Press, 1975); Christine Stansell, "Women, Children, and the Uses of the Streets: Class and Gender Conflicts in New York City, 1850–1860," *Feminist Studies* 8 (Summer 1982): 309–36. Also see Stansell, *City of Women,* 204–5, 50, 53; Priscilla Ferguson Clement, *Growing Pains: Children in the Industrial Age, 1850–1890* (New York: Twayne Publishers, 1997), 186–218.

87. SPCC, *First Annual Report,* 1877 (1878), 8.

88. SPCC, *Thirteenth Annual Report,* 1889 (1890), 25; *Fourth Annual Report,* 1880 (1881), 37, #1569; Brace, *Dangerous Classes,* 154, 116–17, 135 for further discussion of street-trading as the path to prostitution.

89. SPCC Board Minutes, March 11, 1889, 429; April 8, 1889, 431; May 14, 1889, 432; Viviana A. Zelizer, *Pricing the Priceless Child: The Changing Social Value of Children* (New York: Basic Books, 1985), 71–72, 115–27; George Behlmer, *Child Abuse and Moral Reform in England, 1870–1908* (Stanford, Calif.: Stanford University Press, 1982), 120–25.

90. SPCC, *Fifteenth Annual Report,* 1891 (1892), 12; *First Annual Report,* 1877 (1888), 8.

91. SPCC, *Ninth Annual Report,* 1885 (1886), 11; *Thirty-Second Annual Report,* 1908 (1909), 13.

92. *Public Ledger,* January 26, 1877.

93. SPCC Board Minutes, vol. 1, March 5, 1883, 260; March 27, 1883, 262.

94. SPCC, *Ninth Annual Report,* 1885 (1886), 11–12.

95. Linda Gordon, *Heroes of Their Own Lives: The Politics and History of Family*

Violence, Boston 1880–1960 (New York: Viking, 1988), 42, makes a similar claim for the Boston SPCC.

96. SPCC, CR, 1880, #1829.

97. Sylvis, *Life*, 209.

98. Kenneth Fones-Wolf, "Trade Union Gospel: Protestantism and Labor in Philadelphia, 1865–1915," Ph.D. dissertation, Temple University, 1985, 164.

99. Montgomery, *Beyond Equality*, 238–49, 239. For a further discussion of transformations in the definition of labor and property, see William Hamilton Sewell, Jr., *Work and Revolution in France: The Language of Labor from the Old Regime to 1848* (New York: Cambridge University Press, 1980), chap. 6, 200–201, 215; Wilentz, "Against Exceptionalism," 10–12; Harring, *Policing a Class Society*, 103.

100. Testimony of Isaac Sturgeon, *Report of the Senate Committee*, 393–94.

101. Sylvis, *Life*, 208–9.

102. Henry George, as cited in *Tocsin*, October 23, 1886; for a discussion of Henry George's complex relation to the labor movement, see Aveling and Aveling, *The Working Class Movement in America*, 236–37; David Scobey, "Boycotting the Politics Factory: Labor Radicalism and the New York City Mayoral Election of 1886," *Radical History Review* 28–30 (1984): 280–325; Thomas, *Alternative America*.

103. F. Waters, "Plea for the Toilers," *Tocsin*, November 3, 1886; "Cruelty to Children," *Tocsin*, February 19, 1887.

104. Waters, "Cruelty to Children."

105. *Tocsin*, September 4, 1886.

106. Richmond noted (*Long View*, 46), that the trade-unionist "refers to us in his labor journals as a lot of canting hypocrites, whose knowledge, motives, and methods are beneath contempt."

Chapter 2. Informing the "Cruelty"

1. *Public Ledger*, January 24–26, 1877.

2. Ibid.

3. Ellen Ross, "'Not the Sort That Would Sit on the Doorstep': Respectability in Pre-World War I London Neighborhoods," *International Labor and Working Class History* 27 (Spring 1985): 39–59; W. E. B. Du Bois, *The Philadelphia Negro: A Social Study* (1899; Philadelphia: University of Pennsylvania Press, 1996), 312–15; Michael Denning, "Cheap Stories," *History Workshop* 22 (Fall 1986): 1–17; Amos Griswold Warner, *American Charities: A Study in Philanthropy and Economics* (New York: Thomas Crowell and Co., 1894), 68.

4. *Public Ledger*, January 24–26, 1877.

5. British historians have most fully explored working-class cultural and social distinctions between "roughness" and "respectability." See Standish Meacham, *A Life Apart: The English Working Class, 1890–1914* (Cambridge, Mass.: Harvard University Press, 1977); Ross, "'Not the Sort That Would Sit on the Doorstep,'" 39–59.

6. Leon Fink, *Workingmen's Democracy: The Knights of Labor and American Politics* (Urbana: University of Illinois Press, 1983); Susan Levine, *Labor's True Woman: Carpet Weavers, Industrialization, and Labor Reform in the Gilded Age* (Philadelphia: Temple

University Press, 1984); David R. Roediger, *The Wages of Whiteness: Race and the Making of the American Working Class* (New York: Verso, 1991); Ava Baron, "On Looking at Men: Masculinity and the Making of a Gendered Working-Class History," in *Feminists Revision History*, ed. Ann-Louise Shapiro (New Brunswick, N.J.: Rutgers University Press, 1994), 146–71, 155; Baron, "An 'Other' Side of Gender Antagonism at Work: Men, Boys, and the Remasculinization of Printers' Work, 1830–1920," 47–69; Mary H. Blewett, "Manhood and the Market: The Politics of Gender and Class Among the Textile Workers of Fall River, Massachusetts, 1870–1880," 92–113; Eileen Boris, "'A Man's Dwelling House Is His Castle': Tenement House Cigarmaking and the Judicial Imperative," 114–41, and Nancy A. Hewitt, "'The Voice of Virile Labor': Labor Militancy, Community Solidarity, and Gender Identity Among Tampa's Latin Workers, 1880–1921," 142–67, all in *Work Engendered: Toward a New History of American Labor*, ed. Ava Baron (Ithaca, N.Y.: Cornell University Press, 1991). For a discussion of the complexity of understanding African American class structure in its historical dimensions, see Deborah Gray White, "The Slippery Slope of Class in Black America: The National Council of Negro Women and the International Ladies' Auxiliary to the Brotherhood of Sleeping Car Porters, a Case Study," in *New Viewpoints in Women's History: Working Papers from the Schlesinger Library 50th Anniversary Conference*, ed. Susan Ware (Cambridge, Mass: Arthur and Elizabeth Schlesinger Library on the History of Women in America, Radcliffe College, 1994), 180–95.

7. Walter Licht, *Getting Work: Philadelphia, 1840–1950* (Cambridge, Mass.: Harvard University Press, 1992; Philadelphia: University of Pennsylvania Press, 1999), 50.

8. Michael Denning, *Mechanic Accents: Dime Novels and Working Class Culture in America* (New York: Verso, 1987); Evelyn Brooks Higginbotham, *Righteous Discontent: The Women's Movement in the Black Baptist Church, 1880–1920* (Cambridge, Mass.: Harvard University Press, 1993), 14, 145, 204; Claudia Tate, *Domestic Allegories of Political Desire: The Black Heroine's Text at the Turn of the Century* (New York: Oxford University Press, 1992), 4, 62; Du Bois, *The Philadelphia Negro*. See also Linda Gordon, "Black and White Visions of Welfare: Women's Welfare Activism, 1890–1945," *Journal of American History* 78, 2 (September 1991): 559–90; Hazel Carby, "Policing the Black Woman's Body in an Urban Context," *Critical Inquiry* 4 (Summer 1992): 738–55; Eileen Boris, "The Power of Motherhood: Black and White Activist Women Redefine the 'Political'," in *Mothers of a New World: Maternalist Politics and the Origins of Welfare States*, ed. Seth Koven and Sonya Michel (New York: Routledge, 1993), 213–47; Elisabeth Lasch-Quinn, *Black Neighbors: Race and the Limits of Reform in the American Settlement House Movement, 1890–1945* (Chapel Hill: University of North Carolina Press, 1993), 117–18, and Kevin Gaines, "Uplifting the Race: Black Middle-Class Ideology in the Era of the 'New Negro,' 1890–1935," PhD dissertation, Brown University, 1991, esp. 10, 11, 20, 23.

9. Roediger, *The Wages of Whiteness*; Higginbotham, *Righteous Discontent*, 194–96.

10. For a discussion of these issues in antebellum America, see Amy Bridges,"Becoming American: The Working Classes in the United States Before the Civil War," in *Working Class Formation: Nineteenth-Century Patterns in Western Europe and the United States*, ed. Ira Katznelson and Aristide R. Zolberg (Princeton, N.J.: Princeton University Press, 1986), 157–96, 186.

11. Christine Stansell, *City of Women: Sex and Class in New York, 1789–1860* (New

York: Knopf, 1986), chap. 3, 41–62; Ardis Cameron, *Radicals of the Worst Sort: Laboring Women in Lawrence, Massachusetts, 1860–1912* (Urbana: University of Illinois Press, 1993), 109; Marjorie Murphy, review of Stansell, *City of Women*, *Women's Review of Books* 4, 7 (April 1987): 15–16; Ellen Ross, "Survival Networks: Women's Neighborhood Sharing in London Before World War One," *History Workshop* 15 (Spring 1983): 4–27.

12. Stansell, *City of Women*, 60–61.

13. John F. Sutherland, "Housing the Poor in the City of Homes: Philadelphia at the Turn of the Century," in *The Peoples of Philadelphia: A History of Ethnic Groups and Lower-Class Life, 1790–1940*, ed. Allen F. Davis and Mark H. Haller (Philadelphia: Temple University Press, 1973; Philadelphia: University of Pennsylvania Press, 1998), 175–202; Maxwell Whiteman, "Philadelphia's Jewish Neighborhoods," in *Peoples of Philadelphia*, ed. Davis and Haller, 231–54, 240.

14. Whiteman, "Philadelphia's Jewish Neighborhoods," 249; Sutherland, "Housing," 175.

15. Murray Friedman, "Introduction: The Making of a National Jewish Community," in *Jewish Life in Philadelphia, 1830–1940*, ed. Murray Friedman (Philadelphia: ISHI Publications, 1983), 1–25, 7–8; Sutherland, "Housing," 175–76; John Sutherland, "The Origins of Philadelphia's Octavia Hill Association: Social Reform in the 'Contented' City," *Pennsylvania Magazine of History and Biography* 99, 1 (January1975): 20–44; Du Bois, *The Philadelphia Negro*, 293.

16. Alan N. Burstein, "Immigrants and Residential Mobility: The Irish and Germans in Philadelphia, 1850–1880," in *Philadelphia: Work, Space, Family, and Group Experience in the Nineteenth Century*, ed. Theodore Hershberg (New York: Oxford University Press, 1981), 174–203, 177, 183; Stephanie W. Greenberg, "Industrial Location and Ethnic Residential Patterns in an Industrializing City: Philadelphia, 1880," in *Philadelphia*, ed. Hershberg, 204–32, 216, 219, 224.

17. Greenberg, "Industrial," 216, 219; Sutherland, "Housing," 180; Michael B. Katz and Thomas J. Sugrue, "Introduction: The Context of *The Philadelphia Negro*: The City, the Settlement House Movement, and the Rise of the Social Sciences," in *W. E. B. DuBois, Race, and the City: The Philadelphia Negro and Its Legacy*, ed. Michael B. Katz and Thomas J. Sugrue (Philadelphia: University of Pennsylvania Press, 1998), 1–37, 8.

18. Friedman, "Introduction," 7–8; Whiteman, "Philadelphia's Jewish," 241; Carroll Wright, Commissioner of Labor, *Fourth Annual Report, 1888: Working Women in Large Cities*, (Washington, D.C.: Government Printing Office, 1889), 31; Howard Gillette, Jr., "The Emergence of the Modern Metropolis: Philadelphia in the Age of its Consolidation, in *The Divided Metropolis: Social and Spatial Dimensions of Philadelphia, 1800–1925*, ed. William Cutler III and Howard Gillette, Jr. (Westport, Conn.: Greenwood Press, 1980), 3–25.

19. "Building Operations of Theodore Starr," in Starr Centre Association, *History of a Street* (Philadelphia, 1901), Octavia Hill Association Collection, Urban Archives, Temple University, Philadelphia.

20. George Rogers Taylor, "'Philadelphia in Slices' by George G. Foster," *Pennsylvania Magazine of History and Biography* 93 (January 1969): 23–72, 25; Deborah Nord, "The Social Explorer as Anthropologist: Victorian Travellers Among the Urban Poor," in *Visions of the Modern City: Essays in History, Art, and Literature*, ed. William

Sharpe and Leonard Wallock (Baltimore: Johns Hopkins University Press, 1987), 122–34.

21. Taylor, "Philadelphia," 62.

22. Herbert Gutman and Ira Berlin, "Class Composition and the Development of the American Working Class, 1840–1890," in *Power and Culture: Essays on the American Working Class*, ed. Gutman with Berlin (New York: Pantheon, 1987), 380–94.

23. Gail Bederman, "'Civilization,' the Decline of Middle-Class Manliness, and Ida B. Wells's Antilynching Campaign (1892–94)," *Radical History Review* 52 (1992): 5–30 and Kevin J. Mumford, "'Lost Manhood' Found: Male Sexual Impotence and Victorian Culture in the United States," in *American Sexual Politics: Sex, Gender, and Race Since the Civil War*, ed. John C. Fout and Maura Shaw Tantillo (Chicago: University of Chicago Press, 1993), 75–99, 86.

24. SPCC CR, 1896, #15446, #15796.

25. Harriet Beecher Stowe, *We and Our Neighbors* (New York: Fords, Howard, and Hulbert, 1875), 277.

26. Du Bois, *Philadelphia Negro*, 81; Higginbotham, *Righteous Discontent*, 204–5; David Levering Lewis, *W. E. B. Du Bois: Biography of a Race, 1868–1919* (New York: Henry Holt, 1993), chap. 8, "From Philadelphia to Atlanta," 179–210. For an analysis of uplift ideology and shifting political strategies of African American reformers, see Ann Holder, "Gender, Sexuality, and the Strategy of Racial Uplift, 1890–1920," presented October 1, 1994 at the Western New England Women's History Conference.

27. Anna Julia Cooper, *A Voice from the South* (1892; New York: Oxford University Press, 1988), 249–50.

28. Du Bois, *The Philadelphia Negro*, 351.

29. George Gunton, *Wealth and Progress: A Critical Examination of the Labor Problem* (New York: D. Appleton and Co., 1887), 210; Levine, *Labor's True Woman*, 110.

30. See Patricia Williams, *The Alchemy of Race and Rights* (Cambridge, Mass.: Harvard University Press, 1991), 22, for a discussion of the right to privacy as a function of wealth.

31. Stansell, *City of Women*; Ellen Ross, "Women's Networks and Collective Childcare in Working-Class London, 1870–1918," unpublished paper, November 1986, 8; Michael B. Katz, *Poverty and Policy in American History* (New York: Academic Press, 1983), 50.

32. Stansell, *City of Women*, 76, 82–85.

33. SPCC CR, Jan. 10, 1896, #15090, #15429, #16967.

34. SPCC CR, Oct. 19, 1887, #8150.

35. SPCC CR, June 18, 1880, #1733.

36. See Ross, "Women's Networks," 6, for a similar discussion of London.

37. SPCC CR, 1887, #7801.

38. SPCC CR, Feb. 28, 1887, #7550; SPCC CR, 1896, #1525.

39. SPCC CR, June 17, 1879, #982; *Public Ledger*, January 5, 1877; Charles Lawrence, *History of the Philadelphia Almshouses and Hospitals* (Philadelphia: Charles Lawrence, 1905; New York: Arno Press, 1976), chaps. 17, 18, 22, 24, on fear of pauper burials and the sale of corpses to medical students.

40. *Public Ledger*, February 2, 1877; SPCC CR, 1887, #7801; Emily K. Abel, "Correspondence Between Julia C. Lathrop, Chief of the Children's Bureau, and a

Working-Class Woman, 1914–1915," *Journal of Women's History* 5, 1 (Spring 1993): 79–88, 88n5. For an example of the stigma involved in accepting public "indoor" relief, see Haven Diary, Nov. 23, 1888, "Mrs. H. called and took M. P. and infant away the latter cried as if her heart would break to think she had to go to the almshouse her husband deserted her."

41. SPCC CR, June 23, 1879, #994; SPCC CR, May 18, 1887, #7747; SPCC CR, 1880, #1439.

42. SPCC CR, 1887, #8211; SPCC CR, #2099, 1880.

43. SPCC CR, 1896, #15079, for a complaint about noise and "growler-running." A growler, or a kettle of beer, cost about ten cents and in practice could be purchased by children running errands for parents, although the sale of beer to children was illegal.

44. SPCC CR, July 8, 1901, #20028.

45. SPCC, *Eighth Annual Report*, 1884 (1885), 22.

46. SPCC, *Eighth Annual Report*, 19; SPCC CR, 1896, #15859; SPCC CR, 1893, #12953; *Madeleine: An Autobiography* (New York: Harper and Brothers, 1919), 81.

47. SPCC CR, 1893, #12596.

48. SPCC CR, 1896, #15412.

49. SPCC CR, 1879, #1153; SPCC CR, 1878, #782; SPCC, *Second Annual Report*, 1878 (1879), 27.

50. Henry Boies, *Prisoners and Paupers: A Study of the Abnormal Increase of Criminals and the Public Burden of Pauperism in the United States* (New York: Putnam,1893; Freeport, N.Y.: Books for Libraries Press, 1972, 5, 99, 101.

51. Stansell, *City of Women*, 209–11; Charles Loring Brace, *The Dangerous Classes of New York and Twenty Years' Work Among Them* (New York: Wynkoop and Hallenbeck, 1872), 246–70; Alice Rhine, "Woman in Industry," in *Woman's Work in America*, ed. Annie Nathan Meyer (New York: Henry Holt and Co., 1891; New York: Arno Press, 1972), 276–322, 314–15; Stephen O'Connor, *The Orphan Trains: The Story of Charles Loring Brace and the Children He Saved and Failed* (Boston: Houghton Mifflin, 2001).

52. SPCC CR, April 5, 1880, #1512.

53. SPCC CR, April 5, 1880, #1512.

54. SPCC CR, Sept. 4, 1879, #1148; SPCC CR Sept. 27, 1893, #13165; SPCC CR, 1887, #7624; SPCC CR. 1878, #451.

55. See Judith Lowder Newton, "History as Usual? Feminism and the 'New Historicism,'" in *The New Historicism*, ed. H. Aram Veeser (New York: Routledge, 1989), 152 67, 160 61.

56. SPCC, *Sixteenth Annual Report*, 1892 (1893), 10; *Thirty-Second Annual Report*, 1908 (1909), 12; SPCC CR, Sept. 28, 1896, #15739.

57. Martin Shefter, "Trade Unions and Political Machines: The Organization and Disorganization of the American Working Class in the Late Nineteenth Century," in *Working Class Formation*, ed. Katznelson and Zolberg, 208; Joseph F. Kett, *Rites of Passage: Adolescence in America, 1790 to the Present* (New York: Basic Books, 1977), 93; David Johnson, "Crime Patterns in Philadelphia, 1840–70," in *Peoples of Philadelphia*, ed. Davis and Heller, 97; Sean Wilentz, *Chants Democratic: New York City and the Rise of the American Working Class, 1788–1850* (New York: Oxford University Press, 1984), 263.

58. Starr Centre, *History of a Street* (Philadelphia: Ivy Leaf in Sansom Street, 1901), 32–34. See Benjamin Sewell, *Sorrow's Circuit, or Five Years' Experience in the Bedford Street Mission* (Philadelphia, 1859), 14, 105, 107–8, on hostility to preachers in Philadelphia on the part of "Painites" and hecklers.

59. SPCC CR, 1877, #69; Stansell, *City of Women*, 36; Gordon, *Heroes of Their Own Lives*, 95.

60. SPCC CR, 1877, #72; SPCC CR, 1878, #683, in *Second Annual Report*, 1878 (1879), 43; Michael Grossberg, *Governing the Hearth: Law and the Family in Nineteenth-Century America* (Chapel Hill: University of North Carolina Press, 1985), 268–80.

61. SPCC CR, Jan. 1880, #1378.

62. These themes figure prominently in Edward W. Townsend, *Near a Whole City Full* (New York: G.W. Dilingham Co., 1897) and in Townsend's earlier novel, *A Daughter of the Tenements* (New York: Lovell, Coryell, and Co., 1895).

63. For background on Pemberton, see Caroline Pemberton, "How I Became a Socialist," *The Comrade* 1, 9 (June 1902): 202; Philip Foner, "Caroline Hollingsworth Pemberton: Philadelphia Socialist Champion of Black Equality," *Pennsylvania History* 43, 3 (1976): 239–46. See Natalie Zemon Davis, *Fiction in the Archives: Pardon Tales and Their Tellers in Sixteenth-Century France* (Stanford, Calif.: Stanford University Press, 1987), 3, for a discussion of the fictive nature of historical records.

64. Pemberton, *The Charity Girl*, chap. 3, 637–50, 637.

65. SPCC, *Sixteenth Annual Report*, 1892 (1893), 12–13; *Thirty-Fourth Annual Report*, 1910 (1911), 9; Michael B. Katz, *In the Shadow of the Poorhouse: A Social History of Welfare in America* (New York: Basic Books, 1986), 58–84; Priscilla Ferguson Clement, *Growing Pains: Children in the Industrial Age, 1850–1890* (New York: Twayne Publishers, 1997), 197.

66. See the following examples of cases where mothers resisted removal of children: SPCC CR, 1880, #2088; SPCC CR, 1887, #8189; SPCC CR, 1896, #15245.

67. SPCC, *Fourteenth Annual Report*, 1890 (1891), 10; SPCC CR, 1887, #8157; SPCC CR, Oct. 27, 1877, #235; SPCC CR, 1901, #20047, #20165; SPCC CR, 1887, #8243; SPCC CR, June 11, 1879, #968.

68. SPCC CR, 1893, #12577, #12467; SPCC CR, 1896, #15791; Judith Walkowitz, *Prostitution and Victorian Society* (New York: Cambridge University Press, 1980), 29–30, 197, 201.

69. SPCC CR, 1901, #19780; SPCC CR, 1893, #121809; SPCC CR, 1893, #12577.

70. SPCC CR, 1896, #15796.

71. SPCC CR, 1879, #787; SPCC CR, 1901, #19561.

72. SPCC Board Minutes, 1881.

73. Katz, *In the Shadow of the Poorhouse*, 136; Sidney Harring, *Policing a Class Society: The Experience of American Cities, 1865–1915* (New Brunswick, N.J.: Rutgers University Press, 1983), 237; Michael B. Katz, Michael Doucet, and Mark Stern, *The Social Organization of Early Industrial Capitalism* (Cambridge, Mass.: Harvard University Press, 1982), 228–29; Allen Steinberg, "'The Spirit of Litigation': Private Prosecution and Criminal Justice in Nineteenth Century Philadelphia," *Journal of Social History* 20, 2 (Winter 1986): 231–49; Allen Steinberg, *The Transformation of Criminal Justice:*

Philadelphia, 1800–1880 (Chapel Hill: University of North Carolina Press, 1992), 33.

74. SPCC CR, Feb. 25, 1880, #1450; SPCC CR,1878, #421; SPCC CR, 1878, 434, #431.

75. SPCC CR, 1880, #1444; SPCC CR,1880, #1811.

76. SPCC CR, May 26, 1896, #15404.

77. SPCC, *Twentieth Annual Report*, 1896 (1897), 24, 27. For a similar account of SPCC clients as "active negotiators in a complex bargaining" see Linda Gordon, "Child Abuse, Gender, and the Myth of Family Independence: A Historical Critique," *Child Welfare* 64, 3 (May–June 1985): 219; Gordon, *Heroes of Their Own Lives: The Politics and History of Family Violence in Boston, 1880–1960* (New York: Viking Press, 1988).

78. Kenneth Fones-Wolf, "Trade Union Gospel: Protestantism and Labor in Philadelphia, 1865–1915," PhD dissertation, Temple University, 1985, 82; Johnson, "Crime Patterns in Philadelphia," 101; Bruce Laurie, *Working People of Philadelphia, 1800–1850* (Philadelphia: Temple University Press, 1980), 53–66; Alan Dawley and Paul Faler, "Working-Class Culture and Politics in the Industrial Revolution: Sources of Loyalism and Rebellion," *Journal of Social History* 9 (1976): 466–80; Sean Wilentz, *Chants Democratic: New York City and the Rise of the American Working Class, 1788–1850* (New York: Oxford University Press, 1984), 255–71.

79. Linda Gordon makes a similar point in "Family Violence, Feminism, and Social Control," *Feminist Studies* 12, 3 (Fall 1986): 467.

80. Walkowitz, *Prostitution*, 29–30, 197, 201.

Chapter 3. Dens of Inequities

1. SPCC CR, 1878, #480, #483.

2. SPCC, *Fourth Annual Report*, 1880 (1881), 22.

3. For discussions of working-class families and reformers engaged in both conflict and collaboration, see Linda Gordon, *Heroes of Their Own Lives: The Politics and History of Family Violence, Boston 1880-1960* (New York: Viking, 1988); Gordon, *Pitied But Not Entitled: Single Mothers and the History of Welfare, 1890-1935* (New York: Free Press, 1994); Mary E. Odem, *Delinquent Daughters: Protecting and Policing Adolescent Female Sexuality in the United States, 1885-1920* (Chapel Hill: University of North Carolina Press, 1995); Christine Stansell, *City of Women: Sex and Class in New York, 1789-1860* (New York: Knopf, 1986); Eric C. Schneider, *In the Web of Class: Delinquents and Reformers in Boston, 1810s-1930s* (New York: New York University Press, 1992); Barbara M. Brenzel, *Daughters of the State: A Social Portrait of the First Reform School for Girls in North America, 1856-1905* (Cambridge, Mass.: MIT Press, 1983); Emily K. Abel, "Valuing Care: Turn-of-the-Century Conflicts Between Charity Workers and Women Clients," *Journal of Women's History* 10, 3 (Fall 1998): 32–52.

4. Natalie Zemon Davis, *Fiction in the Archives: Pardon Tales and Their Tellers in Sixteenth-Century France* (Stanford, Calif.: Stanford University Press, 1987), 112; George Lipsitz, "Listening to Learn and Learning to Listen: Popular Culture, Cultural Theory, and American Studies," *American Quarterly* 42, 4 (December 1990): 615–36, 618, 621.

5. SPCC CR, 1878, #480, #483.

6. Ellen Ross, "'Not the Sort That Would Sit on the Doorstep': Respectability in Pre-World War I London Neighborhoods," *International Labor and Working Class History* 27 (Spring 1985): 39–59; W. E. B. Du Bois, *The Philadelphia Negro: A Social Study* (1899: Philadelphia: University of Pennsylvania Press, 1996), 310, 312–13; Amos Griswold Warner, *American Charities: A Study in Philanthropy and Economics* (New York: Thomas Crowell and Co., 1894), 68.

7. See Linda Gordon, "Family Violence," in *Gender and American History Since 1890*, ed. Barbara Melosh (New York: Routledge, 1993), 296–97; Joan W. Scott, Review of Linda Gordon, *Heroes of Their Own Lives*, *Signs* 15, 4 (Summer 1990): 848–53; Linda Gordon, "Response to Scott," *Signs* 15, 4 (Summer 1990): 852–53.

8. See Maureen A. Mahoney and Barbara Yngvesson, "The Construction of Subjectivity and the Paradox of Resistance: Reintegrating Feminist Anthropology and Psychology," *Signs* 18, 1 (Autumn 1992): 44–71. Also see Robin G. Kelley, " Notes on Deconstructing 'The Folk'," *American Historical Review* 97, 5 (December 1992): 1400–1408.

9. See Elizabeth Pleck, *Domestic Tyranny: The Making of American Social Policy Against Family Violence from Colonial Times to the Present* (New York: Oxford University Press, 1987), 84, 244n31. Based on her statistical analysis of the cases handled by the Pennsylvania Society to Protect Children from Cruelty, Pleck determined that, from 1878 until 1935, 12 percent of the cases handled concerned physical abuse of children.

10. The term "deserted" was often used in the Haven for Unwed Mothers and Infants diary and house records to refer to women without economic support, even when such women had left their husbands voluntarily. See Haven House Records 1884–1890, 56, and Haven Diary 1883–1887, Jan. 3, 1885. For a discussion of informal working-class patterns of marriage and divorce, see United States Senate *Report on the Condition of Woman and Child Wage-Earners in the United States*, vol. 15, *Relation between Occupation and Criminality of Women* (Washington, D.C.: GPO, 1911), 24–25; Ellen Ross, "'Fierce Questions and Taunts': Married Life in Working-Class London, 1870–1914," *Feminist Studies* 8, 3 (Fall 1983): 581.

11. SPCC CR, 1901, #19542.

12. Pamela Walker, "Domestic Violence in Working-Class London, 1870–1980," unpublished paper presented at the Seventh Berkshire Conference on the History of Women, Wellesley College, Wellesley, Mass., June 21, 1987.

13. Ellen Ross, *Love and Toil: Motherhood in Outcast London, 1870-1918* (New York: Oxford University Press, 1993); Stansell, *City of Women*; Patricia Hill Collins, "Shifting the Center : Race, Class, and Feminist Theorizing About Motherhood," in *Representations of Motherhood*, ed. Donna Bassin, Margaret Honey, and Meryle Mahrer Kaplan (New Haven, Conn.: Yale University Press, 1994), 56–74.

14. See Claudia Goldin, "Household and Market Production of Families in a Late Nineteenth Century American City," *Explorations in Economic History* 16 (1979): 111–31; and Goldin, "Family Strategies and the Family Economy in the Late Nineteenth Century: The Role of Secondary Workers," in *Philadelphia: Work, Space,*

Family, and Group Experience in the Nineteenth Century, ed. Theodore Hershberg (New York: Oxford University Press, 1981): 277–310; Susan Levine, *Labor's True Woman: Carpet Weavers, Industrialization, and Labor Reform in the Gilded Age* (Philadelphia: Temple University Press, 1984), 16, 97, on patterns of women's work in Philadelphia; Jeanne Boydston, *Home and Work: Housework, Wages, and the Ideology of Labor in the Early Republic* (New York: Oxford University Press, 1990); Stansell, *City of Women;* Du Bois, *The Philadelphia Negro,* 193–94.

15. Frank F. Furstenberg, Jr., Theodore Hershberg, and John Modell, "The Origins of the Female-Headed Black Family: The Impact of the Urban Experience," in *Philadelphia,* ed. Hershberg, 444.

16. Furstenberg, Hershberg, and Modell, "Origins," 442–47; Du Bois, *Philadelphia Negro,* 67–68. Separation, divorce, and single motherhood combined accounted for only 25 percent of female-headed households. For a synthetic analysis of historical accounts of African American families in the late nineteenth century, see Stephanie Coontz, *The Way We Never Were: American Families and the Nostalgia Trap* (New York: Basic Books, 1992), 237–41.

17. Eudice Glassberg, "Philadelphians in Need: Client Experiences with Two Philadelphia Benevolent Societies, 1830–1880" (PhD dissertation, University of Pennsylvania, 1979), 195–97, 340.

18. SPCC CR, Dec. 1879, #1351; SPCC CR, 1887, #1193.

19. SPCC CR, Jan. 10, 1896, #15090, #15429, #16967; SPCC CR, Nov. 3, 1880, #2094, #2067.

20. SPCC CR, Jan. 26, 1887, #7460.

21. SPCC CR, April 26, 1877, Oct. 15, 1877, #41, p. 51.

22. SPCC CR, April 26, 1877, Oct. 15, 1877, #41, p. 51.

23. SPCC CR, 1896, #15446, #15796.

24. SPCC CR, 1901, #19909.

25. Joan W. Scott, in exchange between Scott and Gordon in *Signs* 15, 4 (Summer 1990): 851.

26. See SPCC CR, July 15, 1880, #1814.

27 SPCC CR, 1887, #7512; Priscilla Ferguson Clement, *Growing Pains: Children in the Industrial Age, 1850-1890* (New York: Twayne Publishers, 1997), 189.

28. Barbara Leslie Epstein, *The Politics of Domesticity: Women, Evangelism, and Temperance in Nineteenth Century America* (Middletown, Conn.: Wesleyan University Press, 1981), 144–45.

29. SPCC CR, Sept. 28, 1878; Linda Gordon, "Family Violence, Feminism, and Social Control," *Feminist Studies* 12, 3 (Fall 1986): 472.

30. Elizabeth Fee, "The Sexual Politics of Victorian Social Anthropology," *in Clio's Consciousness Raised: New Perspectives on the History of Women,* ed. Mary S. Hartman and Lois Banner (New York: Harper and Row, 1974), 86–102, 89–90, 101.

31. Helen Campbell, Thomas Knox, and Thomas Byrnes, *Darkness and Daylight, or Lights and Shadows of New York Life* (Hartford, Conn.: A.D. Worthington and Co., 1899), 170.

32. See Ida B. Wells, *Crusade for Justice: The Autobiography of Ida B. Wells,* ed. Alfreda

M. Duster (Chicago: University of Chicago Press, 1970); Pauline Hopkins, *Contending Forces: A Romance Illustrative of Negro Life North and South* (Boston: Colored Co-Operative Publishing Co., 1900); and Claudia Tate, *Domestic Allegories of Political Desire: The Black Heroine's Text at the Turn of the Century* (New York : Oxford University Press, 1992).

33. See SPCC CR, June 1901, #19922.

34. In *Love and Toil*, 74, Ross argues that in Victorian London working-class wives did not want separations, but appealed to men in positions of authority to make their husbands give them more of their wages.

35. Allen Steinberg, *The Transformation of Criminal Justice: Philadelphia, 1800-1880* (Chapel Hill: University of North Carolina Press, 1992), 46–48, 69.

36. SPCC CR, July 18, 1879, #1044.

37. SPCC CR, Mar. 19, 1896, #15247.

38. SPCC CR, May 22, 1901, #19870.

39. Mary P. Ryan, *Cradle of the Middle Class: The Family in Oneida County, New York, 1790-1865* (New York: Cambridge University Press, 1981), chap. 4; Stuart M. Blumin, *The Emergence of the Middle Class: Social Experience in the American City, 1760-1900* (New York: Cambridge University Press, 1989).

40. Stansell, *City of Women*.

41. Gordon, *Heroes*, 56.

42. Karin Calvert, *Children in the House: The Material Culture of Early Childhood, 1600-1900* (Boston: Northeastern University Press, 1992), and Viviana A. Zelizer, *Pricing the Priceless Child: The Changing Social Value of Children* (New York: Basic Books, 1985).

43. See Hasia R. Diner, *Erin's Daughters in America: Irish Immigrant Women in the Nineteenth Century* (Baltimore: Johns Hopkins University Press, 1983); Kathy Lee Peiss, "'Charity Girls' and City Pleasures: Historical Notes on Working Class Sexuality, 1880–1920," in *Powers of Desire: The Politics of Sexuality*, ed. Ann Snitow, Christine Stansell, and Sharon Thompson (New York: Monthly Review Press, 1983), 74–87; Elizabeth Ewen, *Immigrant Women in the Land of Dollars: Life and Culture on the Lower East Side, 1890-1925* (New York: Monthly Review Press, 1985).

44. SPCC CR, 1896, #15603. See Stansell, *City of Women*, 208.

45. SPCC CR, 1879, #1315.

46. SPCC CR, Aug. 23, 1879, p. 101.

47. SPCC CR, 1880, #1592.

48. SPCC CR, 1880, #1610.

49. SPCC CR, Mar. 17, 1887, #7588; see SPCC CR, 1896, #15803.

50. SPCC CR, Mar. 1877, #11.

51. SPCC CR, Aug. 2, 1879, #1091; Stansell, *City of Women*, 207.

52. SPCC CR, Mar. 14, 1877, #15, p. 22.

53. SPCC CR, 1877, #161.

54. SPCC CR, Feb. 19, 1896, #15179.

55. SPCC CR, May 18, 1887, #7748.

56. SPCC CR, 1887, #8123.

57. SPCC CR, July 22, 1879, #1060.

58. SPCC CR, 1887, #8204.

59. SPCC CR, July 10, 1901, #20039.

60. SPCC CR, Aug. 24, 1901, #20220; see Stansell, *City of Women*, 53–54.

61. See Kathy Lee Peiss, *Cheap Amusements: Gender Relations and the Use of Leisure Time in New York City, 1820 to 1920* (Philadelphia: Temple University Press, 1986); Stansell, *City of Women*, for a discussion of the antebellum period.

62. Carroll Wright, *Fourth Annual Report of the Commissioner of Labor, 1888, Working Women in Large Cities* (Washington, D.C.: Government Printing Office, 1889), 22, 31–32.

63. Campbell, *Darkness and Daylight*, 233.

64. SPCC CR, Aug. 24, 1893, #13067, #10251, #12620.

65. SPCC CR, Apr. 27, 1893, #12,707; SPCC CR, 1880, #1497; William Isaac Thomas, *The Unadjusted Girl, with Cases and Standpoint for Behavior Analysis* (Boston: Little, Brown, 1923), 109, on girls judged delinquent in the early twentieth century.

66. See Judith R. Walkowitz, *Prostitution and Victorian Society: Women, Class, and the State* (New York, Cambridge University Press, 1980).

67. Ross, *Love and Toil*; Stansell, *City of Women*; Gordon, *Heroes*; and Judith R. Walkowitz, *City of Dreadful Delight: Narratives of Sexual Danger in Late-Victorian London* (Chicago: University of Chicago Press, 1992), 114.

68. SPCC CR, Jan. 3, 1877, #3.

69. See Stansell, *City of Women*, chap. 9, "Women on the Town," 171–92 for an account of sexual exchange that highlights women's agency; Gordon, *Heroes*, 215, points to the links between previous sexual abuse and the creation of an overly sexualized identity.

70. Walkowitz, *Prostitution and Victorian Society*, 21.

71. William Elsing, "Life in New York Tenement Houses as Seen by a City Missionary," in *The Poor in Great Cities: Their Problems and What Is Doing to Solve Them*, ed. Robert A. Woods et al. (1895; New York: Garrett Press, 1970), 72.

72. Ellen K. Rothman, *Hands and Hearts: A History of Courtship in America* (New York: Basic Books, 1984), 209; Peiss, *Cheap Amusements*; Marcia Carlisle, "Prostitutes and Their Reformers in Nineteenth Century Philadelphia" (Ph.D. dissertation, Rutgers University, 1982), 101; Rothman, *Hands and Hearts*, 207; Peiss, "Charity Girls," 76, 77, 78, 81. The theory that some prostitutes began their careers as girls in search of a good time would become the basis for the Progressive emphasis on the provision of wholesome amusements for working girls. See Haven, *Thirty-First Annual Report*, 1912 (1913), 8.

73. See Peiss, *Cheap Amusements*, for a discussion of "treating."

74. SPCC CR, 1896, #15823.

75. SPCC CR, 1887, #7718, #7723. See Regina G. Kunzel, *Fallen Women, Problem Girls: Unmarried Mothers and the Professionalization of Social Work, 1890-1945* (New Haven, Conn.: Yale University Press, 1993), 104–5, for a discussion of the ways alcohol and knock-out drops figured into single women's narratives of their pregnancies.

76. SPCC CR, June 18, 1878, #464.

77. SPCC CR, March 15, 1887, #7585.

78. SPCC CR, 1887, #7714; SPCC CR, 1887, #7603; SPCC CR, Feb. 10, 1887, #7498; SPCC CR, April 1896, #15285.

79. SPCC CR, 1878, #450; Michael B. Katz, *Poverty and Policy in American History* (New York: Academic Press, 1983); Katz, *In the Shadow of the Poorhouse: A Social*

History of Welfare in America (New York: Basic Books, 1986); Brenzel, *Daughters of the State*; Stansell, *City of Women*, 53–54.

80. SPCC CR, 1887, #19914. Also see SPCC CR, 1893, #12, 707.

81. Campbell, *Darkness and Daylight*, 219–20.

82. SPCC CR, 1887, #7738; SPCC CR, Jan. 27, 1893, #12497.

83. SPCC CR, March 22, 1878, #367. Ruth Rosen, *The Lost Sisterhood : Prostitution in America, 1900-1918* (Baltimore: Johns Hopkins University Press, 1982), 144; *Senate, Report on the Relation between Occupation and Criminality in Women*, 102.

84. SPCC CR, 1893, #13217; SPCC CR, 1887, #8149; Gordon, *Heroes*, 215.

85. SPCC CR, 1878, #549, p.78.

86. SPCC CR, 1877, #10.

87. SPCC CR, 1879, #1103; Kunzel, *Fallen Women*, 108–9.

88. Walkowitz, *City of Dreadful Delight*, esp. chaps. 4, 5; Kunzel, *Fallen Women*, 108–9.

89. Gordon, *Heroes*, 18.

90. SPCC, *Fourth Annual Report*, 1880 (1881), 14.

91. Gordon, *Heroes*.

92. Gordon, *Heroes*, 215; Elizabeth Lunbeck, *The Psychiatric Persuasion: Knowledge, Gender, and Power in Modern America* (Princeton, N.J.: Princeton University Press, 1994); and Kunzel, *Fallen Women*.

93. SPCC CR, 1893, #12978. In *Heroes*, 215, Gordon argues that reformers' "ability to recognize incest" was partially based on the belief that incest was "exclusively a vice of the poor."

94. SPCC Board Minutes, Dec. 20, 1909; Sheila Jeffreys, *The Spinster and Her Enemies: Feminism and Sexuality, 1880-1930* (London: Pandora Press, 1985); Ruth Bordin, *Women and Temperance: The Quest for Power and Liberty, 1873-1900* (Philadelphia: Temple University Press, 1980); Estelle Freedman, *Their Sisters' Keepers: Women's Prison Reform in America, 1830-1930* (Ann Arbor: University of Michigan Press, 1981).

95. Gordon, *Heroes*, 212 and chap. 7, "'Be Careful About Father': Incest, Girls' Resistance, and the Construction of Femininity," for an excellent discussion of incest; Anthony Wohl, "Sex and the Single Room: Incest Among the Victorian Working Class," in *The Victorian Family: Structure and Stresses*, ed. Wohl (New York: St. Martin's Press, 1978), 205; Linda Gordon and Paul O'Keefe, "Incest as a Form of Family Violence: Evidence from Historical Case Records," *Journal of Marriage and the Family* 46, 1 (February 1984): 30; Stansell, *City of Women*, 182–85.

96. SPCC CR, Sept. 7, 1880, #1976.

97. Gordon, *Heroes*, 205; Janet Liebman Jacobs, "Victimized Daughters: Sexual Violence and the Empathic Female Self," *Signs* 19, 1 (Fall 1993): 126–45, 141.

98. Gordon, *Heroes*, 227.

99. SPCC CR, June 22, 1887, #7846.

100. SPCC CR, June 22, 1887, #7846.

101. See Gordon, *Heroes*, 215, on Massachusetts SPCC's awareness of the link between previous sexual abuse and prostitution.

102. See Kunzel, *Fallen Women*, 108, for the argument that the language of seduction and betrayal "could also be modified to tell stories of sexual violence and rape."

103. SPCC CR, April 25, 1893, #12703.

104. Allen Steinberg, " 'The Spirit of Litigation': Private Prosecution and Criminal Justice in Nineteenth Century Philadelphia," *Journal of Social History* 20, 2 (Winter 1986): 231–49; Katz, *In the Shadow of the Poorhouse*, 136; Katz, *Poverty and Policy*, 198–99; Brenzel, *Daughters of the State*; Michael B. Katz, Michael J. Doucet, and Mark J. Stern, *The Social Organization of Early Industrial Capitalism* (Cambridge, Mass.: Harvard University Press, 1982), 362.

Chapter 4. Illegitimate Mothers, Redemptive Maternity

1. Barbara Sicherman, ed., *Alice Hamilton: A Life in Letters* (Cambridge, Mass.: Harvard University Press, 1984), 49. In this chapter I use the nineteenth-century term "unwed mother" rather than the more recent term single mother to refer to women who were not married at the time of childbirth.

2. Gianna Pomata, "Unwed Mothers in the Late Nineteenth and Early Twentieth Centuries: Clinical Histories and Life Histories," in *Microhistory and the Lost People of Europe*, ed. Edward Muir and Guido Ruggiero (Baltimore: Johns Hopkins University Press, 1991), 159–204, 182–83.

3. Homes for unwed mothers grew out of the "failure" of refuges for prostitutes. See Otto Wilson, *Fifty Year's Work with Girls, 1883–1933* (Alexandria, Va.: National Florence Crittenton Mission, 1933); Regina G. Kunzel, *Fallen Women, Problem Girls: Unmarried Mothers and the Professionalization of Social Work, 1890–1945* (New Haven, Conn.: Yale University Press, 1993),17.

4. This chapter does not address the situation of women in common-law marriages. See Hendrik Hartog, *Man and Wife in America: A History* (Cambridge, Mass.: Harvard University Press, 2000), 23–31; Nancy Cott, *Public Vows: A History of Marriage and the Nation* (Cambridge, Mass.: Harvard University Press, 2000), 39–40, for discussion of common-law marriage.

5. George Rogers Taylor, "'Philadelphia in Slices' by George G. Foster," *Pennsylvania Magazine of History and Biography* 93 (January 1969): 41.

6. Dr. John Parry, "Infant Mortality and the Necessity of a Foundling Hospital in Philadelphia," lecture to the Social Science Association of Philadelphia, May 5, 1871, 9; Stuart Blumin, "Explaining the New Metropolis: Perception, Depiction, and Analysis in Mid-Nineteenth Century New York City," *Journal of Urban History* 11, 1 (November 1984): 9–38.

7. Judith Walkowitz, *Prostitution and Victorian Society: Women, Class, and the State* (New York: Cambridge University Press, 1980), 18; Ruth Rosen, *The Lost Sisterhood: Prostitution in America, 1900–1918* (Baltimore: Johns Hopkins University Press, 1982), for a discussion of prostitution in America during the Progressive Era. One nineteenth-century American prostitute who wrote her autobiography relied heavily on the sentimental interpretation of women's downfall when she recounted her turn to prostitution in 1887: "I, an attractive young girl, homeless, defenseless, hungry, and in a few months to become a mother, had no choice between the course I took and the Mississippi River." See *Madeleine: An Autobiography* (New York: Harper and Bros., 1919; New York: Persea Books, 1986), 36; see Marcia Carlisle's introduction for a discussion of the probable authenticity of this account.

8. Rosen, *The Lost Sisterhood*, 99; Roger Lane, *Violent Death in the City: Suicide, Accident, and Murder in Nineteenth-Century Philadelphia* (Cambridge, Mass.: Harvard University Press, 1979), 94, for a discussion of prostitutes and abortion in nineteenth-century Philadelphia.

9. Harriet Beecher Stowe, *We and Our Neighbors, or, Records of an Unfashionable Street* (New York: Fords, Howard, and Hulbert, 1875), 329.

10. See Joan Brumberg, "'Ruined' Girls: Changing Community Responses to Illegitimacy in Upstate New York, 1890–1920," *Journal of Social History* 18, 2 (Winter 1984): 247–72; Michael Sedlak, "Young Women and the City: Adolescent Deviance and the Transformation of Educational Policy, 1870–1960," *History of Education Quarterly* 23, 1 (1983): 1–28; Marion Morton, "Seduced and Abandoned in an American City: Cleveland and Its Fallen Women, 1869–1936," *Journal of Urban History* 11, 4 (August 1985): 443–69; Susan E. Harari and Maris Vinovskis, "Adolescent Sexuality, Pregnancy, and Childbearing in the Past," in *The Politics of Pregnancy: Adolescent Sexuality and Public Policy*, ed. Annette Lawson and Deborah L. Rhode (New Haven, Conn.: Yale University Press, 1993), 23–45.

11. See Robert V. Wells, "Illegitimacy and Bridal Pregnancy in Colonial America," 349–61, and Daniel Scott Smith, "The Long Cycle in American Illegitimacy and Prenuptial Pregnancy," 362–78, esp. 370–71, both in *Bastardy and Its Comparative History*, ed. Peter Laslett, Karla Oosterveen, and Richard M. Smith (Cambridge, Mass.: Harvard University Press, 1980); Patricia Cline Cohen, *The Murder of Helen Jewett: The Life and Death of a Prostitute in Nineteenth-Century New York* (New York: Knopf, 1998), 180–201.

12. SPCC CR, 1901, #20193. See SPCC CR, Oct. 29, 1896; SPCC CR, 1901, #19631. See Helen Parrish Diary, Octavia Hill Association Collection, Urban Archives, Temple University, Philadelphia; United States Senate, *Report on Condition of Woman and Child Wage-Earners in the United States*, vol. 15, *relation between Occupation and Criminality of Women* (Washington, D.C.: Government Printing Office, 1911), 24–25.

13. See Kathy Lee Peiss, *Cheap Amusements: Gender Relations and the Use of Leisure Time in New York City, 1820 to 1920* (Philadelphia: Temple University Press, 1986).

14. Brumberg, "'Ruined' Girls," 258.

15. SPCC CR, 1893, #12724; SPCC CR, June 1901, #19983; Leslie J. Reagan, *When Abortion Was a Crime: Women, Medicine, and Law in the United States, 1867–1973* (Berkeley: University of California Press, 1997); Hugh L. Hodge, *Foeticide or Criminal Abortion* (Philadelphia: Lindsay and Blakiston, 1869), 27; Carroll Smith-Rosenberg, *Disorderly Conduct: Visions of Gender in Victorian America* (New York: Knopf, 1985), 218; James Mohr, "Patterns of Abortion and the Response of American Physicians, 1798–1930," in *Women and Health in America: Historical Readings*, ed. Judith Walzer Leavitt (Madison: University of Wisconsin Press, 1984), 117–23; Michael Grossberg, *Governing the Hearth: Law and the Family in Nineteenth-Century America* (Chapel Hill: University of North Carolina Press, 1985), 159–94.

16. Janet Farrell Brodie, *Contraception and Abortion in Nineteenth-Century America* (Ithaca, N.Y.: Cornell University Press, 1994).

17. Brodie, *Contraception and Abortion*, 166–68, 180, 188; Andrea Tone, "Black Market Birth Control: Contraceptive Entrepreneurship and Criminality in the Gilded Age," *Journal of American History* 87 (September 2000): 435–59, 438, 456.

18. Ellen K. Rothman, *Hands and Hearts: A History of Courtship in America* (New York: Basic Books, 1984), 123–24; also see Karen Lystra, *Searching the Heart: Women, Men, and Romantic Love in Nineteenth-Century America* (New York: Oxford University Press, 1989).

19. Harari and Vinovskis, "Adolescent Sexuality," 27.

20. Cited in Peiss, *Cheap Amusements*, 171; see also 174. See Kathy Lee Peiss,"'Charity Girls' and City Pleasures: Historical Notes on Working Class Sexuality, 1880–192," in *Powers of Desire: The Politics of Sexuality*, ed. Ann Snitow, Christine Stansell, and Sharon Thompson (New York: Monthly Review Press, 1983), 83.

21. Ellen Ross, "'Not the Sort That Would Sit on the Doorstep'": Respectability in Pre-World War I London Neighborhoods," *International Labor and Working Class History* 27 (Spring 1985): 45. Also see Peggy Pascoe, *Relations of Rescue: The Search for Female Moral Authority in the American West, 1874–1939* (New York: Oxford University Press, 1990), 151.

22. Catherine Clinton, "Reconstructing Freedwomen," in *Divided Houses: Gender and the Civil War*, ed. Catherine Clinton and Nina Silber (New York: Oxford University Press, 1992), 307, 312, 318; Peggy Cooper Davis, *Neglected Stories: The Constitution and Family Values* (New York: Hill and Wang, 1997), 28–80; Cott, *Public Vows*, 89–90; Amy Dru Stanley, *From Bondage to Contract: Wage Labor, Marriage, and the Market in the Age of Slave Emancipation* (New York: Cambridge University Press, 1998); Claudia Tate, *Domestic Allegories of Political Desire: The Black Heroine's Text at the Turn of the Century* (New York: Oxford University Press, 1992), 92; Eileen Boris, "The Power of Motherhood: Black and White Activist Women Redefine the 'Political,'" in *Mothers of a New World: Maternalist Politics and the Origins of Welfare States*, ed. Seth Koven and Sonya Michel (New York: Routledge, 1993), 213–45; Evelyn Brooks Higginbotham, *Righteous Discontent: The Women's Movement of the Black Baptist Church, 1880–1920* (Cambridge, Mass.: Harvard University Press, 1993), 192, 203; Linda Gordon, "Black and White Visions of Welfare: Women's Welfare Activisms, 1890–1945," *Journal of American History* 788 (September 1991): 559–90, 579; Linda Gordon, *Pitied But Not Entitled: Single Mothers and the History of Welfare, 1890–1935* (New York: Free Press, 1994), 130, on race-specific meanings of sexual purity.

23. Gail Bederman, "'Civilization,' the Decline of Middle-Class Manliness, and Ida B. Wells's Antilynching Campaign (1892–94)," *Radical History Review* 52 (1992): 5–30, 14–15; Ida D. Wells-Barnett, *Crusade for Justice: The Autobiography of Ida B. Wells*, ed. Alfreda M. Duster (Chicago: University of Chicago Press, 1970), Higginbotham, *Righteous Discontent*, 193.

24. W. E. B. Du Bois, *The Philadelphia Negro: A Social Study. Together with a Special Report on Domestic Service*, by Isabel Eaton (1899; Philadelphia: University of Pennsylvania Press, 1996), 193.

25. Gordon, *Pitied But Not Entitled*, 126; Hazel V. Carby, *Reconstructing Womanhood: The Emergence of the Afro-American Woman Novelist* (New York: Oxford University Press, 1987), 98, 141; Molly Ladd-Taylor, *Mother-Work: Women, Child Welfare, and the State, 1890–1930* (Urbana: University of Illinois Press, 1994), 61.

26. Marion Morton, *And Sin No More: Social Policy and Unwed Mothers in Cleveland, 1855–1990* (Columbus: Ohio State University Press, 1993; Kunzel, *Fallen Women,*

Problem Girls, 71; Rickie Solinger, *Wake Up Little Susie: Single Pregnancy and Race Before Roe v. Wade* (New York: Routledge, 1992).

27. See Pascoe, *Relations of Rescue*, 69, for a study of women's institutions that recognizes conflict and cooperation between reformers and inmates; Kunzel, *Fallen Women, Problem Girls*, chap. 4, also explores this theme.

28. For a description of the neighborhood in which the Haven was located, see Maxwell Whiteman, "Philadelphia's Jewish Neighborhoods," in *The Peoples of Philadelphia: A History of Ethnic Groups and Lower-Class Life, 1790–1940*, ed. Allen F. Davis and Mark H. Haller (Philadelphia : Temple University Press, 1973; Philadelphia: University of Pennsylvania Press, 1998), 231–54, 246–47.

29. Haven, *Sixth Annual Report* (1888).

30. When the Haven for Unwed Mothers and Infants was established, the only other "infant home" in Philadelphia was the West Philadelphia Home for Infants, which could receive about thirty to forty children at a time. See SPCC, *Fifth Annual Report*, 1881 (1882), 14; *Ninth Annual Report*, 1885 (1886), 14.

31. See Ellen Smith, "Institutions: Wide and Fruitful Fields," in *Send Us a Lady Physician: Women Doctors in America, 1835–1920*, ed. Ruth J. Abram (New York: W.W. Norton, 1985), 182.

32. The agreement made with the holders of the Haven's records prohibits my stating which denomination.

33. Haven, *Twelfth Annual Report* (1894).

34. Haven, *Sixth Annual Report* (1888); *Boyd's Blue Book: A Society Directory Containing a List of the Names and Addresses of the Elite of the City of Philadelphia* (Philadelphia: Boyd Publishing Co., 1879–81).

35. See Ellen DuBois and Linda Gordon, "Seeking Ecstasy on the Battlefield: Danger and Pleasure in Nineteenth-Century Feminist Sexual Thought," in *Pleasure and Danger: Exploring Female Sexuality*, ed. Carole S. Vance (Boston: Routledge and Kegan Paul, 1984), 38, for an analysis of the conceptualization of sexuality in the nineteenth-century woman's movement; Linda Gordon, *Woman's Body, Woman's Right: A Social History of Birth Control in America* (New York: Penguin, 1975), chap. 5, on voluntary motherhood.

36. Brumberg, "'Ruined Girls,'" 254. Also see Nancy Hewitt, *Women's Activism and Social Change: Rochester, New York, 1822–1872* (Ithaca, N.Y.: Cornell University Press, 1984).

37. See Christine Stansell, *City of Women: Sex and Class in New York, 1789–1860* (New York: Knopf, 1986), 219.

38. See SPCC CR, May 8, 1878, #409, "The infant has been left with the mother temporarily, in hopes that it may be the means of bringing her to a knowledge of her situation and condition"; Charles Loring Brace, *The Dangerous Classes of New York and Twenty Years' Work Among Them* (New York: Wynkoop and Hallenbeck, 1872; Montclair, N.J.: P. Smith, 1967), 416–17; Linda Gordon, "Single Mothers and Child Neglect, 1880–1920," *American Quarterly* 37, 2 (Summer 1985): 188; SPCC, *Ninth Annual Report*, 1885 (1886), 16; Amos Griswold Warner, *American Charities: A Study in Philanthropy and Economics* (New York: Thomas Crowell and Co., 1894), 212.

39. Haven Diary, Dec. 1885, 137.

40. Karin Calvert, *Children in the House: The Material Culture of Early Childhood,*

1600–1900 (Boston: Northeastern University Press, 1992), 109.

41. SPCC Board Minutes, 1894; SPCC CR, Dec. 5, 1879, #1325; Michael Grossberg, *Governing the Hearth: Law and the Family in Nineteenth-Century America* (Chapel Hill: University of North Carolina Press, 1985), 279; Robert Bremner, *The Public Good: Philanthropy and Welfare in the Civil War Era* (New York: Knopf, 1980), 163; "Report of the Committee on the History of Child-Saving Work" in *History of Childsaving in the United States*, Twentieth National Conference of Charities and Corrections, June 1893; Elizabeth Pleck, "Feminist Responses to 'Crimes Against Women,' 1868–1896," *Signs* 8, 3 (Spring 1983): 468.

42. Morton, *And Sin No More*; Kunzel, *Fallen Women, Problem Girls*.

43. Julie Berebitsky, *Like Our Very Own: Adoption and the Changing Culture of Motherhood, 1851–1950* (Lawrence: University Press of Kansas, 2000), 9, 18, 20.

44. Haven Diary, March 25, 1886; Haven Diary, Aug. 9, 1884; Haven Diary, Jan. 13, 1885.

45. Haven Diary, Sept. 24, 1883; Haven Diary, Sept. 26, 1883; Haven Diary, July 1, 1884; Haven Diary, Aug. 15, 1884; Haven Diary, Jan. 20, 1885; Haven Diary, March 21, 1885.

46. Haven Diary, May 18, 1885.

47. Emphasis in original. See Haven Diary, Dec. 19, 1883; Haven Diary, March 19, 1884. The fewest vacancies occurred in winter and during economic downturns.

48. Haven Diary, July 2, 1884.

49. Haven House Records, 1884–1890, pp.56, 73.

50. Ruth Abrams, "Affiliations," unpublished manuscript, Urban Archives, Temple University, Philadelphia.

51. Haven House Records, Jan. 10, 1885, March 12, 1885.

52. Haven Diary, July 28, 1884.

53. Haven Diary, Sept. 6, 1884.

54. Haven Diary, January 1884.

55. See Kunzel, *Fallen Women, Problem Girls*, 87; for working-class families' use of institutions, see Barbara M. Brenzel, *Daughters of the State: A Social Portrait of the First Reform School for Girls in North America, 1856–1905* (Cambridge, Mass.: MIT Press, 1983); Stansell, *City of Women*; Steven L. Schlossman, *Love and the American Delinquent: Theory and Practice of "Progressive" Juvenile Justice, 1825–1920* (Chicago: University of Chicago Press, 1977).

56. Haven Diary, Jan. 1884; Haven Diary, Dec. 11, 1883; Haven Diary, Oct. 4, 1884.

57. Haven Diary, Aug. 28, 1883.

58. Haven Diary, June 14, 1884.

59. Haven Board Minutes, June 1891, p. 62.

60. Haven Diary, September 1, 1883; Brumberg, "'Ruined' Girls, " 258.

61. Haven Diary, April 26, 1885.

62. Haven Diary, Sept. 22, 1883; Haven Diary, January 17, 1885; Haven House Records, Dec. 30, 1884; Haven House Records, Jan. 10, 1885.

63. Haven House Records, June 30, 1885.

64. Haven House Records, April 21, 1885.

65. John K. Alexander, *Render Them Submissive: Responses to Poverty in Philadelphia, 1760–1800* (Amherst: University of Massachusetts Press, 1980); Priscilla Clement,

Welfare and the Poor in the Nineteenth-Century City: Philadelphia, 1800–1854 (Rutherford, N.J.: Fairleigh Dickinson University Press, 1985), 68; Morris Vogel, *The Invention of the Modern Hospital: Boston, 1870–1930* (Chicago: University of Chicago Press, 1980), 5.

66. Haven, Diary, June 4, 1884; Haven Diary, Feb. 1, 1885.

67. Haven House Records, Nov. 17, 1886, p.114.

68. Kunzel, *Fallen Women*, 102–12, for an excellent analysis of the tales applicants told to gain admission to maternity homes.

69. Haven Diary, May 1888.

70. See Anna Clark, *Women's Silence, Men's Violence: Sexual Assault in England, 1770–1845* (New York: Pandora, 1987), 77, on the different meaning of the term "seduction" in middle- and working-class language; Reagan, *When Abortion Was a Crime*, 32.

71. See Michael Denning, *Mechanic Accents: Dime Novels and Working-Class Culture in America* (New York: Verso, 1987), chap. 10; Joanne J. Meyerowitz, *Women Adrift: Independent Wage Earners in Chicago, 1880–1930* (Chicago: University of Chicago Press, 1985), chap. 3.

72. Meyerowitz, *Women Adrift*, 58–60.

73. Denning, *Mechanic Accents*, 191.

74. Nan Enstad, *Ladies of Labor, Girls of Adventure: Working Women, Popular Culture, and Labor Politics at the Turn of the Twentieth Century* (New York: Columbia University Press, 1999), 74.

75. Pauline E. Hopkins, *Contending Forces: A Romance Illustrative of Negro Life North and South* (1900; New York: Oxford University Press, 1988), 100–101; Du Bois, *Philadelphia Negro*, 67.

76. Carby, *Reconstructing Womanhood*, 144; Tate, *Domestic Allegories*, 161.

77. Haven Board Minutes, 1898.

78. Parry, "Infant Mortality," 24, noted "the great difficulty in procuring women willing to suckle foundlings." It is very likely that this rule was one reason that some inmates felt stigmatized by their experience at the Home. Also see Patricia T. Rooke and R. L. Schnell, *Discarding the Asylum: From Child Rescue to the Welfare State in English Canada* (Lanham, Md.: University Press of America, 1983), 119; Janet Golden, *A Social History of Wet Nursing in America: From Breast to Bottle* (New York: Cambridge University Press, 1996).

79. Haven Board Minutes, Jan. 1894, 150; Haven Board Minutes, Feb. 1895.

80. Pascoe, *Relations of Rescue*, 106 and Kunzel, *Fallen Women*, 102, for accounts of conflict in other late nineteenth-century women's institutions.

81. Haven, *Twelfth Annual Report* (1894), 11.

82. Haven Diary, Jan. 1884.

83. Haven Diary, Jan. 7, 1884.

84. Haven Diary, March 21, 26, 27, 1884. Also see Haven Diary, Dec. 28, 1883.

85. Haven Diary, April 1884.

86. Dr. Charlotte Abbey of the Women's Directory noted that if postpartum women were required to perform arduous domestic tasks they would become rebellious. See Annual Report of the Women's Directory of the City of Philadelphia, 1899, 9, and Haven Board Minutes, March 1895, 214–15.

87. See Haven Diary, June 21, 1885; Aug. 12–14, 1884. Earlier Elizabeth had caused

trouble by her refusal to nurse a black child. She returned to the Home seeking work, however, possibly as a laundress if not as a wetnurse. See Haven Diary, Jan. 22, 1885.

88. Pascoe, *Relations*, 79; Meyerowitz, *Women Adrift*.

89. Haven Diary, June 1896; Haven Board Minutes, April 1890.

90. Haven Diary, September 1883.

91. Haven Diary, 1884; Haven Board Minutes, May 1897, p. 281.

92. Haven Board Minutes, February 1894, p. 165; Haven Board Minutes, June 1898.

93. Haven Diary, June 29, 1885; Haven House Records, March 9, 1888; Haven Diary, June 4, 1884.

94. Haven House Records, June 8, 1885, 93; Haven Diary, April 28, 1884; Haven Diary, Dec. 8, 1884; Haven House Records, Feb. 17, 1885; Haven House Records, Feb. 24, 1888.

95. Elizabeth Clark-Lewis, *Living In, Living Out: African American Domestics in Washington, D.C., 1910–1940* (Washington, D.C.: Smithsonian Institution Press, 1994), 48–49; Faye E. Dudden, *Serving Women: Household Service in Nineteenth-Century America* (Middletown, Conn.: Wesleyan University Press, 1983), 206–19; Barbara Meil Hobson, *Uneasy Virtue: The Politics of Prostitution and the American Reform Tradition* (New York: Basic Books, 1987), chap. 5, and Pascoe, *Relations of Rescue*, 171, for a discussion of the reform strategy of placing inmates as domestic servants. Although reformers believed that domestic service provided a sheltered work environment for women who had already become unwed mothers, domestic servants were disproportionately represented among women who became pregnant out of wedlock. See U.S. Senate, *Report on Condition of Women and Child Wage Earners*, vol. 15, *Relation between Occupation and Criminality of Women*, (Wash. D.C.: Government Printing Office, 1911), 86–87.

96. Haven Diary, Feb. 21,1884.

97. Haven Diary, Dec. 1886.

98. Pascoe, *Relations of Rescue*, 149, 151.

99. Haven Board Minutes, Feb. 1898, pp. 296–97.

100. Haven Diary, Nov. 10, 1884; Haven Diary, June 1892; Haven House Records, Nov. 6, 1885.

101. Russell Conwell's speech Acre of Diamonds is quoted in Henry F. May, *Protestant Churches and Industrial America* (1949; New York: Octagon Books, 1963), 199–200. See Haven, *Twelfth Annual Report* (1884), 11.

Chapter 5. Murderous Mothers and Mercenary Baby Farmers?

1. SPCC CR, July 29, 1879, #1080, #877.

2. SPCC, *Third Annual Report*, 1879 (1880); SPCC CR, July 29, 1879, #1080. See Viviana Zelizer, *Pricing the Priceless Child: The Changing Social Value of Children* (New York: Basic Books, 1985), 115–27, on working-class mourning rituals and the controversy over children's life insurance policies; Jacob Riis, *Children of the Poor* (1892; New York: Johnson Reprint Corporation, 1970), 24, on working-class mourning rituals in New York City. Mourning rituals were an important part of ethnic and working-class culture in poor neighborhoods. See Karen Halttunen, *Confidence Men and Painted*

Women: A Study of Middle Class Culture in America, 1830–1870 (New Haven, Conn.: Yale University Press, 1982), chap. 5, 124–52 for a discussion of middle-class mourning in Victorian America; George Behlmer, *Child Abuse and Moral Reform in England, 1870–1908* (Stanford, Calif.: Stanford University Press, 1982), 120, and Ellen Ross, "'Not the Sort That Would Sit on the Doorstep': Respectability in Pre-World War I London Neighborhoods," *International Labor and Working Class History* (Spring 1985): 46, on working-class mourning in Victorian England.

3. Behlmer, *Child Abuse and Moral Reform*, 25, notes that the use of the term multiplied in England in 1867. The term baby farming was in use in the United States by at least the 1850s; by the 1870s it was widely used although generally placed in quotation marks in printed sources.

4. Dr. John Parry, "Infant Mortality and the Necessity of a Foundling Hospital in Philadelphia," paper read to the Philadelphia Social Science Association, May 5, 1871, 9. Pamphlet Collection, Urban Archives, Temple University, Philadelphia.

5. SPCC, *Seventh Annual Report*, 1883 (1884), 19.

6. SPCC, *First Annual Report*, 1877 (1878), 36.

7. Anna Julia Cooper, *A Voice from the South* (1892; New York: Oxford University Press, 1988), 248–49.

8. David I. Macleod, *The Age of the Child: Children in America 1890–1920* (New York: Twayne Publishers, 1998), 40; Samuel H. Preston and Michael R. Haines, *Fatal Years: Child Mortality in Late Nineteenth-Century America* (Princeton, N.J.: Princeton University Press, 1991), 86, 146, 159.

9. George G. Bradford, "Reports from the City of Washington," in "Mortality Among Negroes in Cities," *Atlanta University Publications* 1 (1896): 15–16; Cooper, *A Voice from the South*, 248–49; Eileen Boris, "The Power of Motherhood: Black and White Activist Women Redefine the 'Political,'" in *Mothers of a New World: Maternalist Politics and the Origins of Welfare States*, ed. Seth Koven and Sonya Michel (New York: Routledge, 1993), 213–45, 216.

10. Parry, "Infant Mortality," 15. See Roger Lane, *Violent Death in the City: Suicide, Accident, and Murder in Nineteenth-Century Philadelphia* (Cambridge, Mass.: Harvard University Press, 1979), 90–91, 98–99, on legal sanctions against infanticide and the slim number of convictions in Philadelphia.

11. Parry, "Infant Mortality," 10–13. For discussions of infanticide and abandonment see Nancy Scheper-Hughes, *Death Without Weeping: The Violence of Everyday Life in Brazil* (Berkeley: University of California Press, 1992); Rachel G. Fuchs, *Poor and Pregnant in Paris: Strategies for Survival in the Nineteenth Century* (New Brunswick, N.J.: Rutgers University Press, 1992), chap. 9; Fuchs, *Abandoned Children: Foundlings and Child Welfare in Nineteenth-Century France* (Albany, N.Y.: SUNY Press, 1984); Paul Gilje, "Infant Abandonment in Early Nineteenth-Century New York City: Three Cases," in *Growing Up in America: Children in Historical Perspective*, ed. N. Ray Hiner and Joseph M. Hawes (Urbana: University of Illinois Press, 1985), 109–17; Linda Gordon, *Woman's Body, Woman's Right: A Social History of Birth Control in America* (New York: Penguin, 1975), 32–35, 49–51; Peter C. Hoffer and N. E. H. Hull, *Murdering Mothers: Infanticide in England and New England, 1558–1803* (New York: New York University Press, 1981).

12. Parry, "Infant Mortality," 5. See Haven House Records, 1882, 101; Haven

House Records, Nov. 30, 1888; Haven House Records, 1883, 113; Gretchen Condran, Henry Williams, and Rose A. Cheney, "The Decline in Mortality in Philadelphia from 1870 to 1930: The Role of Municipal Services," *Pennsylvania Magazine of History and Biography* 108, 2 (April 1984): 155–57; Joyce Antler and Daniel M. Fox, "The Movement Toward a Safe Maternity: Physician Accountability in New York City, 1915–1940," in *Sickness and Health in America: Readings in the History of Medicine and Public Health*, ed. Judith Walzer Leavitt and Ronald L. Numbers (Madison: University of Wisconsin Press, 1978), 375–92. Infant mortality statistics for the city of Philadelphia as a whole hide the extent to which infant mortality rates varied in different neighborhoods and differed according to the variables of class, race, and marital status of the mother.

13. Lane, *Violent Death*, 99–100.

14. Lane, *Violent Death*, 99.

15. Philadelphia Society for Organizing Charitable Relief and Repressing Mendicancy, *Manual for Visitors Among the Poor* (Philadelphia: J.B. Lippincott and Co., 1879), 33.

16. In Parry's examination of coroner's inquests in Philadelphia from November 1863 to October 31, 1866 and from November 1869 to March 31, 1871, race is used as a category but the number of inquests is too small to be a reliable indicator of causes of infant mortality in Philadelphia. Also see the 1879 life tables for Baltimore and Washington, D.C., in U.S. Bureau of the Census, *Mortality and Vital Statistics, 1880* (Washington, D.C.: Government Printing Office, 1883), pt. 2, 773–77, for differential mortality by race. In *The Free Black in Urban America, 1800–1850: The Shadow of the Dream* (Chicago: University of Chicago Press, 1981), 143, Leonard P. Curry notes that in Washington, D.C. and Charleston blacks made up 2/5–2/3 of those whose deaths were attributed to unknown causes.

17. Lane, *Violent Death*, 110.

18. Fuchs, *Poor and Pregnant in Paris*, 202.

19. *Public Ledger*, January 17, 1877.

20. *Public Ledger*, February 28, 1877.

21. *Public Ledger*, January 15, 1877.

22. Haven House Records, 1885–1890, esp. April 29, 1888.

23. Haven House Records, April 29, 1888;. see also Haven House Records, March 8, 1889.

24. Harry Dowling, *City Hospitals: The Undercare of the Underprivileged* (Cambridge, Mass.: Harvard University Press, 1982), 81, Regina Morantz-Sanchez, *Sympathy and Science: Women Physicians in American Medicine* (New York: Oxford University Press, 1985), 226; David Rosner, *A Once Charitable Enterprise: Hospitals and Health Care in Brooklyn, New York, 1885–1915* (New York: Cambridge University Press, 1980); Morris Vogel, *The Invention of the Modern Hospital: Boston, 1870–1930* (Chicago: University of Chicago Press, 1980), 1; Richard Wertz and Dorothy Wertz, *Lying-In: A History of Childbirth in America* (New York: Free Press, 1977); Parry, "Infant Mortality," 8.

25. Amos Griswold Warner, *American Charities: A Study in Philanthropy and Economics* (New York: Thomas Crowell and Co., 1894), 68, 204–6. The link between illegitimacy and high infant mortality rates persists today. Historian George Sussman found a similar correlation in nineteenth-century France. See Sussman, "The

End of the Wet-Nursing Business in France, 1874–1914," in *Family and Sexuality in French History*, ed. Roger Wheaton and Tamara K. Hareven (Philadelphia: University of Pennsylvania Press, 1980), 245, and Sussman, *Selling Mothers' Milk: The Wetnursing Business in France, 1715–1914* (Urbana: University of Illinois Press, 1982).

26. Ross, "'Not the Sort That Would Sit on the Doorstep,'" 45, on premarital pregnancy in nineteenth-century London; John Gillis, *For Better, For Worse: British Marriages, 1600 to the Present* (New York: Oxford University Press, 1985).

27. Haven Diary, Nov. 12, 1883; Haven House Records, Nov. 1887.

28. Haven Diary, 1883–1887, Sept. 10, 1884. Also see Haven House Records, 1884, 147.

29. An example recorded in the records of the Society to Protect Children from Cruelty documents how the loss of respectability due to the birth of an illegitimate child could serve to label a woman and her children as unworthy of financial assistance. See SPCC CR, Oct. 28, 1896, #15817.

30. Haven Diary, Nov. 3, 1884.

31. Haven Diary, 1883–1887, May 12, 1884.

32. Haven House Records, 1884, p. 119.

33. Haven House Records, Nov. 5, 1885, p. 52.

34. Haven House Records, Feb. 2, 1885.

35. See Christine Stansell, *City of Women: Sex and Class in New York, 1789–1860* (New York: Knopf, 1986), 56–57, on the backfiring of various forms of mutual aid. For a discussion of con games and crime in nineteenth-century Philadelphia, see David R. Johnson,"Crime Patterns in Philadelphia, 1840–70," in *The Peoples of Philadelphia*, ed. Allen F. Davis and Mark H. Haller (1973; Philadelphia: University of Pennsylvania Press, 1998), 89–110. Roger Lane discusses strategies of abandonment in *Violent Death*, 95.

36. Haven Diary, March 15, 1885, and June 18, 1885.

37. Haven House Records, March 5, 1885, p. 18.

38. Haven House Records., Oct 8, 1887.

39. Haven House Records, Aug. 30, 1887, p. 147.

40. Haven House Records,1882, p. 65; Haven House Records,1883, p. 109; Haven Diary, April 3, 1885.

41. Haven House Records, April 22, 1885.

42. Haven House Records, Oct. 21, 1887; Haven Diary, Jan. 2, 1884.

43. Haven House Records, Aug. 7, 1885, 39; Haven House Records, Jan. 8, 1882.

44. Haven Diary, Nov. 3, 1885; Haven Diary, Oct. 26, 1884.

45. *Fifth Annual Report of the Women's Directory of Philadelphia* (Philadelphia, January 1898), 6–7; Parry, "Infant Mortality." See also Virginia Quiroga, *Poor Mothers and Babies: A Social History of Childbirth and Childcare Hospitals in Nineteenth Century New York City* (New York: Garland, 1989). For a discussion of foundling homes in nineteenth-century Italy, see David Kertzer, *Sacrificed for Honor: Italian Infant Abandonment and the Politics of Reproductive Control* (Boston: Beacon Press, 1993.) For a discussion of European social policies toward foundlings, see Fuchs, *Abandoned Children*; Rosalind Petchesky, *Abortion and Woman's Choice* (Boston: Northeastern University Press, 1985); and John Gillis, "Servants, Sexual Relations and the Risks of Illegitimacy in

London, 1801–1900," in *Sex and Class in Women's History*, ed. Judith Newton, Mary Ryan, and Judith Walkowitz (Boston: Routledge and Kegan Paul, 1983).

46. *First Annual Report of the Women's Directory of Philadelphia* (Philadelphia, 1894), 5; Warner, *American Charities*, 204–6; Charles Loring Brace, *The Dangerous Classes of New York and Twenty Years' Work Among Them* (New York: Wynkoop and Hallenbeck, 1872), 416–17; Janet Golden, *A Social History of Wet Nursing in America: From Breast to Bottle* (New York: Cambridge University Press, 1996), 113–16.

47. Priscilla Clement, *Welfare and the Poor in the Nineteenth-Century City: Philadelphia, 1800–1854* (Rutherford, N.J. : Fairleigh Dickinson University Press, 1985), 120; Lane, *Violent Death*, 95. In 1883 Pennsylvania passed a law that prohibited the retention of children between the ages of two and sixteen years in poorhouses (unless "feeble-minded or defective") for a period of longer than sixty days. See Homer Folks, *The Care of Destitute, Neglected, and Delinquent Children* (1900; New York: Arno Reprints, 1971), 49; SPCC CR, 1893, #13298.

48. Claudia Goldin, "Family Strategies and the Family Economy in the Late Nineteenth Century: The Role of Secondary Workers," in *Philadelphia: Work, Space, Family, and Group Experience in the Nineteenth Century*, ed. Theodore Hershberg (New York: Oxford University Press, 1981), 281; Michael Haines, "Poverty, Economic Stress, and the Family in a Late Nineteenth-Century American City: Whites in Philadelphia, 1880," in *Philadelphia*, ed. Hershberg, 244, 261.

49. Haines, "Poverty," 266; John Modell, Frank Furstenberg, Jr., and Theodore Hershberg, "Social Change and Transitions to Adulthood in Historical Perspective," in *Philadelphia*, ed. Hershberg, 335; Goldin, "Family Strategies," 284.

50. Haven Diary, Sept. 17, 1884.

51. Sonya Michel, "The Limits of Maternalism: Policies Toward American Wage-Earning Mothers During the Progressive Era," in *Mothers of a New World: Maternalist Politics and the Origins of Welfare States*, ed. Seth Koven and Sonya Michel (New York: Routledge, 1993), 277–320, 282, and Sonya Michel, *Children's Interests/Mothers' Rights: The Shaping of America's Child Care Policy* (New Haven, Conn.: Yale University Press, 1999); Elizabeth Rose, *A Mother's Job: The History of Day Care, 1890–1960* (New York: Oxford University Press, 1998).

52. See Ellen Smith, "Institutions: Wide and Fruitful Fields, " in *"Send Us a Lady Physician": Women Doctors in America, 1835–1920*, ed. Ruth Abrams (New York: W.W. Norton, 1985), 188; Susan Porter, *Engendering Benevolence: Orphan Asylums in Antebellum America* (Baltimore: Johns Hopkins University Press, forthcoming).

53. Haven Diary, Sept. 29, 1884, July 24, 1884, and Jan. 9, 1884.

54. See Louisa May Alcott, *Work* (1873, New York: Schocken Books, 1977), 139.

55. Golden, *A Social History of Wet Nursing*, 98.

56. Janet Golden, "Trouble in the Nursery: Physicians, Families, and Wet Nurses at the End of the Nineteenth Century," in *"To Toil the Livelong Day": America's Women at Work*, ed. Carol Groneman and Mary Beth Norton (Ithaca, N.Y.: Cornell University Press, 1987), 125–37; Harvey Levenstein, "'Best for Babies' or 'Preventable Infanticide'? The Controversy over Artificial Feeding of Infants in America, 1880–1920," *Journal of American History* 70 (June 1983): 75–94; S. Rima Apple, "'To Be Used Only Under the Direction of a Physician': Commercial Infant Feeding and

Medical Practice, 1870–1940," *Bulletin of the History of Medicine* 54 (Fall 1980): 402–17; Patricia T. Rooke and R. L. Schnell, *Discarding the Asylum: From Child Rescue to the Welfare State in English Canada* (Lanham, Md.: University Press of America, 1983), 118–19.

57. Haven Diary, Jan. 14, 1884.

58. This discussion is based on Golden, *A Social History of Wet Nursing.*

59. SPCC CR, Dec. 11, 1896, #15911.

60. SPCC CR, Dec. 11, 1896, #15911.

61. See Patricia Hill Collins, "Black Women and Motherhood," in *Rethinking the Family: Some Feminist Questions,* ed. Barrie Thorne and Marilyn Yalom (Boston: Northeastern University Press, 1992), 215–45, for a discussion of traditions of informal adoption in African American communities in the United States; Dorothy E. Roberts, "Mothers Who Fail to Protect Their Children: Accounting for Private and Public Responsibility," in *Mother Troubles: Rethinking Contemporary Maternal Dilemmas,* ed. Julia E. Hanigsberg and Sara Ruddick (Boston: Beacon Press, 1999), 31–49, 42–43.

62. SPCC CR, Oct. 14, 1893, #13209.

63. SPCC CR, 1896, #15698.

64. SPCC CR, Oct. 1893, #13212.

65. Even trusted relatives who provided childcare could occasionally deceive a mother. See Haven House Records, May 13, 1885, p. 39, "Jacob S. was taken away by his mother Kate S.— This child was placed with the woman's step-mother to board, but she having two other children to support could give but a mite toward the baby's maintenance, so the step-mother unknown to the mother brought the child here."

66. SPCC CR, May 4, 1893, #12721, and #6824. See Ellen Ross, *Love and Toil: Motherhood in Outcast London, 1870–1918* (New York: Oxford University Press, 1993), 135–36, on baby farming in Victorian and Edwardian London as an alternative to taking in laundry or doing daily charring, generally engaged in by widows or older women with grown children.

67. Rima D. Apple, *Mothers and Medicine: A Social History of Infant Feeding, 1890–1950* (Madison: University of Wisconsin Press), 7.

68. Parry, "Infant Mortality," 26–28.

69. David I. Macleod, *The Age of the Child: Children in America, 1890–1920* (New York: Twayne Publishers, 1998), 41; Samuel H. Preston and Michael R. Haines, *Fatal Years: Child Mortality in Late Nineteenth-Century America* (Princeton, N.J.: Princeton University Press, 1991); Richard A. Meckel, *Save the Babies: American Public Health and the Prevention of Infant Mortality, 1850–1929* (Baltimore: Johns Hopkins University Press, 1990).

70. Parry, "Infant Mortality," 8–9; Golden, "Trouble in the Nursery," 135.

71. Helen Campbell, with Thomas Knox, and Thomas Byrnes, *Darkness and Daylight, or Lights and Shadows of New York Life* (Hartford, Conn.: A.D. Worthington and Co., Hartford Publishing Co., 1899), 140.

72. *First Annual Report of the Women's Directory of Philadelphia* (Philadelphia, 1894), 11.

73. Haven House Records, Sept. 9, 1884, "One woman called to get a deserted infant in as she had taken it to board and then the mother deserted it."

74. Haven Diary, Jan. 5, 1885.

75. Haven Diary, Sept. 24, 1884.

76. Haven House Records, April 22, 1885, p. 25.

77. Haven House Records, Dec. 10, 1881, p. 18; Allen Steinberg, *The Transformation of Criminal Justice: Philadelphia, 1800–1880* (Chapel Hill: University of North Carolina Press, 1992), 20.

78. Haven Diary, Feb. 9, 1884, 35.

79. SPCC, *Seventh Annual Report*,1883 (1884), 19. See Howard O. Sprogle, *The Philadelphia Police: Past and Present* (Philadelphia, 1887; New York: AMS Press, 1974), 290.

80. SPCC *Seventh Annual Report*, 20.

81. *Public Ledger*, June 1896.

82. SPCC CR, July 2, 1896, #15505.

83. SPCC CR, 1877, #183.

84. Haven HR, Dec. 10, 1885, 56.

85. SPCC CR, Sept. 3, 1877, #183, p.191.

86. SPCC CR 1896, #59111.

87. See Anna L. Tsing, "Monster Stories: Women Charged with Perinatal Endangerment," in *Uncertain Terms: Negotiating Gender in American Culture*, ed. Faye Ginsburg and Anna L. Tsing (Boston: Beacon Press, 1990), 282–99, on contemporary constructions of nonassisted childbirth and charges of medical noncompliance. Also see Ross, *Love and Toil*, 172, for a discussion of working-class attitudes toward medical treatment of infants in Victorian London.

88. SPCC, *Ninth Annual Report*, 1885 (1886), 8.

89. SPCC CR, 1893; also see SPCC CR, 1896, #59111, in which Emma, a baby farmer under investigation after the death of a child in her home, told the coroner that she had called a doctor and that there was nothing amiss.

90. Behlmer, *Child Abuse and Moral Reform*, 33, cited 34. The opposition to the regulation of baby farms paralleled opposition to the regulation of prostitution, although the baby farm bills did not provoke as sustained an opposition as the Contagious Diseases Acts did. In the U.S., reformers opposed to the regulation of prostitution supported the regulation of baby farming. For legislation in France, see Sussman, "The End of the Wetnursing Business in France," 224–52.

91. SPCC CR 1896, #15698.

92. Ellen Ross, "Labour and Love : Rediscovering London's Working-Class Mothers, 1870–1918," in *Labour and Love: Women's Experience of Home and Family, 1850–1940*, ed. Jane Lewis (New York: Blackwell, 1986), 83.

93. Ross, "Labour and Love," 83: "Crowds of women mobbed and hooted women accused of starving 'farmed-out' infants when they appeared in court, and extra police guards were sometimes required."

94. For a discussion of adoption in the nineteenth century, see Michael Grossberg, *Governing the Hearth: Law and Family in Nineteenth-Century America* (Chapel Hill: University of North Carolina Press, 1985); Zelizer, *Pricing the Priceless Child*; Julie Berebitsky, *Like Our Very Own: Adoption and the Changing Culture of Motherhood, 1851–1950* (Lawrence: University of Kansas Press, 2000); and Jamil Zinaldin, "Child Exchange in Boston: The Origins of Modern Adoption, 1851–1900," PhD dissertation, University of Chicago, 1976.

95. Also see Leslie J. Reagan, *When Abortion Was a Crime: Women, Medicine, and Law*

in the United States, 1867–1973 (Berkeley: University of California Press, 1997), 52, on the variety of reproductive services provided by midwives.

96. Women's Directory, *Sixth Annual Report* (1899), 10.

97. Women's Directory, *Sixth Annual Report*, 11.

98. SPCC, *Seventeenth Annual Report*, 1893 (1894), 20.

99. Women's Directory, *Sixth Annual Report*, 11; SPCC CR 1901, # 19640. Advertisements were listed in the *Item* and the *Stern*, a German newspaper. For an investigation of baby farming in New York in 1905, see Linda Gordon, *Heroes of Their Own Lives: The Politics and History of Family Violence* (New York: Viking, 1988), 44–45.

100. SPCC, *Ninth Annual Report*, 1885 (1886), 24.

101. SPCC CR, 1901, #19640; SPCC, *Twenty-Fifth Annual Report*, 1901 (1902), 30.

102. SPCC, *Twenty-Fifth Annual Report*, 29.

103. SPCC, *Twenty-Fifth Annual Report*, 30.

104. SPCC CR, 1893, #13298.

105. Women's Directory. *Sixth Annual Report*, 8.

106. SPCC, *Ninth Annual Report*, 1885 (1886), 24. See SPCC CR 1893, # 12724, for the case of a woman charged with "performing a criminal opperation" [sic] who also ran a lying-in home; Golden, *A Social History of Wet Nursing*, 76, on lying-in homes.

107. Daniel Scott Smith, "Family Limitation, Sexual Control, and Domestic Feminism," in *A Heritage of Her Own: Toward a New Social History of American Women,* ed. Nancy Cott and Elizabeth Pleck (New York: Simon and Schuster, 1979), 226.

108. Golden, "Trouble," 133, 135.

109. Mary Poovey, *Uneven Developments: The Ideological Work of Gender in Mid-Victorian England* (Chicago: University of Chicago Press, 1988), 144.

110. Tsing, "Monster Stories," 283.

111. See Eileen Boris, *Home to Work: Motherhood and the Politics of Industrial Homework in the United States* (New York: Cambridge University Press, 1994), 114.

112. James Sylvis, ed., *The Life, Speeches, Labors, and Essays of William H. Sylvis* (Philadelphia: Claxton, Remsen, and Haffelfinger, 1872), 208–9; Isaac Sturgeon, Testimony of Issac Sturgeon, *U.S. Senate Report of the Committee of the Senate upon the Relations between Labor and Capital, and Testimony Taken by the Committee, between Labor and Capital*, 2: 393–94.

113. Parry, "Infant Mortality," 26–28; Hugh Hodge, *Foeticide or Criminal Abortion* (Philadelphia, 1869). Doctors did not form a monolithic bloc; see Morantz-Sanchez, *Sympathy and Science: Women Physicians in American Medicine* (New York: Oxford University Press, 1985) for an account of differences within the nineteenth-century medical profession; William Leach, *True Love and Perfect Union* (New York: Basic Books, 1980), 297–99, 323 on the American Social Science Association, and 319 on the Philadelphia Social Science Association, which apparently had no female members.

114. Parry, "Infant Mortality," 26–28.

115. Carroll Smith-Rosenberg, *Disorderly Conduct: Visions of Gender in Victorian America* (New York: Knopf, 1985), 221; Reagan, *When Abortion Was a Crime*, 58; Hodge, *Foeticide or Criminal Abortion*.

116. Hodge, *Foeticide*, 30–32.

117. Helen Miller, "Foeticide," thesis submitted to the Woman's Medical College of Pennsylvania, 1884 and Mary V. Mitchell, "Infanticide—Its Moral and Legal

Aspects," thesis submitted to the Woman's Medical College of Pennsylvania, 1884; John D'Emilio and Estelle Freedman, *Intimate Matters: A History of Sexuality in America* (New York: Harper and Row, 1988), 146–47; Cynthia Eagle Russett, *Sexual Science: The Victorian Construction of Womanhood* (Cambridge, Mass.: Harvard University Press, 1989), 116–25; Rosalind Rosenberg, *Beyond Separate Spheres: Intellectual Roots of Modern Feminism* (New Haven, Conn.: Yale University Press, 1982), 1–28, for discussions of the scientific debate over women's reproductive health and higher education in the late nineteenth century.

118. Haven Board Minutes, Oct. 1892, 109; SPCC, *Fifth Annual Report* 1881 (1882), 14–15.

119. See Molly Ladd-Taylor and Lauri Umansky, eds., *"Bad" Mothers: The Politics of Blame in Twentieth-Century America* (New York: New York University Press, 1997) and Roberts, "Mothers Who Fail," 31–49, for an examination of this phenomenon in the twentieth century.

Conclusion

1. Women's Committee of One Hundred, *New York Times* advertisement, August 8, 1995; Gara La Marche, "Compassionate Aversionism," *The Nation* 272, 18 (May 7, 2001): 27–32.

2. Dorothy E. Roberts, *Killing the Black Body: Race, Reproduction, and the Meaning of Liberty* (New York: Pantheon, 1997); Roberts, "Welfare's Ban on Poor Motherhood,"152–67, 152 and Gwendolyn Mink, "Aren't Poor Single Mothers Women? Feminists, Welfare Reform, and Welfare Justice," both in *Whose Welfare*, ed. Mink (Ithaca, N.Y.: Cornell University Press, 1999), 171–88.

3. Roberts, "Welfare's Ban," 157, 164; Martha Albertson Fineman, *The Neutered Mother, the Sexual Family, and Other Twentieth Century Tragedies* (New York: Routledge, 1995), 178.

4. Diane Dujon and Ann Withorn, eds., *For Crying Out Loud: Women's Poverty in the United States* (Boston: South End Press, 1996).

5. Roberts, "Welfare's Ban," 153.

6. Frances Olsen, "The Myth of State Intervention in the Family," in *Family Matters: Readings of Family Lives and the Law*, ed. Martha Minow (New York: New Press, 1993), 277–82.

7. Julia E. Hanigsberg and Sara Ruddick, "Introduction," in *Mother Troubles: Rethinking Contemporary Maternal Dilemmas*, ed. Hanigsberg and Ruddick (Boston: Beacon Press, 1999), xi; Dorothy E. Roberts, "Mothers Who Fail to Protect Their Children: Accounting for Private and Public Responsibility," in *Mother Troubles*, ed. Hanigsberg and Ruddick, 31–49, 47.

Index

to, 3, 12, 23–24, 48; childhood norms and, 37–39, 104–5, 194; children's wages, 21, 39, 46–47, 103–5, 108–10; class and, 77, 193; as destructive, 193; domestic disputes, 84–85, 90–93, 94–103; domesticity and respectabil-ity, 55, 57, 75; economic inequality of life, 193–94; erosion and disintegration of, 1–4, 16, 72; female-headed households, 93–94, 227n16; gender roles in, 7–8, 16–17, 21, 25–26, 92–95, 135; historical study of, 7–8, 12–13; incest and, 72–73; kin ties and chil-drearing, 178–79; labor movement and, 2–4, 11–13, 49–50, 134–35, 193–94; marriage and, 113, 130–33, 154, 168; normative view of, 49–50; parent-child relations, 38–40, 103–10; parenting, 37–38, 77–78, 104–5; pre-sent-day, 202; privacy issues, 64, 66; public lifestyles, 63–64; reformers' view separat-ing, 81–83; reformers' views of, 1–6, 11–13, 16, 37–39, 49–50, 72, 81–83, 134–35, 193; and reform intervention, 89, 123–24, 207n1; resi-dence patterns, 59–60, 62; self-representa-tions and negotiation of, 5–6, 7–8, 87, 89–92, 92, 124; separation of, 81–83; sexual attitudes, 112–13; social science view of, 100–101; and stability of Republic, 11–12; threats to, 11–13; unwed mothers excluded, 175; values of, 92; views of threats to, 11–13; wage earners in, 15, 21, 93–94, 174–75; women's rights efforts, 134–35. *See also* African Americans; immigrants and immigrant families

Family Story Paper, 147
family wage, 193–94
Fee, Elizabeth, 100
Fireside Companion, 147
Foeticide (Hodge), 194
Fones-Wolf, Kenneth, 86
"Fortunes of a Street Waif" (Brace), 41–44
Foster, George G. "Gaslight," 60, 128
foundlings: desertion locations, 170–73; at Haven, 138–40, 141, 149, 167–73; health of, 168; hospital births, 167–68; infant survival, 170–71; naming of, 169, 170; and policies of reformers, 173. *See also* child abandonment

gender roles: class and, 25–26, 134–35; girls and boys, 92; Haven highlighting of, 134–35, 143; husbands and wives, 92–95; as innate, 25–26; labor and, 13, 19–20, 33–34, 193–94; of men, 16–17, 25–26, 92–93, 135; provider roles, 21; racialization of, 26; reformers' view of, 16–17, 21, 27, 94–95; of women, 16–17, 21, 25–26, 34, 90–95, 135, 166; in working-class family, 7–8, 16–17, 21, 25–26, 92–95, 135

Gingrich, Newt, 202
girls: gender roles, 92; incest and dutiful daughterhood, 120–21; institutionalization of, 116; portents of future immorality, 112; and prostitution of mothers, 70–71, 117–18; reformers' roles in protecting, 118–20; and sexual abuse, 118, 120; and sexual propri-ety, 110–17, 229n72; use of SPCC, 117–18, 124; wages of, 109–10. *See also* child labor; children, working-class
Gordon, Linda, 113, 117, 119, 120, 207n4, 230n93
Great Railroad Strike of 1877, 14
Guardians of the Poor, 173–74, 190
Gunton, George, 63

Hamilton, Alice, 18–19, 125
Haven. *See* Haven for Unwed Mothers and Infants
Haven for Unwed Mothers and Infants: admission decisions, 138–41, 143–46, 173, 175; as adoption agency, 138; African American women at, 141, 152–53; appli-cants to, 143–46, 175; baby farmers and, 181–82, 184–85, 191; case records of, 7, 169–73; charity supporters of, 135–36, 141; child abandonment at, 167–73, 181–82; and class conflict, 134–35, 143; and class con-tact, sisterhood, 135, 137; conflicts between inmates and staff, 149–51; demands made on, 139–40; departing inmates, 153–55; deserted and abused women in, 144–45, 175, 226n10; discharges and expulsions, 150–52; and domesticity, 137, 149–51; domestic servants, 137, 146, 154; establish-ment of, 134–35, 234n30; failures of, 133–34, 150, 152, 155; fees for, 181; foundlings at, 138–40, 141, 149, 167–73; gender roles and, 134–35, 143; goals of, 133–35, 143; illegiti-macy and, 155, 168–69, 175; infanticide per-spective, 135, 138; inmates mending reputations, 142; inmates' perceptions of, 149–50, 153–54; institutional life at, 148–53; labor movement and, 134–35; Lady Man-agers, 136, 143, 144, 145–46, 147, 149, 150–51, 152–53, 154, 182; medical care at, 141; and motherhood, bond of, 134, 137–39, 143; mothers and babies kept together, 137–40, 173, 175; name of, 208n5; and Philadelphia charity network, 136; prosti-tution concerns, 137, 144; racial tensions at, 141, 152–53; rebellion and misconduct at, 148, 151–52; redemptive maternity, 135, 138, 140–41, 150, 155; reform strategy of, 134–38, 148–53; religious conversion at, 139; as resource for women, 197;

Acknowledgments

It is a pleasure to acknowledge those whose help and encouragement have enabled me to research and write this book. My parents, Irwin and Ruth Broder, first encouraged my interest in history as a child, taking family trips to historical sites in New Jersey and—on hot humid days before air conditioning was ubiquitous—to the Paterson Falls, where dyes from the silk mills used to color the spray from the waterfalls when the mills were still running. Their interest in telling and retelling our family stories and in the history and ongoing communal life of the Jewish community of Passaic, New Jersey when I was a child sparked my own curiosity about the intertwined social histories of people from diverse backgrounds. Janice Broder and Michael Broder have long supported my writing, reading chapters and offering suggestions and encouragement regarding this and other aspects of my life. Alfreda Natowicz and David Natowicz offered enthusiastic encouragement while I prepared the manuscript for publication.

My oldest intellectual debts are to the remarkable group of scholars in the School of Social Science at Hampshire College in Amherst, Massachusetts in the 1970s, where I spent my undergraduate years. I have vivid memories of being one of a small group of students from a class in Capitalism and Empire crowded into Laurie Nisonoff's office, engaged in a lively discussion of Alice Clark's *Working Life of Women in the Seventeenth Century* and Ivy Pinchbeck's *Women Workers and the Industrial Revolution, 1750–1850* in a period when these early works of women's history were not widely available and the very notion of the economic contribution of women as a subject worthy of study was open to debate. In these years Margaret Cerullo, Joan Landes, Laurie Nisonoff, Miriam Slater, and Anson Rabinbach encouraged me to think of myself as a historian and pursue graduate work in history. At Brown University, I benefited from the creative scholarship of Mari Jo Buhle, Joan Scott, and John Thomas. Each offered thoughtful comments and astute guidance throughout the process of researching and writing a dissertation, while challenging me to meet their high standards of scholarship. Joan Scott encouraged me to continue writing and revising during a period when I was consumed by other obligations.

From 1994 through 2001 the Women's Studies Research Center at Brandeis University provided me with a congenial and stimulating home and engagement with a lively and supportive group of scholars.

Gail Bederman, Andrew Buni, Wendy Chmieleweski, Kenneth Fones-Wolf, Janet Golden, Sandra Hackman, Nancy Hewitt, Ann Holder, Regina Kunzel, Barbara Machtinger, Martha Nichols, Susan Porter, Nancy Palmer, and Miriam Slater read individual chapters and in some cases, the entire manuscript. I thank them for their insightful comments and suggestions about both content and style. Susan Porter generously shared her own work on nineteenth-century social welfare institutions for children with me, meeting to exchange chapters and advice.

I could not have completed the research for this book without the guidance and friendship of archivists. Ken Fones-Wolf, the late Fred Miller, and David Weinburg, all formerly of the Urban Archives at Temple University in Philadelphia, made me welcome while I pored over crumbling volumes from the Pennsylvania Society to Protect Children from Cruelty. Ken Fones-Wolf kindly shared his own compelling work on the Philadelphia labor movement and showed me where to look for archival material on the Philadelphia labor press in the Gilded Age.

I was fortunate to receive a number of grants and fellowships while working on this project. I am grateful to the American Historical Association for a Littleton-Griswold fellowship, the Woodrow Wilson National Fellowship Foundation for the Charlotte W. Newcombe and Woodrow Wilson Women's Studies fellowships, and for a Boston College Faculty Research Grant that provided support for a summer.

The Urban Archives of the Temple University Libraries in Philadelphia, the Philadelphia Society for Services to Children, and the Philadelphia Jewish Archives Center kindly granted me permission to quote from original documents in their possession or to reproduce photographs in their collections. *Radical America* and Sage Publications allowed me to use materials from my earlier articles.

I am grateful to the reference and interlibrary loan staff at the Winchester Public Library in Winchester, Massachusetts for their friendly and prompt assistance in procuring books and articles.

For their graciousness, insight, patience, and dedication throughout the process of turning my manuscript into a book, I thank Bob Lockhart and Alison Anderson of the University of Pennsylvania Press.

During the years that I worked on this book, a medical catastrophe changed the lives of my family and in particular that of my oldest son. Against my will, I was transformed from a scholar of social welfare history and critic of local and federal social services for families to an appreciative yet still critical beneficiary of such services as well. Over the years I have been privileged to know many dedicated individuals whose commitment to children with disabilities and their siblings and parents has led me to a more nuanced outlook on the state and the provision of social services to families in need. Among them Susan Lunn of Fidelity House Human Services Inc. in Lawrence, Massachusetts stands out for her unwavering commitment to creatively supporting families. Thanks also to the dedicated staff at the May Center for Education and Neurorehabilitation in Randolph, Massachusetts; Eileen Buckley; the faculty and staff at the Lesley Ellis School in Arlington, Massachusetts; and the terrific group of students from Tufts University and Lesley College who have contributed greatly to our family life with energy, enthusiasm, and good humor over the past ten years. I would also like to thank Alba Garcia, Colleen Manning, Diana Mazzaglia, Katie McGinigle, Meredith Nichols, Olga Schedrina, and Teri Torchia for their assistance and friendship. Marybeth Barker, Susan Ireland, Paula Shields, and Paula Tirrell also sustained me with their friendship and support.

One spring day while browsing in a library at NYU I came across a notice Fred Miller had placed in *International Labor and Working-Class History*, informing readers of a wealth of material contained within the SPCC collection at the Urban Archives at Temple University in Philadelphia. Immediately intrigued, I planned a trip to the Urban Archives, where I was fascinated by the materials I discovered. Two years later in Philadelphia I met Marvin Natowicz, whose help in negotiating the family and much more has enriched my life ever since. This book is dedicated to him and to our children, Samuel, Rebecca, and Jacob.